CHARLIE'S ANGELS
CASEBOOK

Charlie's Angels casebook

David Hofstede

Jack Condon

foreword by
Jaclyn Smith

POMEGRANATE PRESS LTD.

BEVERLY HILLS   LONDON

Library of Congress Card Number: 00-101704

Softcover: ISBN 0938817-20-5

Cover and Interior Design:
Cheryl Carrington

Photography Credits:

Cover, page 241, color insert—second page bottom:
© *Copyright Peter Kredenser. All rights reserved.*

*Charlie's Angels, Honey West, The Rookies,
J. Kennedy, Jack & Mike* and *Dynasty*
ABC Archives—© Copyright 2000 ABC, Inc. All rights reserved.

Author photo with collectibles—color insert:
© *Copyright Jeff Werner/Incredible Features. All rights reserved.*

Photos: pages vi and x:
© *Copyright Charles Bush*

First Printing 2000

2 4 6 8 10 9 7 5 3 1

Printed and bound in the United States of America

POMEGRANATE PRESS, LTD.
P.O. Box 17217
Beverly Hills, CA 90209
fax: 310·271·4930
http://www.pompress.com

Acknowledgments

The authors wish to thank the following people and organizations for their invaluable contributions: Ronald Austin, Jay Bernstein, Robert S. Biheller, Theodore Bikel, John D.F. Black, Charles William Bush, Les Carter, the Center for Motion Picture Study at the Academy of Motion Picture Arts & Sciences, Collectors Bookstore, David Doyle, Robert Earll, John Forsythe, Ron Friedman, Brett Garwood, Kevin Goff, Trevor Goff, Sabin Gray, Mark Grogan, Shelley Hack, Bo Hopkins, Rick Husky, Peter Kredenser, Suzenna Kredenser, Cheryl Ladd, Edward Lakso, Lee Lakso, David Levinson, Chris Mann, Kim Manners, Ben Martin, Nolan Miller, Esther Mitchell, Tanya Roberts, Barney Rosenzweig, Cis Rundle, Kathryn Leigh Scott, Jaclyn Smith, Hilary Thompson, Alana Voeller, Mark S. Willoughby, and Mary Woronov.

Foreword

WHEN MY GOOD FRIEND JACK ASKED ME TO WRITE A FOREWORD to this book, I immediately accepted as I felt that *Charlie's Angels* certainly changed my life. It's a memory I own. I really owe most of the success I have obtained in the entertainment field to the show's creator, Aaron Spelling.

So much has happened since 1976 when we commenced filming our first episode. Little did I realize that five years of starring in so many different and unusual situations would provide a magnificent training ground for my future.

It was during this extraordinary period of sudden fame that I recognized that I might become "Kelly Garrett" in the minds of television audiences—never able to shake that role for the rest of my acting career. So many actors have had to continue portraying characters similar to ones that made them famous; fortunately the show's success enabled me to tackle so many offbeat roles that the specter of being typecast never materialized.

As I read this book, so many memories came to the fore, as each episode had a life of its own. I am sure those of you who were fans of the series will relive some of the stories, and recognize what an innovative show Aaron Spelling created.

I only hope that reading this book will create nostalgic feelings of a time long past. It created the opportunity to start a wonderful career—hopefully entertaining those who have watched and supported me through the years.

With gratitude,

OCTOBER 1999   LOS ANGELES, CALIFORNIA

Contents

Jaclyn Smith with coauthor Jack Condon.

Introduction

by

Jack Condon

"Money, mystery, murder.
They're in it up to their
gorgeous private eyes . . ."

WHAT COULD BE MORE PROMISING THAN AN ADVERTISEMENT like that! And who knew that one *TV Guide* ad from March 21, 1976, would spark an interest in and a dedication to one television series, and its stars, that would last more than two decades?

Charlie's Angels captured the hearts of America—men, women, children of all ages, and, in particular, one eleven year old boy, who was living in the suburbs of Boston. Already having an interest in Kate Jackson, from her four-year stint on *The Rookies*, I was intrigued to see her in an ad for a new mystery movie that promised lots of excitement. Having been a fan of another ABC detective drama, *Get Christie Love*, I was hoping this show would deliver the same action and appeal Teresa Graves ignited during her series' brief run.

After watching the pilot, what impressed me most was the chemistry of the three leads. There was something interesting in how well they worked together, how each woman had a style all her own, yet meshed well with her partners. And, of course, they were all dazzling. This was never more apparent to me than when they graced the cover of *TV Guide*, for the week of September 25, 1976. I was so captivated that I saved that *TV Guide*. It became the first item in what is now the largest collection of *Charlie's Angels* memorabilia in the world.

Charlie's Angels was a sensation right from the start. It was one of the first shows of it's time to debut in the top ten and remain there—praised by the public and dismissed by the critics. Never has a show been analyzed so closely to discover the secret of it's popularity. Dubbed "Jiggle TV" (apparently by those who never really watched it), its appeal for me was much more than just three girls running around in bikinis.

Kate Jackson, Farrah Fawcett, Jaclyn Smith (and later Cheryl Ladd, Shelley Hack and Tanya Roberts) were larger than life. They had charisma, style and charm, yet they always seemed approachable. These were ladies you could invite into your living room every week. Away from the series, they also appeared frequently on talk shows and variety specials, giving the public a chance to get to know them as individuals.

The "Angels" subsequent work in television—movies, series and specials—is what has sustained my interest in their careers, and my collection of them. While many television stars wind up in "syndication heaven" when their series is cancelled, these ladies continued to showcase their talents in challenging and diverse roles. Along the way they surprised some of their harshest critics, and overcame any typecasting from the series that provided a springboard for their success.

To this day, I am not sure how I became so enthralled with collecting in such a serious fashion at such an early age—after I saved that first *TV Guide*, I kept *Angel* covers from *People* and *Time* magazine, and I bought a poster, and a T-shirt. I had a grandmother and an aunt who loved to shop, so during the summer it gave me something to hunt for. When my older brother got his license and needed any excuse to drive, it was off to the mall again in hope of finding something I didn't already have.

Over the years, it has been the enthusiasm of family and friends that continues to make my collection special. Almost every piece has a memory to go with it or a story behind it. So many people participated in my quest, and were so supportive, and for that I am grateful: Janice

Antonelli, Tom Appel, Diane Barow, Rueben Castillo, Miles Clark, Joy Corneliussen, Greg Davis, Giovanna Del Buono, Rose Feick, Sabin Gray, Sandy Hahn, Thomas Hof, Margaret Jahn, David Kuebler, Terry Lee, Leon Lejda, Frank Lombardi, Terry Longanecker, Chris Mann, Bill Morgan, John Racyn, Evelyn Reina, Kevin Sanford, Dan Steindi, Scott Toschlog, Edward Winkler, Joan Wilson, Ali Wisseman—I appreciate you all. A special thanks to Virgil Novotny, who has endured the enthusiasm for my hobby longer than anyone I know. Thank you for always being there.

My family tolerated a lot during those "trying teenage years"—my mother, Joyce Condon (who let me ruin the bedroom walls), my brother, James, sister Jill, my cousins, especially Bill Timmins, Jr. and my uncle and aunt, Bill and Mary Timmins. You always made shopping fun. My aunt, Betty Hurnowicz, you are always so supportive. Phillip Billan, you are just like family to me, truly the greatest friend anyone could have. And a special dedication to my father, Joseph Condon and my beloved grandmother, Anna Condon. You were always my strength.

This has been a project I have often been asked to do, but I never wanted to take on the task alone. It wasn't until December of 1995 when a collectibles magazine commissioned a writer to do a piece on me and on *Charlie's Angels* that I knew it would happen. This writer had style and a sense of what this series was all about, and I knew then that this was the person with whom I wanted to share the experience. David Hofstede, the bumps were many, but you always made it seem like a smooth ride.

Jaclyn Smith, you are everything I have always envisioned and more. You opened your heart to me, and I cherish all the wonderful things you have done for me over the years. You have shared so much with me, including your family–your wonderful mother Margaret Ellen, your terrific husband, Dr. Bradley Allen, and your two beautiful children, Gaston Anthony and Spencer Margaret, who I've had the pleasure of seeing emerge into fine young adults. You should be as proud of your personal and professional accomplishments, as I am of you.

Alana Voeller, you are the greatest support system any one person could have. You are truly the rarest find from my collecting, and the most priceless. You are the reason I am most glad that I started collecting so many years ago. This one is for you.

One of the first team photos of Charlie's original Angels—
Jaclyn Smith (left), Farrah Fawcett-Majors, and Kate Jackson.

CHAPTER ONE

Hello, Angels

Once upon a time, there were three little girls who went to the police academy.

AMERICANS NOW RECALL THE 1970S WITH NOSTALGIC FOND-ness, but those who lived through the decade remember that it didn't get off to an auspicious start. By 1975, the country had been subjected to fuel shortages, an energy crisis, the leisure suit as a fashion statement, and the Watergate scandal that ended Richard Nixon's presidency. And disco music hadn't even peaked yet!

But in 1976, a few rays of sunshine parted the dark clouds of the past five years, bringing an assortment of diversions that finally gave people something to smile about. It was the year of the nation's bicentennial, which prompted a variety of patriotic celebrations across the United States. The Summer Olympics introduced the world to Romanian gymnast Nadia Comaneci, who scored the first perfect "10"s in the history of the Olympic Games. At the movies, Sylvester Stallone's *Rocky* won the Academy Award for Best Picture, and had audiences standing and cheering in the theater for underdog club fighter Rocky Balboa. And on March 21, 1976, America met *Charlie's Angels*. Some guys are still trying to wipe the smiles off their faces.

Anne Francis (left) as Honey West, and Diana Rigg (below) as *The Avengers'* Emma Peel, television's first sexy female crimefighters.

Detective shows dominated the three major networks, and no one was watching cable because it wasn't available yet. Television offered sleuths of all shapes and styles, with little in common except an ability to capture a criminal in less than 60 minutes. A partial roll call would include married detectives Rock Hudson and Susan Saint James in *McMillan and Wife*, Buddy Ebsen as geriatric private eye *Barnaby Jones*, Robert Blake as *Baretta*, Karl Malden and Michael Douglas patrolling *The Streets of San Francisco*, Jack Lord saying "Book 'em, Dano" on *Hawaii Five-O*, Peter Falk as the ever-rumpled *Columbo*, Telly Savales as *Kojak*, and the Torino-driving duo of *Starsky and Hutch*, played by Paul Michael Glaser and David Soul.

Considering the proven popularity of the private eye genre among '70s era couch potatoes, it's not surprising that someone would ask, "How about a show featuring beautiful women as detectives? Do you think anybody would watch?" After that, Nadia's perfect 10s wouldn't be the only ones on television.

■   ■   ■

*I*n the days before Xena and Buffy and Nikita, female action heroes were still a novelty. The prototype was Emma Peel, the leather-clad, high-kicking British super-spy played by Diana Rigg on *The Avengers* (1965-1968). American television introduced Cinnamon Carter (Barbara Bain) on *Mission: Impossible* (1966-1973), and Julie Barnes (Peggy Lipton) on *The Mod Squad* (1968-1973), but the only American woman who approximated Mrs.

Peel's enticing blend of beauty and brass was *Honey West*, as played by Anne Francis.

Honey was a resourceful investigator, a judo expert, and a lovable eccentric. She kept an ocelot named Bruce as a pet, used her lipstick as a radio transmitter, and wore a trenchcoat on cases because it seemed like the right thing for a detective to do. Anne Francis played TV's first lady gumshoe with tongue firmly in cheek. *Honey West* debuted in 1965 but lasted only one season, which was a great disappointment to the series' executive producer, an ambitious, rail-thin dynamo named Aaron Spelling. Apparently, he thought, America wasn't ready for sexy sleuths . . . yet.

Spelling didn't dwell on the setback for very long. At the age of forty-one, he had already spent more than ten years in television as an actor, writer, and producer, and he was familiar with the fickle nature of the medium. Born in Dallas, Texas to Russian-Polish immigrant parents, Aaron was the youngest of five children whose Jewish heritage made him an outsider in cowboy country. Young Aaron retreated to the school library, where he devoured great novels and pulp paperbacks, and discovered the power of a good story when confronted by anti-Semitic bullies. Threatened with a butt-kicking every day, Spelling tried telling stories to his attackers to diffuse the situation. Sometimes it worked, sometimes it didn't, but at least he learned what types of stories people liked, and the benefits of giving an audience what it wanted.

After serving in the Air Force, Spelling attended Southern Methodist University, where he spent most of his time in the theater department. Upon graduation he left Dallas for New York City, where he learned his college credits didn't count for much on Broadway. Three months later, he moved to Los Angeles. He tried to break into show business by writing spec scripts for TV shows, but was sidetracked into an acting career after landing a small role on *Dragnet*. *Nick at Nite* and *TV Land* viewers can still catch the early Spelling *oeuvre* in episodes of *Gunsmoke*, in which he played a retarded Civil War soldier, and *I Love Lucy*, where he played a gas station attendant who gives directions to Lucy and Ricky.

Spelling's acting career came to an abrupt end after he worked three weeks on the MGM musical *Kismet* (1955) to deliver one line—

"Alms for the love of Allah." Realizing he could finish a half-dozen scripts in that time, Spelling refocused on writing. He made his first sales in 1955 to two anthology series, *Fireside Theater* and *Dick Powell's Zane Grey Theater*. His friendship with *Zane Grey* producer Dick Powell opened many doors in Hollywood, where Spelling gained a reputation for his ability to turn out good formula scripts at a rapid pace.

The first television series created by Aaron Spelling was *Johnny Ringo* (1959-1960). The title character, played by Don Durant, was a gunfighter turned lawman who carried the first "seven-shooter" in the old west. The extra bullet gave Ringo the edge in every duel. During the series' brief run, Spelling also produced a popular spinoff of *The Dick Powell Show* called *Burke's Law*, starring Gene Barry. Honey West originated as a spinoff of *Burke's Law*.

During a routinely busy day of working on a variety of shows for Powell's Four Star Productions, Aaron Spelling met a young advertising executive named Leonard Goldberg, whose agency had purchased commercial time on several Four Star shows. They had dinner together that night, beginning a friendship that would ultimately generate a series of hit shows that defined television in the 1970s: *The Rookies*, *Starsky and Hutch*, *Family*, *Hart to Hart*, *Fantasy Island*, *S.W.A.T.*, and, of course, *Charlie's Angels*.

Their professional collaboration, however, did not commence after that first dinner. While Spelling continued to write and produce for Four Star and, later, with Danny Thomas at Thomas-Spelling Productions, Leonard Goldberg became director of development at ABC in New York. He was promoted to vice-president of daytime programming (where he helped launch *The Dating Game* and *The Newlywed Game*), and then president of programming. The first show he purchased from Aaron Spelling was the counterculture cop series *The Mod Squad* (1968-1972), which became the biggest hit of Spelling's career.

The series proved so popular that Spelling was offered an exclusive four-year contract to create and develop shows for ABC. At the time, the network was running third in a three-way race, and needed all the help it could get. Ratings were so abysmal that comedian Milton

Berle once quipped, "Put the Vietnam War on ABC and it will be over in thirteen weeks."

Before Spelling signed the contract, Leonard Goldberg left ABC to become head of production at Screen Gems, the television division of Columbia Pictures. But he hated the job and returned soon after, to reunite with his friend Aaron and to officially form Spelling-Goldberg productions. Their first series was *The Rookies*, for which Aaron had already produced the pilot.

The Rookies debuted in 1972 and ran for four years. As he did with *The Mod Squad*, Spelling explored the dramatic possibilities of a trio of lead characters, in this case three rookie cops in southern California: Officer Terry Webster (George Stanford Brown), Officer Willie Gillis (Michael Ontkean), and Officer Mike Danko (Sam Melville). The shifting alliances in the three-character dynamic opened up a world of stories. The majority of the show's fan mail, however, went to Kate Jackson, a tall, slim brunette who played Jill Danko, Officer Mike's wife. When *The Rookies* was cancelled, Spelling and Goldberg exercised an option in Jackson's contract to put her in another series.

In a scenario that seems too Hollywood cliché to be true, Spelling and Goldberg first concocted the idea for *Charlie's Angels* over lunch at the famous Polo Lounge of the Beverly Hills Hotel. Goldberg, a fan of *The Avengers*, revived a concept he had years earlier about three Emma Peel-like women in leather jackets who worked as freelance crimefighters. Since most of the detective shows on the prime-time schedule were serious, hard-edged dramas, they decided to take this series in the opposite direction, and emphasize glamorous escapism over gritty realism.

From that premise, they developed *The Alley Cats*, a show featuring three gorgeous female detectives named Allie, Lee, and Catherine (Al-Lee-Cat). They pitched the show to two men on their way to global domination in the entertainment media; Michael Eisner, ABC's Senior Vice President for Prime Time Production and Development, and Barry Diller, Eisner's mentor at ABC, who by 1975 had left the network to become Chairman of the Board at Paramount Pictures.

Demonstrating their infallible instinct for the public taste, the two moguls studied the proposal and pronounced their judgment. "That's the worst idea I've ever heard," said Eisner. "You've got to be crazy," echoed Diller. "Three beautiful girls running around, chasing criminals. It's not believable. It's terrible. Forget it."

Undaunted, Spelling and Goldberg refused to let the idea drop. One year earlier, they had produced a TV movie called *The Affair* (1974), starring Robert Wagner and Natalie Wood. In the contract, they inserted a clause enabling them to produce a series pilot for ABC with Wagner and Wood. The terms forced ABC to pay $25,000 to the quartet, whether they made a pilot or not. After listening to Spelling's pitch for *The Alley Cats*, Wagner echoed the derisive assessments of Eisner and Diller. "But what do I know?" he added. "You're the producer." That was all the encouragement Spelling needed. Thus, Robert Wagner and Natalie Wood acquired 45 percent ownership of the new show.

Spelling and Goldberg then presented the idea to Kate Jackson. "I didn't think the title would work, so I met with them to give them my ideas," Jackson recalled in 1979. "At the meeting, I saw a squawk-box on Aaron's desk, and suggested the girls work for a guy they never see; he only talks to them on the phone or squawkbox. Then I noticed a picture of three angels on Aaron's wall; so I said, let's call the girls 'angels.'"

Leonard Goldberg hired screenwriter Ernest Tidyman to write the pilot, which was now called *Harry's Angels*. Five years earlier, Tidyman had won the "Best Screenplay" Academy Award for *The French Connection* (1971), and had also penned winning scripts for the black exploitation classic *Shaft* (1971), and the Clint Eastwood western *High Plains Drifter* (1973). But his efforts on behalf of *Angels* didn't impress anybody, so the producers turned to the veteran writing team of Ivan Goff and Ben Roberts, who had recently ended an eight-year stint as executive producers of the detective series *Mannix* (1967-1975).

The partnership of Ivan Goff and Ben Roberts began in the 1930s. Roberts, who with writer Sidney Sheldon had penned three successful Broadway shows (*Merry Widow*, *Dream With Music*, and *Jackpot*), first teamed with Goff on the murder-mystery *Portrait in Black* (1945), which played on both London and Broadway stages before being adapted into a 1960 film starring Lana Turner. The success of the play led to a contract offer from Warner Bros. From 1936 to 1957, they wrote more than two dozen films, including the Lon Chaney movie biography *Man of a Thousand Faces* (1957), for which they earned an Oscar nomination. Their script for the James Cagney classic *White Heat* (1949), contained one of Cagney's most indelible final scenes; as psychotic gangster Cody Jarrett, Cagney stood atop a flaming oil tank, shouting the movie's most famous line "Look ma, I made it. Top of the world!" before being blown to smithereens.

Goff and Roberts created *The Rogues* for television in 1964. It was an urbane, playful series about two aristocratic families who, for three centuries, had survived as con artists and jewel thieves. Gig Young, David Niven, and Charles Boyer led a prestigious international cast. "Ben and my father were brought into the *Angels* project by (ABC programming head) Fred Silverman, who was a fan of *The Rogues*, and wanted a similar concept for *Angels*—stories with sophisticated cons," said Ivan Goff's son, Kevin.

The Rogues lasted only one season, but Goff and Roberts enjoyed telling multilayered con stories, and contributed several scripts to *Mission: Impossible* (1966-1973), the standardbearer for complex espionage adventures. When they received the *Angels* assignment, they wrote a story comparable to their earlier work, in which the Angels used their intelligence and guile to solve a murder mystery at a northern California winery.

Fred Silverman was the first network executive to share Spelling-Goldberg's enthusiasm for the new show. "I only saw the one-line description—*Harry's Angels*. That's the show I'm excited about. I smell a hit," he told the producers. He suggested, however, that the title be changed to avoid confusion with another ABC detective series, *Harry O* (1974-1976). Spelling and Goldberg settled on "Charlie" instead, a name then associated with a popular line of perfume.

The first actress to be cast in *Charlie's Angels* was, of course, Kate Jackson, for whom the series was created.

The Smart One

always wanted to sign autographs," said Kate Jackson early in her career. "I'd lie in bed at night fantasizing about people coming up and asking me for my autograph, and during the day I'd practice signing my name." Over the years, she's had plenty of opportunity to do just that.

Born October 29, 1948, in Birmingham, Alabama, the eldest daughter of Hogan and Ruth Jackson, Kate made her acting debut at Brooke Hill High School, where she starred in *The Mad Woman of Chaillot*. She attended the University of Mississippi for two years and played a season of summer stock at the Stowe Playhouse in Vermont, before venturing to New York to enroll in the American Academy of Dramatic Arts. She appeared in such plays as *Royal Gambit*, *Night Must Fall*, *Constant Wife*, and *Little Moon of Alban*. To help pay her tuition, Kate conducted the NBC studio tour at Rockefeller Center, and also tried modeling. "I hated it," she later said, "there's nothing worse than wondering if a snip of hair is out of place."

Kate Jackson played Daphne Harridge on *Dark Shadows* and a nurse on Spelling-Goldberg's *The Rookies* prior to becoming an Angel.

Kate's first big break came when she auditioned and won a continuing part in the hit daytime drama *Dark Shadows* (1966-1970). She played Daphne Harridge, the ghost of a 19th century governess who tries to protect two children from her murderous lover. "I started as a ghost and wasn't given a single line of dialogue for the first two months," she recalls. "But I was grateful to be drawing a paycheck and getting experience; besides, at that time I was too scared to open my mouth." Jackson reprised the role in the MGM film adaptation of the series, *Night of Dark Shadows* (1971).

A television talent scout encouraged Kate to move to Hollywood, and upon arriving she found work almost immediately, playing guest roles on *Bonanza* and *The Jimmy Stewart Show*. She appeared in a failed television pilot called *The New Healers* (1972), but it was her part as Nurse Jill Danko in *The Rookies* that brought her television fame, and the notice of Aaron Spelling and Leonard Goldberg. "I recall doling out medical reassurances," she remembers, "but I would have more to do when the scripts called for me to be kidnapped, which happened often."

Her generous contract on *The Rookies* allowed for time off to pursue other roles. She starred in a theatrical film for Universal Studios, *Limbo* (1972) about Vietnam POW wives, and earned glowing reviews. She then became the television equivalent of scream queen Jamie Lee Curtis, by appearing in such horror movies-of-the-week as 1973's *Satan's School for Girls* (also featuring Cheryl Stoppelmoor [Ladd]), *Killer Bees* (1974), *Death Cruise* (1975), and *Death at Love House* (1976).

In 1977, her first year on *Charlie's Angels*, Kate Jackson received the first of two Emmy nominations for Best Actress in a Dramatic Series. She was also nominated as Best Supporting Actress for the NBC series pilot *James at 15*.

■   ■   ■

"A blonde" was the only qualification for employment as Charlie's second Angel, which hardly narrowed down the field in California, the ancestral home of the blonde. But Farrah Fawcett-Majors had the inside track for the role of athletic thrillseeker Jill Munroe. "I knew Farrah from when I double-dated with her and (her husband) Lee Majors," Aaron Spelling told *TV Guide* in 1977. Majors had starred in the *Four Star Western* series *The Big Valley* (1965-1969), and Farrah had already appeared in three Spelling-Goldberg TV movies, most notably as a stewardess in *Murder on Flight 502* (1975). The producers were certain that the stunning twenty-eight-year-old beauty was on the verge of a breakthrough. No one could have guessed how enormous that breakthrough would become.

The Phenomenon

arrah Leni Fawcett was born on February 2, 1947, the younger of two daughters born to James and Pauline Fawcett in the coastal city of Corpus Christi, Texas. James, an oil field contractor, and Pauline, a housewife, named Farrah after an old friend of the family's. Pauline liked the way it sounded with "Fawcett".

Just 28 days after her birth, a life-threatening tumor was discovered between her upper and lower stomach. Surgery to remove the tumor was a serious matter for an infant, and there was no guarantee

Farrah Fawcett's dazzling smile made her one of TV's top commerical actresses in the 1970s.

of success, or of her survival. But the little girl was a fighter, and she survived the operation with no more than a scar.

Farrah attended St. Patrick's parochial school, where she studied hard, earned good grades and was always eager to please her parents. The nuns took to Farrah right away, and Farrah once told her mother that she wanted to be a nun, but that didn't last very long. In 1962, she attended W.B. Ray High School, where every year she was voted "Most Beautiful Girl in School." She was popular and outgoing, and while Farrah had many suitors, she continued to excel in her academics, particularly biology.

She entered The University of Texas at Austin in 1965, pledged the Delta Delta Delta sorority, and majored in microbiology. After she was voted one of the ten most beautiful students during her freshman year, her photograph was spotted by Hollywood publicist David Mirisch, who suggested she come to California and try her hand at modeling. Her parents were against the idea, but Farrah was intrigued by the possibilities.

During her sophomore year, Farrah finally convinced her parents that Hollywood was worth a try. She intended to stay only through the summer, and return to Texas to finish school. Her parents drove her to California, and checked her into the Hollywood Studio Club, a boarding house for women. Within two weeks of her arrival, Mirisch signed her to a $350.00 a week contract with Screen Gems/Columbia, for modeling and commercials.

Farrah played bit parts in *I Dream of Jeannie*, *The Flying Nun* and *The Partridge Family*. She made her film debut in the 1970 camp classic, *Myra Breckinridge*, opposite Mae West and Racquel Welch. That same year, she appeared in the French/Italian production *Love is a Funny Thing* with Jean-Paul Belmondo. But she first became known to the public as the California blond with the sunny smile in a series of commercials for Ultra-Brite toothpaste. The success of that campaign led to more than 100 other commercials, including spots for Noxema, Max Factor, Lady Schick, Winchester Cigarettes, Mercury Cougar, and Wella Balsam.

Farrah's face also caught the attention of actor Lee Majors, who saw Farrah's photograph in his publicist's office, and insisted on meeting her. The couple married in 1973.

Lee took an active interest in Farrah's career, and helped her land guest roles on *Apple's Way*, *Harry O*, *S.W.A.T.* and both of his own series, *Owen Marshall, Counselor at Law* (1971-74) and *The Six Million Dollar Man* (1974-78). Farrah also appeared in the made-for-TV movies *The Feminist and the Fuzz* (1971), *The Girl Who Came Gift-wrapped* (1974) and *Murder on Flight 502* (1975).

Farrah enjoyed acting, but her first priority was her marriage, and the support of her husband's career. She was earning $100,000 a year for commercial work and bit parts, and was content to remain one of the most successful unknowns in Hollywood. But when *Charlie's Angels* came along, it seemed like too much fun to pass up.

The original plan to cast a blond, a brunette, and a redhead was abandoned when no suitably carrot-topped candidate came forward. By the summer of 1975, however, word of *Charlie's Angels* had spread through the actors' community, and hundreds of would-be Angels were clamoring for an audition. "Every gorgeous girl in town was coming in at that point," recalled Rick Husky, a producer of the series' first season. "Studio executives would lean out their window and see a parade of beautiful women." Among the hopefuls: Suzanne Somers, who landed a role on *Three's Company* (1977-1984) one year later, actress/model Susie Coelho, who was encouraged to audition by her friend, Farrah, and Veronica Hamel, later a four-time Emmy nominee for her performance as attorney Joyce Davenport on *Hill Street Blues* (1981-1987).

Husky had already worked with Aaron Spelling, first as a story editor on *The Mod Squad* and later as a producer on *The Rookies*. "During that period I remember being in a Beverly Hills nightclub, turning a corner and running face to face into Jaclyn Smith. I was struck dumb by her beauty," he recalls. "She was very gracious and sweet, and I knew she was an actress because we had a mutual friend. Some months later I cast her in the role of an airline stewardess on *The Rookies*. We went to lunch during filming, and after that we started dating."

At the time the *Angels* pilot was being cast, Husky and Jaclyn Smith were still an item, and had become friends with

Would-be Angels over the years include: Michelle Pfeiffer, Kim Basinger, Shari Belafonte, Catherine Bach, Veronica Hamel, Connie Selleca, Deborah Shelton, Jayne Kennedy, Kathie Lee Gifford and Suzanne Somers.

Leonard Goldberg and his wife, Wendy. But Smith's invitation to read for *Charlie's Angels* came not from Rick Husky but from Robert Wagner, who remembered her from her guest appearances on his series, *Switch*. "R.J. (Wagner) told Aaron, 'Forget the redhead, you've got to go with her,'" recalls Smith.

"Jaclyn told me she was reading for the pilot," said Husky. "Afterward, she called me because she hadn't received the script in advance and wasn't prepared. I asked if she'd like to go in and read again, and she said yes."

"I don't like readings," Smith explains. "I'd rather memorize the part then act it out. But I read, and I didn't think I was very good." Husky told Leonard Goldberg, "I think you're making a mistake if you don't have her in again." Goldberg agreed, and Jaclyn received a second chance. "This time, she knocked them out," said Husky. "As you can see in the pilot, her face just jumped off the screen."

The Southern Belle

Jaclyn Ellen Smith was born in Houston, Texas, on October 26, 1947. "Jaclyn" was for her father, Jack Smith, a prominent dentist; "Ellen" was for her mother, Margaret Ellen, a homemaker. Jaclyn and her older brother, Tommy, both learned many of their early life lessons from their grandfather, Gaston, a minister of the Methodist Church. "Paw-Paw," as Jaclyn called him, was one of her most profound childhood influences. "My family was and always will be my greatest source of strength and security," she said.

An early publicity still of dancer-turned-Angel Jaclyn Smith.

When she was just three years old, Jaclyn fell in love with ballet. Throughout her childhood she dreamed of becoming the next Maria Tallchief or Margot Fonteyn, and spent countless hours perfecting her grande jetés and double pirouettes. By her eleventh birthday, she was a stand-out in her class.

Captivated by ballet, Jaclyn found little time for socializing and making new friends. "I was strictly a wallflower," she said. "I was never one to attend parties and football games like the rest of my peers." To ease her shyness, she began performing in a number of high school productions. When she discovered that she wasn't shy on stage, she joined the Houston Community Playhouse and started building up a resumé of acting credits.

Smith studied drama at Trinity University in San Antonio, where she majored in psychology, though her heart was not in her studies. "I was homesick all the time, and I could not stop thinking about dancing," she explained. She dropped out after one year and, with her parent's blessing, she headed to New York to live in the famed Barbizon Hotel for Women, and to enroll in Balanchine's School of American Ballet.

Switching from Balanchine to Broadway, she danced in the chorus line of several musicals, summer stock, and off off-Broadway productions. During that time she received a "test option" from Paramount Pictures to star in a remake of *Roman Holiday* (1953), opposite Robert Redford. The film was never made, and Smith returned to New York.

Smith answered a *Backstage Magazine* ad looking for commercial actors, and auditioned for a Listerine commercial. "I also auditioned for a show in Las Vegas, and I got a part in a dance company backing up Tony Bennett. It was $300.00 a week," Jaclyn laughed, "to me that could have been a million. I weighed the idea of traveling to Las Vegas. In the end I declined but, one month later, I got a phone call telling me I got the Listerine commercial. I was very nervous—but, it was a beginning!"

After performing in a musical revue in Central Park, she was approached by Harry Abrams, an agent for actors in television commercials. He thought Jaclyn had the perfect look, and immediately landed her a role on a Camay commercial. Other commercials followed, including

Diet-Rite, English Leather, and Woolite. Her first measure of fame was a result of her appearance as a "Breck Girl" (see sidebar page 16).

While still under contract to Paramount, Smith appeared as a model in *Goodbye, Columbus* (1969), and was cast in *The Adventurers* (1970). "This was a huge picture," Jaclyn recalled. "I went in and read for director Lewis Gilbert (*Alfie, Educating Rita*). The part called for a 'Texas girl.' I read with an accent. He said 'you are going to be in this movie.' I didn't really believe it. The next thing I knew, I got a call saying I had to go to Rome. It was a small part, a reporter. At that point, Mia Farrow bowed out of her role and Gilbert offered it to me. It was the starring role, but I couldn't do a part that required nudity. So, I had to pass." The role was played by Leigh Taylor Young.

In 1968, Jaclyn married actor Roger Davis, who proposed on their second date. She continued to work in commercials, while he continued a stint on the Gothic daytime serial *Dark Shadows*. Two years later, while Roger played the lead in the western series *Alias Smith and Jones* (1971-73), Jaclyn commuted between Los Angeles and New York to work in commercials and television guest spots, among them *The Partridge Family*, *McCloud, Get Christie Love, The Rookies* and *Switch*. The travel and long hours put a strain on the relationship, which ended in divorce in 1976.

That same year, she auditioned for *Charlie's Angels*. After winning the role of Kelly Garrett, Smith was accused in a *Time* magazine article of being hired as a result of her relationship with the show's producer, Rick Husky.

"As a part of the Spelling-Goldberg company I was aware the auditions were going on, but I had no direct involvement in them," said Husky. "I fired off a telegram, which was printed in the Letters to the Editor the following week. The letter stated that 'an injustice was done a lovely, gentle lady,' and that Miss Smith 'garnered that role on her talent alone.'"

■　　■　　■

When the show was conceived, Kate Jackson was supposed to play Kelly Garrett. "Kelly was written for Kate, Jill was definitely Farrah, and there was only one character left, so I figured I was going to be Sabrina," Smith

Breck-ing into Show-biz

*B*efore she was cast as Kelly Garrett, Jaclyn Smith was most familiar to television viewers as the "Breck Girl." Breck Shampoo had created the popular Breck Girl advertising campaign more than a decade earlier, and the models chosen for the company's commercials were regarded as among the most beautiful on television.

The Wella Corporation, Breck's foremost competition in the shampoo business, had used Farrah Fawcett-Majors as its spokeswoman for Wella Balsam Hair Conditioner. But in 1975, when Wella introduced a new combination shampoo/conditioner, tests revealed viewer confusion between the two products. Wella's advertising firm, James Neal Harvey Inc., suggested using a different model to help the product create a separate identity.

James Harvey, president of the agency, bumped into Jaclyn Smith while shopping at New York's Saks Fifth Avenue. He asked what she was working on. "Nothing," she said. "I haven't been going out on as many calls." Harvey was shocked; Smith was one of television's top spokesmodels, and was beginning to establish a career as an actress. He asked about her status as the Breck Girl. "I'm free and clear of that contract," she replied.

Harvey couldn't believe his luck. Usually when a firm hires a model to represent its product, there is a stipulation in the contract that the model cannot switch to a rival sponsor for a certain number of years. In this instance, however, the provision was overlooked. She was able to work for another shampoo company. Harvey signed her immediately.

The agency cast Jaclyn Smith in a commercial originally written for Farrah—with one significant change. Unable to resist a shot at Breck, Harvey changed the beginning of the script so that Jaclyn says "I switched." By hiring Jaclyn Smith, the Wella Corporation achieved two triumphs—getting one up on a business rival, and having a product endorsed by two Angels. ◣

recalled. "But Kate changed it (when) we got a description of each girl in the pilot script; Sabrina was described as the girl who had everything—beautiful, a fashion plate, educated, refined, and elegant." ("When you bump into Sabrina, you might wonder if Prince Rainier knows she's missing from the palace," was the Goff/Roberts description). "Kate thought that would be more of a stretch for her at the time," said Smith. "Instead of the more down-to-earth characters she usually played, she wanted to be the girl that walked across a room, and everybody faints."

As a result of Jackson's last-minute role change, the third-cast, third-billed Jaclyn Smith plays the most prominent role in the pilot. The first half-hour of the ninety minute film is practically a solo outing for Kelly, who lays the groundwork for an elaborate double-switch con scheme. Jackson, as Sabrina, then follows Kelly into the winery, dressed by Nolan Miller and wrapped in furs.

Jackson, however, soon tired of the cosmetic demands of the role. "She didn't like fittings," said Smith. "Farrah and I would gladly shop all day for our wardrobe, but Kate wanted to wear the same turtleneck all the time, and would stand behind the bar in the Townsend office so she wouldn't have to change her pants!" When the series began, Jackson reverted to wearing blue jeans, and Sabrina Duncan became the least flamboyant Angel. Jaclyn Smith, as Kelly, played dress-up in almost every episode.

"No matter what description they put in the script, the actress dictates what the character becomes," Smith said.

■ ■ ■

Rounding out the regular cast were David Doyle as John Bosley, and David Ogden Stiers as Scott Woodville, two associates of Charlie's who served as liaisons between the Angels and their elusive boss. "I don't exactly remember how I got the role," said Doyle. "I never auditioned—someone just called and asked if I wanted the job." Doyle hadn't worked for Spelling-Goldberg before, but he suspects that his good fortune was due to producer Douglas Cramer, who created *The Love Boat* (1977-1986) with Aaron Spelling. Doyle spent one year on *Bridget*

Loves Bernie (1972-1973), a sitcom produced by Cramer. "He might have said something to Aaron about me," Doyle said.

Good Old Dependable Bos

orn December 1st, 1925 in Lincoln, Nebraska, David Doyle grew up predestined for a career as an attorney—his grandfather, father, brother and nephew all practiced law. Although his interest in acting began at the age of ten with community theatre, Doyle still had thoughts of following in his family's footsteps where he enrolled at the University of Nebraska as a pre-law student. But after spending the summer of 1950 performing at Virginia's Barter Theatre, he decided to switch schools and majors. He moved to New York to train at the prestigious Neighborhood Playhouse, where he was a classmate of Joanne Woodward.

David Doyle played the Angels' friend and colleague, John Bosley

After a brief stint in the Navy as an air controller and a radio deejay, he returned to the stage in 1962, to appear on Broadway in *Something About a Soldier*. Other plays followed, including *Here's Love, I was Dancing*, and a revival of *South Pacific*, where he met his second wife Anne Nathan, a former singer-dancer (his first wife, Rachel, died in a fall in 1968, leaving David to raise their daughter, Leah).

His successful stage career continued with performances in *Will Success Spoil Rock Hunter?*, where he replaced Walter Matthau, and

The Angels and The Partridges

*P*rior to being cast in *Charlie's Angels*, Farrah Fawcett-Majors, Jaclyn Smith, and Cheryl Ladd all made guest appearances on a variety of television series. By sheer coincidence, all three future Angels turned up in episodes of *The Partridge Family*.

In episode 2, "The Sound of Money," (October 2, 1970) Willie Larkin (Harry Morgan) cries whiplash after a minor fender-bender with the Partridge bus, and files a lawsuit. Danny (Danny Bonaduce) hires Farrah Fawcett, billed as "Pretty Girl," to prove there's nothing wrong with Willie's back and neck. She is asked to pass him in the street and drop her handkerchief. When Harry bends over to pick it up, Danny will take the picture that will end the lawsuit.

Jaclyn Smith appears in episode 5, "When Mother Gets Married" (October 23, 1970). The Partridge kids are happy for their mom (Shirley Jones) when she rekindles a romance with old friend John McMartin (Larry Metcalf), a handsome doctor. But when the kids spot John buying a ring for Tina, played by Jaclyn, they confront their mother's boyfriend. John explains that Tina is his niece, and the ring is a present for her college graduation.

Billed as Cheryl Stoppelmoor, Cheryl Ladd plays San Pueblo dreamgirl Johanna Houser, who agrees to a date with Keith Partridge (David Cassidy) in episode 80, "Double Trouble" (October 20, 1973). Keith becomes so excited about the thought of a date with Johanna that he forgets having already invited another girl to the same beach party.

"Six Partridges and Three Angels," a compilation tape of the three episodes, has been released by Columbia/TriStar. ◼

The Beauty Part with Bert Lahr. In 1967, he moved to Hollywood, and costarred in the Clint Eastwood drama *Coogan's Bluff* (1968).

"I did guest shots on television as crooked lawyers, priests, fathers, and killers, and then I did *Charlie's Angels*," said Doyle. "I'm the luckiest guy with the best job in the world."

■ ■ ■

The guest cast for the pilot consisted of several familiar television faces, including Bo Hopkins, Diana Muldaur, and an intense young actor named Tommy Lee Jones. John Llewelyn Moxey, a veteran of British mystery and horror films, was hired to direct. Filming on the ninety-minute pilot began in July of 1975.

"I thought it was a unique, interesting concept—three girls, the man you don't see—I thought it had all the elements, and could be an interesting show," remembers Jaclyn Smith.

David Doyle met Aaron Spelling, Jaclyn Smith and Kate Jackson on the first day of shooting. "I realized this was probably the last real good chance I had to put any money away," he remembered. "I was never that (crazy) about the trappings of this business; working is all that really counts. The rest is window-dressing. I knew if this were to run for awhile, it could be very important to me. It also turned out to be a great job."

The three actresses cast in the series had all met prior to shooting the pilot. Jaclyn and Kate were first introduced on an audition for a different series. "I thought she was an interesting actress and a beautiful girl," said Smith. Farrah and Jaclyn had both shot commercials for Max Factor prior to becoming Angels. "We both came from Texas, so there was a common history, and we got along immediately," recalls Smith.

One of the most important post-production tasks was to add the voice of Charlie, the Angels' wealthy, mysterious boss. Spelling hired former Rogues star Gig Young, a debonair leading man in several Doris Day films, and an Oscar winner for 1969's *They Shoot Horses, Don't They?* But on the day he was to record his lines, Young, who battled alcoholism throughout his career, was too drunk to perform the role. In desperation, Spelling called his friend John Forsythe, whom he had first met when he was still a writer for Dick Powell.

"It was on a Friday, at 11:30 at night. I was sitting in bed, reading, when I got the call from Aaron," Forsythe recalled. "He said, 'John, I need your help. I'm in terrible trouble. I have a show, and I think it's a good show, and it has to be in New York on Monday. We had a fellow to play the part of Charlie, and unfortunately he's drunk, and he just can't handle it. Would you come over and do it for me? I'd be very grateful.'

Forsythe lived near 20th Century Fox, where the taping was to take place, so he agreed to take the job. "I didn't even take my pajamas off—I just put on my top coat and drove over to Fox." Spelling gave him the script, and a brief overview of what the story was about. "When it was finished, Aaron said, 'That's perfect.' And I went home and went back to bed."

The Boss

*D*espite a distinguished career in motion pictures, television, and the Broadway stage, one of John Forsythe's most recognizable roles was as a voice on the telephone.

Born on January 29, 1918, in Penn's Grove, New Jersey, Forsythe began his show business career in radio. A college job as a public announcer at Ebbets Field, home of the Brooklyn Dodgers, led to announcing Dodger games and eventually to radio acting. Trained at New York's famed Actor's Studio, he performed a variety of roles on stage, and then headed for Broadway, where he was spotted by a talent scout, and signed to a film contract with Warner Bros.

In 1944, Forsythe made his movie debut opposite Cary Grant in *Destination Tokyo*. Soon after, he served a brief stint in the U.S. Army Air Corps, but was pulled from cadet training and put into the cast of *Winged Victory*, the Moss Hart stage musical staffed by Air Corps personnel with theatrical backgrounds. The members of the cast later became members of a Sidney Howard play, *Yellow Jack*, in which Forsythe had the starring role.

After his discharge from military service, Forsythe appeared in George Abbott's *It Takes Two* and Arthur Miller's *All My Sons*. During the "Golden Age" of television, he performed in episodes of such "live" telecasts as *Studio One*, *Philco Playhouse*, *Kraft Theatre*, and *Robert Montgomery Presents*.

His next major theatrical appearance was in the road company of *Mr. Roberts*. Replacing Henry Fonda in the title role, Forsythe toured

Who Is Charlie?

*C*harlie Townsend was the envy of every American male; he owned a successful detective agency, an opulent mansion, a luxurious yacht (The Wayward Angel), and a Rolls Royce. And whenever he was seen (which wasn't often) he was always in the company of a beautiful woman.

But who was this elegant mystery man who sat in an overstuffed leather chair behind a large oak desk? A man that was so elusive that even his team of dazzling detectives couldn't crack the case of seeing him face to face? Here are just a few of the facts that the series let slip about the man behind Charles Townsend Associates.

He served in the Army O.S.S during World War II, and helped command a special Army Allied Intelligence Unit overseas, where he acted as the General's aide. After serving in the war, he toyed with a career in show business, appearing opposite the actress Eve La Deux in Shakespeare's *A Midsummer Night's Dream*. But then he enrolled in the police academy, and graduated swiftly through the ranks from beat cop to Lieutenant of Detectives. Some time later, he left the force to open his own detective agency, with the help of his friend, John Bosley.

During his years as a detective, Townsend helped convict many notorious murderers, thieves, and saboteurs, and he knew that some would eventually be released from prison. When he retired from the field and hired new operatives to continue his practice, he decided to remain anonymous, to avoid being kidnapped, or used as bait to lure his Angels into danger. Though the Angels jumped at every opportunity to catch a glimpse of their boss, Charlie knew that his detectives would be safer if they couldn't identify him.

Retiring from active casework left Charlie with plenty of time to indulge in a variety of recreational pursuits. He was an avid skier and sailor, but spent much of his free time entertaining a medley of lovely female guests at his luxurious home, located at 674 Vinewood Lane in Beverly Hills. Charlie was married once, but realized early on that he was not cut out for monogamy. ◼

for two years before joining the New York production. He followed up *Mr. Roberts* on Broadway by starring in the Pulitzer Prize-winning play, *Teahouse of the August Moon*.

Forsythe resumed his film career in 1955, as the star of Alfred Hitchcock's bizarre black comedy *The Trouble with Harry*. After choos-

John Forsythe provided the voice of Charlie Townsend. Producers kept Forsythe's identity confidential, but the secret didn't last long.

ing to make California his permanent address, he became one of Hollywood's busiest character actors, finding equal success in both film and television. At the movies, Forsythe appeared in *Captive City* (1952), *Madame X* (1966), *In Cold Blood* (1968), *Topaz* (1969), and *The Happy Ending* (1969). In 1979, he was critically acclaimed for his performance as a villainous judge in *And Justice for All*.

Forsythe's most successful television venture was *Bachelor Father* (1957-1962), in which he starred as Bentley Gregg, a wealthy Hollywood attorney who becomes the legal guardian of his niece, Kelly (Noreen Corcoran), after her parents' death. His next two sitcoms, *The John Forsythe Show* (1965-1966) and *To Rome with Love* (1969-1971), did not fare as well. While still lending his voice to *Charlie's Angels*, Forsythe began an eight-year run on the hugely popular series *Dynasty* (1981-1989) as Blake Carrington, the dynamic head of an oil-rich Denver family.

■　　■　　■

The cast of *Charlie's Angels* from the pilot movie, which also featured
David Ogden Stiers (standing, rear) as Scott Woodville.

With filming and post-production complete, the pilot was subjected to
the same exhaustive research and audience testing as any other potential series. *Charlie's Angels* received a score of 73 from the first test audience—a good score, but one that also expressed reservations. The ABC
research department sifted through the comment cards and verbal reactions and presented a report to Spelling, Goldberg, and Fred Silverman,
with the following recommendations:

1. Develop the three female leading characters so they can be made more distinctive, different, and recognizable from each other.
2. Strengthen the appeal and credibility of the three women by making each more skilled and adept at handling themselves in different situations. Further, these women should be portrayed as more intelligent and capable rather than what viewers perceived were three dumb models who got themselves into trouble.
3. Incorporate more action into future stories.
4. Improve future storylines by developing plots that are more plausible and straightforward, have greater mystery and suspense, are less corny and predictable and far less contrived.
5. Improve the dialogue in future storylines by avoiding "stock cops-and-robbers phrases" and "sexual allusions or cliches" in the talk with Charlie.
6. Enhance the believability of future stories by developing villains who are a bit more dangerous or menacing and far less stupid and gullible.
7. Enhance Charlie's role in the series by providing viewers more information about who and what Charlie is, (and) how he came to be so rich. Also tone down considerably Charlie's womanizing and playboy personality so that he appears less "like a silly Hugh Hefner who controls a harem of female servants."
8. Eliminate entirely the continuing role of Woodville and Bosley, or have Woodville's role in each story end after giving the three women their assignments.

The producers listened to the suggestions, but made very few alterations, though the request for more action appealed to Spelling. Network executives, however, still had concerns, especially about who was going to "rescue" the *Angels*. The debut of *Police Woman* (1974-1978), starring Angie Dickinson as sexy Los Angeles cop Pepper Anderson, proved that a female lead in an action series could attract viewers. But every female action hero had a male partner to bail her out of trouble. Even Pepper was assisted by the studly Sergeant Bill Crowley (Earl Holliman). The producers insisted that the Angels

Relaxing between scenes of the pilot movie—Kate Jackson (left), Jaclyn Smith and Farrah Fawcett-Majors.

would not need rescuing—if they got themselves into trouble, they would get themselves out.

A series featuring a team of lady crimefighters journeyed even further into uncharted territory on the television landscape. Silverman was no stranger to new ideas and remained the series' biggest network supporter, but his enthusiasm was not shared by Fred Pierce, the President of ABC and Silverman's boss. He balked at the bizarre concept of three girls working for a guy on the telephone. How do they know what to do? Where did they come from?

According to Spelling's autobiography, he ad-libbed a response that the Angels' background would be explained in the series' main title sequence, which would show them as former members of the police department who joined Charlie for more adventures. "I made that up on the spot and it did the trick. Fred was excited. 'Oh, they went to the police academy? Great. Let's go.'"

The debut of *Charlie's Angels* on March 21, 1976, was overshadowed in the news by the conviction of Patricia Hearst, the kidnapped heiress who joined her terrorist abductors in committing an armed robbery. Compared to that true-life crime story, the Angels' first adventure seemed downright mundane. Critics agreed. "Overall, the pilot was a trifle too slick to generate complete acceptance, but it might do in a pinch," wrote *Variety*. A more harsh assessment was offered by Tom Shales in *The Washington Post*: "The real challenge to this trio is how to keep their hair looking fresh, even while schlepping around a synthetic swamp. Why anyone would have the slightest interest in any of this is one of the questions the defense would like to put to the network and to Spelling-Goldberg Productions, which is trying to pass off another styleless blank as entertainment."

But then the ratings came in, and a shockwave of delight passed through the ABC executive offices when the pilot drew a phenomenal 54 share; of every television in use that Sunday night, more than half were tuned to *Charlie's Angels*. The movie ranked third among all made-for-TV movies that year; when it was aired again on September 14, it finished fourth in the same ranking. With a public endorsement that overwhelming, there was no doubt that the *Angels* would be back.

Charlie's Angels began its first season as a top ten hit; a few weeks later, it was the most popular and controversial show on television.

CHAPTER TWO

The Angels Soar

CHARLIE'S ANGELS DEBUTED WITH A DEGREE OF TELEVISION RATINGS dominance that was unprecedented in 1976, and is achieved now only by special events such as the Super Bowl. The next challenge was to create a series that would build on that beginning, and bring viewers back every week for new adventures.

One of Spelling's first tasks was to retain John Forsythe, his eleventh-hour substitute Charlie. "I asked what the job would entail, and Aaron said, 'Not too much, because the character is never seen.' So I said I'd do it, but I didn't want any billing," Forsythe recalled. Spelling liked that idea. "That makes it even better, because there will be an air of mystery about it," he said. But the mystery was short-lived—several reviews mentioned Forsythe by name as the voice of Charlie, and viewers figured it out right away. "I guess I have a unique voice, because the whole world knew it was me." he said.

Once a week, for five seasons, Forsythe reported to a small room in what he called "the bowels of 20th Century Fox" and recorded his lines for each episode of *Charlie's Angels*. Most sessions lasted no more than fifteen minutes. If he was working on another project, or in

What Might Have Been

On November 19, 1975, Ivan Goff and Ben Roberts presented ten story ideas for the *Charlie's Angels* series to Aaron Spelling and Leonard Goldberg. These shows developed the style they introduced in the pilot, which presented the Angels in complex, sophisticated con stories. When Spelling-Goldberg opted for a more action-oriented series, Goff and Roberts departed. These story ideas, revealed for the first time, were never used.

"The Champagne Bullet" (Writer: Shimon Wincelberg)
Adopting various identities, the Angels, Woodville, and Bosley board the L.A. to Las Vegas Celebrity Express to protect a man's wife who believes she may be the target of a hired killer.

"The Walls Came Tumbling Down" (Writer: David Harmon)
To prove a reclusive financier guilty of murder, the Angels, Woodville and Bosley establish a publishing firm whose first best-seller promises to be an explosive unauthorized biography of the financier. Any similarity to the Clifford Irving—Howard Hughes affair is, hopefully, intentional.

"The Deep End" (Writer: John Meredyth Lucas)
The Angels and company are hired to find the missing assistant of a shipping tycoon, who may have been kidnapped by rival interests to discover industrial information about his company which only he possesses.

"Original Sin" (Writer: Harold Livingston)
An older woman, a widow, finds when she goes to sell her late husband's favorite painting (in order to keep the business afloat) that it is a forgery. To recover the money from the fraudulent dealer, the Angels and company pose as master forgers and distributors (using Charlie's real paintings as evidence of their counterfeiting skills). They con the dealer into giving them enough money to repay the widow, and at the same time make the venture profitable for the Townsend Agency.

UNTITLED (Writers: Arnold & Lois Peyser)
Someone has tried to kill a J. Paul Getty-like billionaire. He hires Charlie and the Angels to find out who. After thirty five years as a recluse on a mountain top in Switzerland, he announces he is coming home to his family (one of whom he believes to be interested in his premature death). It is Bosley who shows up in Los Angeles as the eccentric, wizened billionaire. Surrounding him are his twenty-five year old intended bride (Kelly), his nurse (Jill), and a Candice Bergen-like photojournalist (Sabrina). Woodville is the officious doctor in attendance. While Bosley staves off attempt after attempt on his life, the Angels try to find the would-be killer.

UNTITLED (Writer: Robert Pirosh)
Someone has stolen four reels of expensive location film from a movie in production. The producer, a friend of Charlie's, is on the brink of financial ruin. The film is impossible to reshoot, and the banks are breathing down his neck. The Angels and company are hired to find out who stole the film and why.

UNTITLED (Writer: Martin Roth)
An aspiring politician (a friend of Charlie's) is being blackmailed. He is afraid to enter an important political race for fear of exposure. The Angels and company go after the blackmailer, convince him that he committed a murder (which in fact never took place) and take over the blackmail evidence as the price of their silence. They discover that the evidence was against the politician's wife all along.

UNTITLED (Writer: Dan Ullman)
Someone believes Hugh Franklin is dead. Someone has every reason to—he ordered the hit, and attended the funeral. But the bullet missed its mark, and Franklin is alive; he staged his death and the funeral to prevent any further attempts. *Charlie's Angels* are hired to find the assassin. They psyche out Franklin's business associates by presenting evidence that he is still alive-or perhaps communicating from the "other side." Bosley, an admitted fraud as a medium, confesses under pressure

that this is the first time he has ever really had any contact with the spirit world. With Franklin's help, the Angels are able to trap the man who wanted Franklin dead.

Untitled (Writer: Shimon Wincelberg)

Someone who's watched too many episodes of *Medical Center* is stalking doctors and patients at a hospital. The Angels and company are hired to find out who's doing what to whom; they go undercover as a nurse (Kelly), a hotshot heart surgeon from Dallas (Sabrina), and an elderly patient (Bosley) and his grasping attorney (Woodville) who lets it be known that he is on the market for someone to knock off his ancient client.

Untitled (Writer: Del Reisman)

Someone seems to have it in for Jack Kent Cooper, sports entrepreneur and manager of super athletes. The Angels, deftly manipulated by that noted puppeteer and director, Charlie, arrive on the scene as a group making a documentary for ABC called "A Day in the Life of Jack Kent Cooper." There may be no film in the camera, but that puts no damper on the uninhibited behavior of the superstars of sport, stage and screen who show up for the filming at the Cooper Estate. Before the Angels are through, their cameras and sound equipment have brought down a would-be assassin. ◣

Europe as he was on one occasion, the studio sent him his lines with a tape recorder, and he would perform them and send the recorder back. "It wasn't much of an assignment, but I enjoyed it," said Forsythe.

Charlie's face never appeared on camera, though the idea was broached several times. "I told them, "This is such a good idea this way. Why would you want to put me on camera? If you use my body, it will cost you a lot more money!" he recalls, laughing. "I was doing *Dynasty* and a lot of other things back then, and I really didn't want to get involved with *Charlie's Angels* beyond that level."

Instead, the producers used various stand-ins for the teasing glimpses of Charlie during the briefing scenes that opened most episodes. David Doyle's stand-in, Rick Warwick, was a frequent choice early in the series run. In later seasons, a production assistant played the role, and signed a document promising to never reveal his identity. But the majority of Charlie's on-screen appearances were performed by E. Duke Vincent, a friend of Spelling's who was asked to do the role by Angels producer Barney Rosenzweig. "I thought he had a great head of hair," said Rosenzweig, explaining his hiring criteria. Vincent later became a producer on Spelling's series *VEGA$* (1978-1981), and the executive producer of *Beverly Hills 90210* and *Melrose Place*.

But while John Forsythe was happy to continue his association with the Angels, the two men who wrote the series pilot wanted nothing more to do with the heavenly trio. "Aaron changed the whole concept from a classy con show to three girls out of the police academy, with lots of tits and ass," said Ivan Goff's son, Kevin. "My father and Ben (Roberts) cared about their writing, and didn't want to be involved in that kind of show."

"I was very disappointed that they didn't stay," said Jaclyn Smith. "They had that whole con thing down, and added flair to the story. The other writers that came in were all very talented and nice to work with, but sometimes the original writers have the pulse of the material."

Ivan Goff and Ben Roberts accepted an offer to work on a new pilot for their old friend from *Mannix*, Mike Connors. They left *Charlie's Angels*, retaining their 12.5% ownership of the series, with no regrets. "They had a deal that allowed them to walk away, but if the show was a success they were supposed to be a success along with it," said Kevin Goff. A dispute over royalties erupted three years later (see Chapter 6).

The Mike Connors pilot flopped, and Goff and Roberts signed on as producers of *Logan's Run*, a television adaptation of the hit 1976 science-fiction film starring Michael York, Jenny Agutter, and Farrah Fawcett-Majors. Gregory Harrison and Heather Menzies played the leads in the series, which lasted only one season.

Charlie's Angels would have required several different writers even if Goff and Roberts had remained. Scripts were solicited from veteran TV scribes, many of whom had worked for Spelling-Goldberg on *The Rookies*. Rick Husky, who wrote or cowrote four first-season shows, also

WRITERS' GUIDELINES FOR "CHARLIE'S ANGELS"

Following are some definitive guidelines:

1. "Charlie's Angels" is a detective show in the classic tradition, but with a new twist; the investigators are three beautiful girls who are bright, athletic and have been trained in police work. The girls will work undercover for their employer, Charlie (whom we never see), on cases that will stress action, adventure and suspense. What we have is Angie Dickinson times _three_.

2. "The Rockford Files" is an example of the type of show we will be doing; i.e., a realistic private eye series with humor.

3. The Angels' "client" in each case must be a sympathetic person whom the audience will root for.

4. The stories must have twists and double-twists in their plot development. We must have _story_ _surprises_ for the audience.

5. We must place the Angels in _personal jeopardy_ each week. It is essential that each of the girls be in jeopardy at least once during every episode.

6. Charlie's office, and the Angels' base of operations, is in Los Angeles. But the locale and settings of our stories must be glamorous, upbeat and colorful. We must avoid the inner-city, precinct look. Like-wise, our guest characters must be colorful, unique, and as glamorous as possible.

    At the same time, we must not deal exclusively with the world of international society and heavy money — or we will be dealing way over the heads of the average television viewing audience and they will be unable to relate to our series.

7. Humor must be a part of every story. The audience likes to laugh; particularly when they're laughing _with_ our people - _at_ the weekly heavies.

    One caution with regard to this element of humor; the humor must come from realistic situations; the heavies must always be real, dangerous, and not comedic. Once again, "The Rockford Files" is an example of the style of humor we want to achieve.

WRITERS' GUIDELINES FOR "CHARLIE'S ANGELS"

8. Insofar as our Angels are concerned, they are the
    three most beautiful girls on television and we
    must afford them an opportunity to display their
    assets each week.

    The audience also enjoys seeing our Angels dressing
    up and playing other parts - particularly when
    they're contrary to their real personalities (i.e.,
    the mousy secretary; the hillbilly, etc.).

9. We should try to develop the individual character
    of our Angels a bit more each week. Get to know
    about their backstories and their current life
    away from the job.

10. We must also include in each episode at least one
    "interplay" scene with our Angels.

11. The Angels, like all private investigators, will
    on occasion be covering the same ground as the
    local police. Good conflict, in the classic
    private eye tradition, would be to pit the Angels
    against both the heavies and a noncooperative
    local police. This to be used when it helps the
    story; also, there is nothing wrong with having
    the Angels work with the police when needed.
    Remember, they all are former police officers
    themselves, and Sabrina is divorced from but still
    seeing her ex, an L.A.P.D. detective.

12. The character of Bosley is to be used whenever
    needed; however, we must remember that it is the
    Angels' show. They are capable of doing practically
    everything a man can do (and more), and each episode
    should spotlight them. Bosley is a supporting
    player and should be written as such; again, to be
    used when needed.

ADDITIONAL NOTES TO WRITERS

1. The pilot you have seen does not reflect the style of
    show we want to do. We want more action and adventure
    than there was in the pilot, plus more character from
    the girls.

2. The sample script you have received does reflect the
    type of series we will be doing; however, this script
    will also be rewritten to add more character for each
    of the Angels per the short character sketches which
    follow this page.

3. Stories can be open or closed. We want to go mostly
    with straight private investigation stories; however,
    an occasional "con" story, if it's unique, will be
    used.

SABRINA DUNCAN (KATE JACKSON)

SABRINA looks like an angel, and is. Tall, lean of limb, with a today sense of humor, her glance is level, her manner clear-headed. An "army brat", educated in Europe where she grew up around military bases, she speaks five languages fluently, and is bright enough to match wits with any adversary. There is imagination in everything she does. And she has that rare ability to be good at anything she tries.

Sabrina can disarm a heavy with her charm or a skilled karate chop. Of the three Angels, she would be considered the intellect (though they are all bright women of today), and the more pragmatic and coolly analytical of the trio in the face of danger (which is often). She's the Angels' unofficial leader. The one who would be the calm in the eye of a storm, and make the final decision if there was conflict among the three.

A private person off the job, Sabrina lives in a high-rise security building. While available for dates with eligible males (her standards are high), there is only one special man in her life: her ex-husband, a plainclothes detective on the L.A.P.D. They went through the Academy together, fell in love, got married, found that two cops in the same household didn't work; but their relationship now is better than it's ever been. When questioned by the other Angels as to why she and her ex don't remarry, Sabrina's answer is the inevitable: "Why spoil a good thing?"

JILL MUNROE (FARRAH FAWCETT-MAJORS)

A California girl with covergirl looks, JILL is gorgeous, open, warm, romantic, a bit kookie. She wears her heart on her sleeve, and since her heart beats within a lovely bosom, men all over the place are eager to be the recipients of those ready emotions.

The most naturally athletic of the trio (though they are all athletic), Jill is dynamite on a tennis court, in a bikini, or scaling the side of a six-story building. And that athletic ability she readily admits has been inherited from a sports crazy family; a mother who was a tennis pro; a father who played minor league baseball. The odds on tomorrow's game, the Super Bowl, the World Series? Jill is Jimmy-the-Greek with curves, is a veritable encyclopedia of sports knowledge and trivia, and has been known to pause in the midst of a hectic investigation to place a wager on a longshot at Santa Anita (with invariably good results).

Jill has a small house at the beach, leads an outdoor life off the job, is devoted to her family, and digs country-and-western music. Her relations with the opposite sex are active, California free, with her love of men equal to their love of her. Marriage? When the right man comes along, according to Jill. But not right now. She's having too much fun.

KELLY GARRETT (JACLYN SMITH)

KELLY is radiantly beautiful, silkily sophisticated on the outside but the most sensitive of the trio on the inside. Born and raised in Houston, Texas, and a touch of that Texas drawl still peeks through now and then. While her past is not as shrouded in mystery as that of her boss, Charlie, there does seem to be more to Kelly than meets the eye; something deeper, hurt from the past, that makes her react more emotionally to situations than the other girls. A model for Kelly's character might be the Peggy Lipton characterization of "Julie" in "Mod Squad".

Of the three Angels, Kelly would be the more cynical. She's not hard, but she's streetwise. Orphaned early in life, she's been around, worked as a stewardess, a cocktail waitress in Las Vegas, etc. Kelly thinks twice about everything she does, and, since she's heard every "line" invented, she's not quick to accept anything on face value. Also, she's the most adept at self-defense and an expert on the police pistol range. Anyone who's tried to tangle with her has quickly discovered those curves are dangerous.

Kelly lives in a small canyon house with a large standard poodle named Albert, who thinks he's a German shepherd. She's crazy about animals, is a mother to every stray pet imaginable, and collects them like some women collect clothes.

JOHN BOSLEY (DAVID DOYLE)

BOSLEY is fiftyish, cheerful, round-faced, with a dryly devastating sense of humor. He's the middle-man between Charlie and the Angels, is their contact in each episode, and should be used whenever needed -- but never in a situation one of the Angels can handle themselves, or in a situation that would overshadow any of the girls dramatically.

Somewhat of a bumbler, Bosley might occasionally (but inadvertently) blow a cover, a clue, etc., to cause the Angels further danger on a case.

And, no matter what, Bosley always wants to ingratiate himself to the Boss, Charlie.

became the series' first producer. "There was nothing like it on TV, and I knew it was going to be a smash hit," he said. But Husky was hesitant when Aaron asked him to produce. "I had done *The Mod Squad* and *The Rookies*, both of which were more reality-based shows; *Angels* seemed lighter than what I wanted to do. But I was going with Jaclyn at the time, so I made a deal to do ten episodes and get the show started, while they had time to find another producer." The couple split shortly before filming began. "It could have been hell under different circumstances," said Husky, "but it was amicable and we were able to work together."

After viewing the pilot, Husky saw no reason for Charlie to have two male liaisons. At his suggestion, David Doyle was retained as Bosley, over David Ogden Stiers. "Having been a director and cast a lot of people myself, I figured that Stiers' character was a little severe, while Bosley was a guy they could have fun with," said Doyle. One year later, David Ogden Stiers began a successful six-year stint as Major Charles Winchester on *MASH* (1972-1983).

Another goal of Husky's was to develop the characters of the Angels in a way that would make them less interchangeable, echoing an observation made by the pilot's test audience. "I talked to each of the girls about their characters, and they all had ideas," he recalled. "In the pilot Kelly was more of a hustler—we decided to soften her and treat her more like a lady. Kate as the smart Angel was easy to come by; she's a very bright lady. Farrah was the California golden girl; we knew she was athletic, and worked that in when we could."

"I tried to play Kelly as very sensitive and tenderhearted. I found her to be the most gentle of the three," said Jaclyn Smith. Over the course of five years, Kelly Garrett became the Angel with the most detailed history. Viewers discovered that she was an orphan, who had a difficult upbringing. An early draft of her biography hinted that she may have done a little street hustling to survive, but Smith vetoed the suggestion.

"You've got to have bits of yourself in a character if you're going to play it for five years, and I didn't think (that) was in my demeanor. I didn't mind being an orphan, and having a rough background—that gave Kelly the sensitivity to reach out to people in trouble. I could relate to that, but (hustling) I didn't find as believable," she explains.

The office of Townsend Investigations, where Charlie briefed
the Angels and Bosley on each new case.

"He was originally more of a nerd," said David Doyle of John
Bosley. "Once we started filming the episodes, the actors have more of a
say in how their character is played. He was still comic relief, but not
broad and foolish. I didn't want him to get trapped behind the desk, and
that didn't happen. He was like an uncle to the girls—he liked his job
because of the adventure, but had no aspirations of running the show."

Husky wrote a set of writer's guidelines that included character
sketches of all three Angels and Bosley. They are reproduced on pages
34-40 by permission.

However, the extent to which Husky's guidelines were followed is
debatable, especially after his departure. True to his word, he produced
the first six shows, then turned the job over to David Levinson. Levinson

lasted only four episodes, but during his short tenure he made an invaluable contribution to the series by hiring Les Carter, a California disc jockey and freelance magazine writer. Though Carter had no prior television experience, he wrote two of the series' most memorable episodes, "Consenting Adults" (#10) and "Dancing in the Dark" (#19).

"To be honest, after I watched the pilot I thought it was unlikely that the show would ever get on the air," Carter said. "It seemed fairly primitive, and I didn't think Jaclyn or Farrah were much in the acting department, though both have come a long way since."

Still, he was grateful for the opportunity, and worked night and day to turn in his first script. "I used to call it 'Huey, Dewey and Louie' dialogue, after the nephews of Donald Duck," Carter said. "If you recall, Huey would start a sentence, Dewey would come in in the middle, and Louie would finish; so you'd have dialogue in *Angels* where one would say, 'Who is that?' and the second Angel would say, 'It looks like the bad guys!' and the third would say, 'and they're headed in our direction!' There were a lot of scenes like that.

"One rule that was passed down to me by Levinson, though I don't remember it being written down, was that it's a lot more fun when the Angels are in danger, and being pursued, than when they're on top of the situation, and doing the pursuing." With that in mind, Carter crafted the series' most famous chase scene, in which Jill hopped on a skateboard and surfed the paths of Los Angeles's Griffith Park, while being chased by an ice cream truck ("Consenting Adults"—#10).

Levinson's replacement was Barney Rosenzweig, who had previously worked for Spelling-Goldberg as producer of the TV movie *One of My Wives is Missing* (1976). When he was twenty-nine, Rosenzweig became the youngest series producer in the business, turning out seventy-six episodes of the frontier drama *Daniel Boone* (1964-1970). After Husky was hired as the Angels' producer, his first call was to Barney, who had hired him as a writer on *Daniel Boone*. "He called me and said 'I beat you out of this job, and I feel terrible about it, but I'm just going to start them off and then I'm out of here,'" recalled Rosenzweig, who expected a call from Aaron Spelling after his protegé's departure.

When David Levinson got the call instead, Rosenzweig enlisted his agent in a campaign to make sure that his was the next name on the list of prospects. "What's the big deal?" the agent asked. "It's just another series." But Rosenzweig knew the show was going to be a hit, and he was delighted that a series featuring female leads would make the concept more viable to network executives. Tucked away in his briefcase was an unfinished script for a show called *Cagney and Lacey*, about two lady cops in New York City. "If (*Angels*) is a hit, and I'm connected to it, there may be a groundswell of interest in doing shows about women, and I've got one," he told his agent.

Three producers in one season is never a good sign, and when Rosenzweig became the latest through the revolving door, he found a series in turmoil, and the first episode hadn't even aired yet. "Nobody quite knew what they had on their hands," said Les Carter. "Some creative forces thought the show was almost a comedy, and should be written tongue-in-cheek, and I was certainly of that school. Other people took it seriously, and made the show more of a procedural police story."

"We didn't know what we were doing,"confessed story editor Edward J. Lakso, who later became the series' fourth producer. The series 'bible' prepared by Rick Husky had already been abandoned. "I never saw it," said Lakso. "When I started they gave me a one-line description of each character, and we winged it for the first few months. You could hand any girl any line."

Rosenzweig watched the first three episodes in a projection room on the Fox lot, before being ushered into Aaron Spelling's office for a meeting. "Yes, Fred. I know, Fred, it's awful. We all agree, it's awful," said Spelling in a phone conversation with Fred Pierce. "They all thought it was a piece of shit," Rosenzweig recalled. "I told them it's not, because the girls are wonderful. They just had some storytelling problems."

His first suggestion was to change the pattern of the show. "The first episodes opened with a crime, or an action scene. Then we'd go to Charlie's office, and Charlie would begin his briefing—'Okay, Angels, this is the bad guy, this is the good guy, this is the client, this is what you're supposed to do. Go get 'em, Angels!' I said to Aaron, 'You're violating some of the major traditions of the private eye genre!"

Quoting everyone from Raymond Chandler to Dashiell Hammett, Rosenzweig asserted that the client should be one of the most interesting characters in the drama. Since most of the clients in the early episodes were associates of Charlie, the audience never met them, and neither did the Angels. "They're like hookers," Rosenzweig told his boss. "They're hired, they do whatever they're told to do, but they have no direct sympathetic feelings toward the caper. It weakens them, because they should have some ideas of their own."

"Do whatever you need to do," Spelling said, "because the show's a disaster."

Rosenzweig made certain that, after the opening action scene, the next scene featured the Angels meeting their client; Sabrina, who developed into the field leader, would sometimes present the case to Charlie, instead of the other way around. "Now they were no longer just bimbos. Charlie was the guy sitting by the pool with models, and the Angels did the brain work. That was a very substantial change in the way the show was presented."

A renewed sense of confidence developed on the set and in the corporate offices; maybe *Charlie's Angels* wouldn't be so bad after all. "Ed Lakso came to work for me as head story guy, and we had a great time spitballing stories," said Rosenzweig. "And Spelling and Goldberg were very happy. We'd get fabulous memos from Leonard Goldberg raving about the scripts, and the direction that the show was going."

And then, just as the first Rosenzweig-produced show began filming, the debut episode of *Charlie's Angels*, "Hellride," was broadcast on September 22, 1976. The plot had the Angels investigating the suspicious death of a female stock car driver, with Sabrina going undercover on the racing circuit to trap the killer.

The reviews were exactly what Spelling-Goldberg expected. "Is any of this believable? Not remotely, and the acting (ranges) from adequate to preposterous . . . Kate Jackson's character is supposed to be the intellectual of the group, which means, I guess, that she can count to ten without taking off her shoes."(*TV Guide*); "one of the most misogynist shows the networks have produced recently."(Judith Coburn); "the dialogue stretches credibility to a transparent sheer for the most part, the

Waiting between takes on "Angels in Chains," the series' most infamous episode.
Note the perfect manicure on prison inmate Jill Munroe (Farrah Fawcett).

acting is on the level of a high school play." (*Seattle Post-Intelligencer*); "If there were a law against bad taste, *Charlie's Angels* would be sentenced to life in prison." (*Dayton Daily News*).

The *Los Angeles Times* offered a mixed assessment, calling the plots "mundane," but praising the Angels as "independent, intelligent, resourceful, and brave." The *Times* was one of the first to observe that the series might appeal to women as well as men, because "the leading characters clearly have more going for them than the way they look." That was as close to a thumbs-up as the series got.

It didn't matter. *Charlie's Angels* exploded out of the gate, finishing eighth in the ratings with a whopping 45 share. "The numbers were so big that people thought it was a mistake," said Rosenzweig. The following week, they went up. "Hey, let's not make this show too good!" Spelling said to his new producer. It sounded like a remark made in jest, but Rosenzweig knew he was serious.

Concerns over the dramatic pattern of each show instantly disappeared. In fact, they now seemed silly. *Charlie's Angels* debuted as a hit and evolved into a phenomenon while other new fall series were still trying to find an audience. One month after "Hellride" aired, a poll conducted by ABC found that 92 percent of those surveyed had seen *Charlie's Angels*. Sixty-two percent of male viewers and a surprising 68 percent of female viewers named the series as their favorite show. No one complained about its story structure or its adherence to the traditions of the detective genre.

"The philosophy became, 'Stop improving the show.' All people care about is seeing tits and ass," said Rosenzweig. "That was devastating—I was no longer in this atmosphere of doing what I thought was right, and taking a little extra time and effort to make the characters more interesting or credible. Suddenly it became 'Is Farrah wearing a bra in this scene or not?' For me, it got to be a very unhappy place to work."

Rosenzweig's relationship with Spelling-Goldberg deteriorated rapidly. He urged them to follow through on the format changes they discussed. "I kept saying, 'Look, guys, this show is a success despite the fact that it's awful, not *because* it's awful!'" But unprecedented ratings numbers and eighteen thousand fan letters every week drained the potency from his argument.

"The show is not just a winner but a certifiable phenomenon," observed *Time* magazine, which put the Angels on the cover of its November 22, 1976 issue. "Seldom has a brand-new entry broken into Nielsen's top ten in its first week and then stayed there, steadily improving its position with each subsequent airing." Every Wednesday night at 10 p.m., nearly 60 percent of television sets in use were tuned to ABC. *Charlie's Angels* ranked fourth among all programs in metropolitan areas, seventh among college graduates, and first with adult viewers across the board—"which may or may not say something about the state of adulthood in the U.S. these days," quipped *Time*.

"I was amazed by the instant popularity," said David Doyle. "We'd go out to shoot on location and so many people would show up that we couldn't move. I had never experienced that kind of rush of enthusiasm from viewers. It was wonderful!"

Sound Stage 8 on the 20th Century Fox lot also became a daily mob scene. "Everyone in the world wanted to come over and see the girls," said Spelling. Photo shoots and interviews began cutting into the work schedule, and by the halfway point of the first season it became nearly impossible to finish an episode in the allotted six days. After episode 17, Spelling ordered the set closed to the press and all visitors. It remained closed for the remainder of the series run.

The immediate impact of the Angels on the popular culture is hard to imagine now, when cable TV and satellite systems have drastically reduced the size of network audiences. Even *Seinfeld*, the most popular series of the last ten years, averaged ratings numbers that were only half of those drawn by *Charlie's Angels*. "The overnight popularity was mind-boggling," remembers Jaclyn Smith. "I was just happy to be working in a situation that was fun, with a group of people I really liked. No one expected it to take off the way it did."

Throughout the fall of 1976 and the spring of 1977, magazines and newspapers were awash in stories about Kate, Farrah, and Jaclyn, the country's new "it" girls. Dozens of articles were devoted to their hair, makeup, and fashion tips. For the record, Kate recommended olive oil as a conditioner, and running an ice cube lightly across the face once a week. Jaclyn advised getting eight hours of sleep every night, and wearing no makeup on weekends, to allow the skin to "breathe." Farrah liked to use vaseline on her eyelashes to keep them shiny.

A burgeoning merchandise business put the Angels' faces on lunchboxes, posters, trading cards, and T-shirts. At one time, three different toy companies were producing Angel dolls simultaneously. (See Appendix C)

"We were like rock stars—we couldn't go anywhere," recalls Jaclyn Smith. "Our lives really changed—career-wise for the better, but personally it was sometimes hard. We were pressured to do too much sometimes, but the fans were so enthusiastic that you couldn't not appreciate them."

"We were told that the number of letters the show received was more than Mickey Rooney, Judy Garland, and all the stars at MGM received in their heyday," said Brett Garwood, an executive coordinator for Spelling-Goldberg. "The first year of *Angels*, we spent $250,000 just to answer mail! Every week we would get five or six large canvas mailbags with letters from all over the world."

In an otherwise negative review of the series, syndicated columnist Lee Winfrey confessed that he couldn't resist watching anyway. "I doubt there has ever been another TV series that displayed, as regular cast members, three women of such stupefying beauty," he gushed.

Other reviews bemoaned the series' lack of any intellectual or emotional depth, and depicted the Angels as poster girls for the exploitation of women in television. The criticism reached its zenith after the airing of episode 4, "Angels in Chains," in which the Angels went undercover in a women's prison. *Time* described several scenes, including one in which the Angels were stripped and fumigated by a sadistic matron, as "family-style porn."

"Big deal. It was so mild," responds Jaclyn Smith. "We liked that show—being chained together and running around. It was fun! There was so much media hype at the time, and the series was being overanalyzed. I'm a conservative girl—if I thought I was doing something that was inappropriate, I wouldn't have done it."

To Spelling-Goldberg, any publicity was good publicity. Instead of denying the charges, they gleefully turned up the heat. "We love to get them wet, because they look so good in clinging clothes," Goldberg confessed to *Time*.

"Leonard would come up with these sexist jokes he wanted to add, and it got to the point where Kate Jackson said, 'I won't say that line,' recalled Barney Rosenzweig. "It's not just boys—girls are watching, women are watching. I've read the mail! I've got three daughters that love the show!" he told Spelling-Goldberg. "These women are role models, and you are insulting over half your audience with these lame sexist jokes!"

Despite its racy reputation, the show was never as scandalous as it was portrayed. Farrah Fawcett never wore a bikini during her season as an Angel, and Kate Jackson never wore a swimsuit in any episode.

"These were clean, straight-arrow girls. They never slept with anybody—they never even had boyfriends!" argues Ed Lakso.

Obviously, the Angels relied on their looks more than their intellect in solving a case. They realized that most guys turn into morons when approached by a beautiful woman, and used the edge provided by their beauty to gather information and catch suspects off-guard. It's a viable, proven formula that has worked in numerous TV series, and in movies from *Double Indemnity* (1944) to *Basic Instinct* (1992).

But Dante J. Francis, a real-life criminal investigator, complained that Sabrina, Jill, and Kelly didn't really act like detectives. He called the Angels "Three female clowns in bikinis." Aaron Spelling's response was quoted in dozens of articles about *Charlie's Angels*; "Anyone who thinks these girls are really private eyes is nuts!"

Much to Barney Rosenzweig's chagrin, Spelling embraced the derision. Pleasing the public was his only goal, and he didn't care if they were laughing with him or at him, as long they tuned in every week. When *TV Guide* penned a typically sarcastic article entitled "Stop the Chase—It's Time for My Comb-Out," Spelling proudly admitted that much of the series' $345,000 per-episode budget was devoted to making the Angels look gorgeous. "On this show we're more concerned with hairdos and gowns than the twists and turns of the plots," he said.

The ABC network had no complaints either. With *Charlie's Angels* in 23 million households on Wednesday nights, and another Tuesday night powerhouse in *Happy Days* and *Laverne and Shirley*, the network vaulted from third to first in the ratings.

Success, however, could not resolve the tensions on the *Angels* set, involving the cast and the creative personnel. The press fueled the sexist stereotype that three women working together had to be a volatile situation, and the Angels' coexistence became another national obsession. Among the headlines of the day: "How the Angels *really* get along"; "We don't hate each other!"; "What the Angels are like without their halos!"; "These Angels were made in Hollywood, not in Heaven!"; "*Charlie's Angels* stars at each others' throats!"; "Angels in name only!", and "*Charlie's Angels*—is three a crowd?" A series featuring three male leads would never inspire such scrutiny.

"The only time we have any conflict is when we knock each other down racing for the doughnut wagon," Farrah told one reporter. But the situation was not quite so benign. "On the Richter scale of 1 to 10, I'd give it a 7," Spelling candidly admitted to *TV Guide*.

Much of the tension emanated from Kate Jackson, whose initial enthusiasm for the series had quickly dissipated. Though she was fond of her costars and just as taken aback by the series' success, Jackson was already an established television star who didn't have as much to prove as Farrah and Jaclyn. When *Time* magazine sent a photographer to shoot the cover for the magazine, Jackson locked herself in her motor home. "She refused to give up her lunch hour," said Smith.

"I liked her a lot, though she was the most difficult and the most troubled," said Barney Rosenzweig. "At the time she was unhappy, and that kind of celebrity always exacerbates those problems." Stories of Kate's dissatisfaction with the scripts were well-known in the TV community, but on the set she had as many defenders as detractors. "Kate was always into making each script and her performance the best they could be in the confines of the premise. She strived to make things better, and I didn't disagree with her," said Rick Husky. "She never complained to me, and if she did I probably would have commiserated with her. There were times I felt the characters *should* be a little smarter."

"When I met Kate for the first time, my reaction was, 'I'm gonna fire the cinematographer.' She was gorgeous, and she didn't look gorgeous on the show," recalls Rosenzweig. Then I found out why—she didn't want to go in the same direction as the other women. She didn't want to be all about hair and makeup. She was the actress—the other two were models."

Rosenzweig's defense of Jackson was emblematic of his fondness for all three girls. "Jackie couldn't be nicer—a very sweet girl. Farrah was my favorite—I was a little smitten with her," he admits. "Beyond being a charismatic person who lit up the screen, she was a lot more talented than anyone was giving her credit for. To my surprise, Farrah was a very good comedienne, and Ed Lakso and I began playing to that."

However, his relationship with Spelling-Goldberg, particularly Leonard Goldberg, had grown more contentious. Goldberg's "If it ain't broke, don't fix it" philosophy remained at odds with Rosenzweig's desire to add credibility to the series. Tempers flared on both sides, and finally exploded during production of episode 15, "Angels on a String."

The climax of the show featured a car chase on a mountain road, and Goldberg asked that Jill's white Cobra be used in the scene. Rosenzweig complied, until a stuntman told him they couldn't risk any damage to the car, as there was no double for the Cobra on the 20th Century Fox lot. The nearest one was in San Francisco. "I said fine, Leonard wants it, so get it from San Francisco." Before the call could be made, Rosenzweig was told by the episode's director, Larry Doheny, that the Cobra wouldn't work anyway. "We've got one girl in back, two girls in front, and nowhere to put the camera—the car's too small!" Doheny requested that Kelly's car be used instead, and Rosenzweig approved the change.

"We're watching the dailies (footage shot that day), and the scene comes on, and Leonard goes crazy," recalls Rosenzweig. "The man broke the door of the screening room. After rejecting his sexist jokes, and resisting his orders not to play with the show's formula, I defied his order. I apologized and explained the situation, but it didn't matter. He fired me."

Aaron Spelling urged Rosenzweig to apologize again. Goldberg refused to meet with the producer for two days, but he accepted the apology and Rosenzweig was back on the payroll, until Goldberg saw the chase scene in the finished episode. "The next time he saw the show, which was a darn good little picture as I recall, he went crazy again! He couldn't get over it, and our relationship was never the same after that."

Rosenzweig's contract ended when the first season was complete, and he was not asked to return. "Leonard had read *Cagney and Lacey* and was interested in coproducing it with me as a theatrical motion picture, but I called my agent and told him to break off the negotiations, because I had no desire to work with him again," Rosenzweig said. "To this day we do not speak."

The first season of *Charlaie's Angels* ended as it had begun, with the series firmly entrenched in the top ten, adored by millions of fans, and loathed by critics and assorted *intelligentsia*. To the surprise of many, both Kate Jackson and David Doyle received Emmy nominations in 1976 for their stellar work on the series. Jackson lost to Lindsay Wagner, star of *The Bionic Woman*, and Doyle was edged out in the Best Supporting Actor race by Gary Frank, from the Spelling-Goldberg series *Family*.

The face of the 1970s: Farrah Fawcett-Majors.

CHAPTER THREE

The Farrah Phenomenon

I N MAY OF 1976, TED TRIKILIS WAS PLANTING TREES ON HIS FARM IN Medina, Ohio, a welcome diversion from his duties as President of the Pro Arts poster company. His neighbor, a college student, dropped by for a visit, and during the conversation he suggested that Trikilis do a poster of Farrah Fawcett-Majors. "The guys at my dorm buy magazines just to clip out her picture," he said.

Trikilis was vaguely familiar with the name—wasn't Farrah one of the stars of that *Charlie's Angels* movie that was being turned into a TV series? If the show becomes as popular as the movie, a poster of the lovely blond Angel might be a good idea.

Farrah accepted the offer to shoot a poster, but dismissed the request that she pose wearing a bikini, while peering seductively from behind a tree. Instead, she followed her own instinct and hired her own photographer, a fellow Texan named Bruce McBroom. Together, they settled on a red one-piece bathing suit, and on doing the photographs around the pool of the Bel Air mansion Farrah shared with her husband, Lee Majors. The session lasted about 90 minutes.

The image selected for the poster was sexy but not nearly as revealing as other cheesecake posters of the day. Farrah appeared in profile, her head tilted slightly back, her smile wide and radiant. The red swimsuit was wet and clinging, but her hair was dry, as requested by Pro Arts, who wanted her cascading mane of blond curls displayed in full bloom. Released in July, two months after Trikilis first heard of Farrah's dormroom popularity, the poster sold well initially. Two months later, after *Charlie's Angels* aired its first episode, retailers couldn't order enough copies to meet the demand.

"When the poster came out, there was just an explosion around Farrah," recalls Rick Husky. "After two episodes of the show had been filmed, Farrah wanted to change her hairstyle. I remember begging her—'Please! Let's do a few more episodes first!'"

Farrah's image graced T-shirts, beanbag chairs, beach towels, pillows and rugs. She topped a *Scholastic Magazine* poll of high school students in a ranking of personal heroes (President Jimmy Carter finished 16th). One entrepreneur even offered her $5 million to bottle water from her kitchen. Her face became so ubiquitous on the pop culture landscape that the June 10, 1977 issue of *New Times* magazine actually ran as its cover headline: "Absolutely nothing in this issue about Farrah Fawcett-Majors."

What was it about Farrah that captivated America? That she was beautiful was obvious; but television in the late 1970s was already a girl-watcher's dream with weekly appearances from Angie Dickinson (*Police Woman*), Lindsay Wagner (*The Bionic Woman*), Lynda Carter (*Wonder Woman*), Suzanne Somers (*Three's Company*), and Farrah's fellow Angels, Jaclyn Smith and Kate Jackson. But Farrah was clearly the girl with something extra, a sex symbol comparable only to Marilyn Monroe in global impact.

"She has enviable cheekbones, green eyes bright with innocent provocation and beguiling enthusiasm, a dentally perfect smile of almost incandescent brilliance, and an identifying mane of long and carefully tousled hair that somehow manages to look sunstruck and breeze-blown even in the still, stale air of a sound stage," swooned film critic Charles Champlin.

"Farrah is a strange combination of the virginal girl-next-door and a vamp, a cross between a Madonna and a Delilah," said Ray W. Browne, a professor of popular culture at Bowling Green State University who spent months researching the phenomenon. "Whenever she flashes that smile, it's almost as if she's saying she has the world by the tail and is enjoying it."

Farrah always downplayed her appearance, and professed not to understand why she had become so beloved. "Why is my mouth so big and why do I have so many teeth?" she said. "I thought Marilyn Monroe was the most beautiful woman in the world. Elizabeth Taylor the most breathtaking. When I look at myself I say 'Oh shoot! What are they all talking about?'"

The ABC publicity department was deluged with requests for Farrah interviews from across America, and from European countries where *Charlie's Angels* had yet to debut. *People* magazine ranked Farrah as one of its "Personalities of the Year" in 1976. By the summer of 1977, her poster had sold an astonishing eight million copies, four times the number of the previous record-holder, Fonzie from *Happy Days*.

Spelling and Goldberg looked forward to riding the wave of Farrah-mania into the second season of *Charlie's Angels*. But that wave crashed on March 7, 1977, when Farrah announced she would not be returning to the show. "It was clear that she had a lot of other things she wanted to do, and a lot of people pulling at her," said Barney Rosenzweig. "I advised her against breaking away from the show. The job was a good job, and a contract is a contract."

Farrah, however, maintained that she didn't have a contract. "At that time the deal had not been closed," said Jay Bernstein, her personal publicist in the 1970s. "There were still things being negotiated in regards to merchandising and a couple of other points. And they were in no rush to close it because no one thought this was going to happen."

Aaron Spelling first learned of Farrah's intentions on the night of the 1977 People's Choice Awards. Farrah was there to receive the "Best Female Newcomer" award, and to honor *Charlie's Angels*' selection as Favorite Television Drama. She was seated at a table with her husband, Lee Majors, Kate Jackson, Jay Bernstein, and Aaron and Candy Spelling.

Farrah's husband, Lee Majors, helped sway her decision to leave *Charlie's Angels*.

"Aaron had gotten up, and Farrah was away from the table, and Candy started mentioning all the fun things Aaron had in mind for the Angels," Bernstein recalls. "That's when Lee first said 'Farrah's not going back to *Charlie's Angels*.' Then he got up from the table and left. We assumed he was kidding—he had had a few beers, and wasn't in a good mood."

The next day, Bernstein called the Majors home and discovered that Lee was serious. "This family makes $55,000 a week, and I make $50,000 of it," said Lee, referring to his salary as star of *The Six Million Dollar Man* (1974-1978). "Farrah makes $5,000 a week and when I get up in the morning she's already gone. When I get home she's still not back."

"Farrah was not unhappy with the series," Bernstein believes. "It wasn't about her being unhappy, it was about Lee being unhappy. And her marriage was more important to her than doing *Charlie's Angels*." Spelling-Goldberg offered to raise their golden girl's salary, but Farrah's counter-offer left little doubt that she had no intention of returning. According to the *New York Post*, she asked for $70,000 a week, and a six-hour-a-day shooting schedule. Neither request was practical; with Jaclyn Smith making $5,000 per episode, and Kate Jackson making $10,000 per show, a raise for Farrah would have necessitated raises for everyone. And 14 hour days are necessary to complete a one-hour episode of dramatic television in eight days. Limiting Farrah's schedule would inevitably have reduced her screen time, which didn't make sense.

The reactions among the series' cast and crew to Farrah Fawcett-Majors' announced departure ranged from reluctant acceptance to intense panic. "I was sad about it, because we had a great chemistry. The success of that first year came from the fact that we all liked each other—there was an ease we had together that showed up on screen," said Jaclyn Smith. "I thought it was a mistake—if you sign a contract you carry it through. But you can't make somebody do what they don't want to do."

"She said to me, I hope this doesn't make you angry," recalled David Doyle. "I said 'Farrah, if you leave, and the show continues, I wish you all the luck in the world. But if you leave and the show goes in the toilet, I'll seriously consider burning your house down.' Then I went home and called the bank to check on my account balance."

The crisis landed on the desk of Ed Lakso, who had been promoted after the departure of Barney Rosenzweig. He was already the series' preeminent scriptwriter, and would remain so for the next four seasons. Lakso's reputation for quality at unbelievable speed began with his first professional writing assignment in 1959, a screenplay for the Korean War drama *Operation Dames*. After he was hired, he went home, borrowed a typewriter, and finished the script in one night.

By the time he joined *Charlie's Angels*, Lakso had written more than 100 hours of television, for such series as *Combat*, *Star Trek*, *The Rookies*, and *Starsky and Hutch*. He could write an *Angels* script in three days, which he often did between races during his frequent visits to the Santa Anita and Hollywood Park racetracks.

With the new season set to begin, Lakso was growing weary of the demands of Farrah's agent, Jay Bernstein, and was ready to move on. "Jay kept saying that she deserved more money, because she was really the star of the show, and that she was going to be a major motion picture star. I knew a lot of TV stars who were going to become big movie stars; almost all of them fell on their ass. I just said, 'Jay, take her and go.' I was fond of her, but the show was a huge hit, and I had a feeling that everybody wanted to be an Angel."

On June 1, 1977, when shooting began on *Charlie's Angels'* second season, Farrah wasn't there. "She feels she doesn't have a contract with the production company and she won't return to the series," wrote Jay Bernstein in a prepared statement.

Spelling-Goldberg countered with their own official declaration: "We'd like to have Farrah come back to work but it isn't the end of the world. No legal action has been taken yet, but it will somewhere down the line." Farrah, meanwhile, had left with her husband for a vacation to Europe and Iran, where they had been invited to dinner by the Shah.

On June 11, production was halted, and Aaron Spelling sued Farrah for $7 million for breach of contract. J. William Hayes, an attorney for Spelling-Goldberg, told the *New York Times* that the company will also seek a court injunction to prevent Farrah from taking any other acting assignments, until the suit is resolved.

With Farrah out of the country, Jay Bernstein became the point man for the negative press. In 1975, Lee Majors had offered him $1,000 a month to handle his publicity, if he would also represent Farrah for free. He now had to deal with the most publicized and contentious departure of an actress from a television series in the history of the medium, for someone he originally agreed to represent without compensation. Bernstein's perceived role in Farrah's departure had made him the first agent to become as well-known as the clients he represented. It also made him the most reviled.

"Everyone had to blame someone, and I had to be the fall guy. " Bernstein said. "You always told me an actor should never be the villain," Lee Majors had told him. "So if you want to be the manager, you have to take the responsibility."

Hollywood also turned against Farrah, who was perceived as a TV sex symbol who wanted to be an actress. Threats of legal action from Spelling-Goldberg also scared away potential job offers. She lost the lead role in Paramount's comedy *Foul Play* (1978) to Goldie Hawn, and lost a role in *Coma* (1978) to Genevieve Bujold.

One month before *Charlie's Angels* would begin its second season, ABC remained publicly optimistic. "We are expecting her to return. "Another offer was submitted to her this week and we are hoping for the best," said a network spokesman. "The scripts have been carefully handled so that should she return to work her character could easily be reworked into the show."

Cheryl Ladd: from "Farrah Fawcett-Minor" to series savior.

CHAPTER FOUR

Hey Little Sister

EXACTLY HOW MUCH OF *CHARLIE'S ANGELS'* EXTRAORDINARY POPULARITY was linked to Farrah Fawcett-Majors was a question that could not be answered until the new season began. However, everyone involved with the show had no doubt that the casting of her replacement would be critical to the series' future.

"When we started recasting, we received photos from all over the world," said Spelling-Goldberg executive coordinator Brett Garwood. "From Africa and Asia and everywhere else. And all the girls always had their hair combed just like Farrah, and they wrote, 'My friends say I look just like her.' Well, that was the last thing we wanted—to duplicate Farrah!"

It was Aaron Spelling who suggested Cheryl Ladd, having remembered her from an audition for another Spelling-Goldberg series, *Family* (1976-1980). Ladd had tested for the role of Nancy Maitland, the ill-fated daughter of matriarch Kate Lawrence (Sada Thompson). "The choice was between Meredith Baxter-Birney and myself. After the third reading, Aaron called me and said 'Congratulations, you got the part.' I was ecstatic," Ladd recalled. "This was exactly the kind of

The Prince and the Angels

he set of *Charlie's Angels* was closed to the press and the public for four of its five seasons, but one exception to the policy was allowed. "When Prince Charles came to Los Angeles, he made it a point to visit the Angels," said Brett Garwood, an executive coordinator for Spelling-Goldberg. In 1977, Buckingham Palace contacted ABC through the British Consulate, requesting a picture of the Angels for the royal television room. Queen Elizabeth and Prince Phillip were regular viewers, and would arrange their dinner and appointments around the series on Wednesday nights.

Garwood was assigned the task of introducing the Prince of Wales to the Queens of Jiggle. "I took him to Stage 8 and presented him to the girls. It was quite an occasion! He was very charming and gracious, and the girls were so enthralled. Back then, you'll remember, he was still an eligible bachelor." ◣

Prince Charles shares a joke with Kate Jackson and Jaclyn Smith. *Charlie's Angels* was the favorite American TV show of the British royal family.

television I wanted to do—great cast, very prestigious. The next day, someone from Aaron's office called and said it was a mistake, and they decided to go with Meredith because she had more experience. That was a very bad morning—I was so devastated."

When Farrah's departure became official, Spelling's first call was to Cheryl Ladd. "She was a year or two too young for the *Family* part, but we felt she'd be interesting to test for *Angels*. We called her agent and word came back that she didn't want to. So, that seemed that," Spelling said.

"The show was not getting the best reviews, and there was such a hullabaloo about it, and I had just been so close to getting *Family*," said Ladd, remembering the reasons for her negative response. At that time, the critically-lauded, Emmy-winning *Family* represented everything that *Charlie's Angels* did not; substance, instead of fluff, with nary a jiggle in sight. "I appreciated the offer, but I really didn't want to do it."

Thus began the first "Angel search," which almost became an annual event in the series' history. Several aspiring Angels were auditioned throughout the summer of 1977, to no avail. Among those who didn't make the cut were Kim Basinger, who appeared in the first season episode "Angels in Chains" (#4). With time running out, a distraught Aaron Spelling shared his dilemma with fashion designer Nolan Miller, over dinner at the Palm Restaurant in Los Angeles.

"I've got this hit show, and I can't find anyone to replace Farrah. What am I going to do? I have to find someone!"

"Come on, Aaron, there are so many beautiful, talented girls in this town. Look at that girl over there," said Miller, gesturing toward a nearby table. "She could replace Farrah." Spelling looked, and saw that Miller had pointed right to Cheryl Ladd, who was having dinner with her husband, David. The exasperated producer sighed. "That's Cheryl—she won't do it!"

But Ladd, her disappointment at losing the *Family* role having receded, was experiencing second thoughts. "All of my friends, and all the people in my acting classes, had said, 'Are you out of your mind? This is your opportunity!'" Ladd sat in on a class and gazed around the room at the 30 students, some of them ten years her senior. They were all talented, but they hadn't yet been in that proverbial right place at the right time. They didn't get the one meeting that led to the one part that would change their lives.

"It started to make sense to me, what they were saying. I wanted to work. I wanted to get on with it," Ladd said. "I had seven years of doing guest parts and building up my resumé`, and I was ready for something to happen." When Spelling called again, still holding a halo for her, she agreed to a meeting.

Once again, Ladd questioned whether she wanted to play the kind of character that *Charlie's Angels* required. "I don't want to be just this glamour-babe. I have no interest in it," she told Spelling. He said, "What if you came in as the rookie, as the kid sister of Jill? Then everybody would be rooting for you."

"Well, that's interesting," said Ladd, now becoming intrigued by the possibilities. "Could I do comedy? And make a lot of mistakes as a detective? I thought if she could be funny, and not just a babe all the time, I would be interested." Spelling agreed, and Kris Munroe was born.

The Girl Next Door

Cheryl Jean Stoppelmoor was born July 12, 1951, in Huron, South Dakota, a state that has produced a surprising number of TV sex symbols (Angie Dickinson and Catherine Bach also hail from there). She grew up in a modest home, with two younger brothers, Brian and Seth, and her older sister, Mary Ann.

"I was singing and dancing before I was talking," Cheryl laughingly recalled, and her parents encouraged her to follow her dream. Money was tight in the household—her father Marion was an engineer with the Chicago Northwest Railroad Company, her mother was a homemaker—so when the family couldn't afford a piano, Cheryl opted for dancing lessons instead.

"I was a little ham, back then." she said. "My sister Mary Ann was good at cooking and sewing, and I was the Otto Preminger on my block." Young Cheryl spent her allowance on clothes at rummage sales and bargain stores so she could play "dress-up." "One summer I was Hayley Mills," she recalled.

Ladd was a cheerleader at Huron High, and a car hop at a the local drive-in restaurant after school. In her senior year, she began singing with a local band called The Music Shop. "I was so young, the leader had to become my legal guardian. We worked so hard, I think I only had two dates in high school, I didn't even have a chance to go to the prom," she recalled.

Before joining the *Angels*, even Cheryl Ladd experimented with Farrah's feathered hairstyle.

Upon graduating from high school in 1969, she toured with the band. They played their opening gig at a steakhouse in Iowa, and moved across the country performing in small taverns and restaurants. After the band parted ways in Thousand Oaks, California, Cheryl headed for Hollywood.

Her first professional break came early, when she was signed as a member of another sexy trio, *Josie and the Pussycats*. Ladd provided the singing voice for the ditzy blond character, Melody. The Hanna Barbera cartoon series spawned an album in 1970, on which Ladd, billed as Cherie Moore, performed several catchy bubblegum tunes with fellow Pussycats Cathy Dougher and Patrice Holloway. The trio was short lived, but Cheryl kept busy by taking drama lessons, doing television commercials for Ford, Max Factor, Ultra Brite, Johnson's Baby Powder, Michelob, and Prell Shampoo, and making guest appearances on such series as *Happy Days*, *Ironside*, *The Partridge Family*, and *Police Woman*.

In 1971, while she was on location in the Caribbean for a film called *Jamaica Reef*, Cheryl met a struggling actor named David Ladd, the son of actor Alan Ladd. The movie was never released, but the couple dated for 18 months before getting married in 1973. Their daughter, Jordan, was born two years later.

■ ■ ■

Spelling's next task was to convince ABC that Ladd could step into Farrah's high heels and chase down the bad guys, while not chasing away any viewers. He prepared a video medley of Ladd's previous TV work for network executives, including a guest spot she did as a rookie cop on *Police Woman*. Ladd first met her future costars during a photo session arranged by ABC. "Once they were convinced that I could do the part, the executives wanted to see how the three of us looked together. So I went to the set, and we stood around and chatted while they took photos," Ladd said.

One month later, amidst lingering network hopes that Farrah might still change her mind, Cheryl Ladd reported to work. Aware that she was walking into an atmosphere of uncertainty, she tried to diffuse the tension of the moment by wearing a t-shirt that read "Farrah Fawcett-Minor."

In the weeks prior to her first day on the set, Ladd admitted to having dreams of walking down the street and being accosted by strangers saying, "Who do you think you are, Farrah?" The insecurity of replacing an icon mounted as the first day of shooting approached, as she realized the future of *Charlie's Angels* rested on her shoulders.

"This whole group of people had worked together for a year on a hit show, and now they were all worried about their jobs. There were also split loyalties—a lot of them were crazy about Farrah, and thought she did the right thing, and others thought she did the wrong thing," said Ladd. "I wanted to unplug from all of that and let them just see me and laugh with me, cause I was really saying 'I don't know, either—let's just take this trip together.'"

Her strategy worked. "She was marvelous from the very beginning," said John D.F. Black, who wrote the episode that introduced Kris Munroe, 'Angels in Paradise.' "She had chutzpa. She had style. Cheryl went in there like she had been doing that large a part on TV forever, and she hadn't."

Ladd also earned a vote of confidence from departed producer Rick Husky. "When I heard Cheryl Ladd was coming in, I figured the show was good for another year, and maybe two. I was glad because I

The Angels go Hawaiian, in the second season opener, "Angels in Paradise."

was still getting some money from the show, and I rooted for them to run until Kate and Jaclyn were in wheelchairs."

Support from her fellow Angels, however, was not as forthcoming. "There were problems with Kate and Cheryl right away," recalls Jaclyn Smith. "I don't know what started it, but it was uncomfortable for me, because I was in the middle and I liked both of them."

"Some days Kate was speaking to me, some days she wasn't," said Ladd, who acknowledged that she wasn't always able to make every effort toward bonding with her costars. "I had a homelife going on, that the other girls didn't have," Ladd explained. "They were single; I wasn't as available to be social, and as much of a girlfriend to them, because I had responsibilities to a daughter and a husband."

"They were unhappy that Farrah left, and they weren't going to make it easy on the new kid," said Ed Lakso. "The directors and the crew all loved Cheryl immediately, but the other girls made her earn her spurs."

"There were friendships formed in that first year that you couldn't just throw overboard for a newcomer," said David Doyle of his costars' trepidation. "I was not privy to everything that went on, but I don't think anyone felt any animosity toward Cheryl. God knows she was pretty enough and talented enough. I found her to be a straight-shooter, honest and forthright."

Between scenes, Cheryl spent time with her husband and her daughter, Jordan. The crew would sometimes invite her and David Doyle over for lunch—something that would never happen with Kate or Jaclyn. "I would not have survived the show without David," she said. "Right away he got me laughing and made me feel like part of the group. When the girls were more careful at first, David was the one that would come over and say, 'Ah, come on, kid.'"

To ease the transition for Ladd and the entire *Angels* company, one episode was filmed in Los Angeles prior to beginning the long and complex location shooting of "Angels in Paradise," the two-hour season premiere that introduced Kris Munroe. By the time the production arrived in Honolulu, Hawaii, several stories had leaked to the press that the Angels weren't getting along. On location, the three stars were forced to share one motor home, and used the opportunity to say, "This has to stop." They spent their off-hours conversing together, and by the time the series returned to Los Angeles, Angel relations were civil, if not entirely cordial.

A more peaceful set eased the first of many challenges facing Cheryl Ladd during her first weeks as an Angel. Not only was she joining a series with a loyal and established fan following, she was doing so with material that was written for another actress. "My scripts still said 'Jill.'" she said. Though it might have been a safer choice to play the scenes as they were envisioned for Farrah, Ladd strived to put a different spin on the character, remembering Aaron Spelling's promise that she could try a comedic approach.

"If the script said 'She walks in and says 'Hi,' and it's supposed to be a seductive scene, I would walk into the room and trip," she recalled. "The writers had nothing to say about it, and the directors had eleven pages a day to get through, so they didn't have time to argue about whether they liked what you were doing or not. (The Angels) don't get much credit for that, but if there were any quirky, interesting elements in the characters that people related to, they came from what we brought as actors."

Ladd was also coping with instant celebrity on a prodigious scale. From the moment Farrah announced she was hanging up her halo, the "Angel Search" dominated entertainment news pages. When Cheryl Ladd got the job, she became one of the most famous women in the country before she filmed her first scene. "Nobody gives you lessons on how to be a celebrity," she said of her sudden notoriety. "I was exactly the same person the day before I said 'yes' to *Charlie's Angels*. But now everything I said was newsworthy, everywhere I went was newsworthy, everything I ate was newsworthy—it's a bizarre phenomenon."

She appeared on the covers of *People* and *TV Guide*, and made the talk show rounds in the fall of 1977 to introduce herself to America. Ladd's dazzling beauty and self-effacing demeanor charmed Mike Douglas and Merv Griffin, but the verdict of *Charlie's Angels* fans would not be known until September 14, when the series opened its second season.

"I was confident in my talent, and I felt I could handle the material," said Ladd. "And I know that people root for the underdog. As long

The Angels and Bosley relax after their Hawaiian adventure.

Smith (left), Kate Jackson and Cheryl Ladd were all smiles in public,
but relations behind the scenes were not always congenial.

as I wasn't full of myself, or didn't try to be Farrah, I thought the audience would at least give me a chance."

As it turned out, Cheryl Ladd had nothing to worry about. *Charlie's
Angels* scored its highest ratings ever in its second season, moving from
fifth overall to fourth in the Neilsen ratings. The audience share earned
by the series in metropolitan areas was astonishing; the *Birmingham*
(Alabama) *News* broke down the numbers for one episode, and discovered that of the 287,000 homes in Birmingham using television, 202,000
of them were turned to *Charlie's Angels*.

The Little Rebel

Farrah Fawcett refused to wear a bikini on *Charlie's Angels*, but Cheryl Ladd had no such reservations. When Kris Munroe donned a two-piece bathing suit, male viewers wept for joy, and teenage boys across America discovered the possibilities of puberty. But when Ladd found her exposure increasing every week, more for the sake of ratings than for the episode's storyline, she decided to make a statement:

"I knew part of my job description was wearing a bathing suit. Being a wife and mother, I have to say that I thought it was flattering, and I went along with the program. But by the second year, I said to Aaron, 'If I'm going to be in a bathing suit, it has to be near water—by the pool, on a boat, at the ocean—some situation where it would be reasonable. I'm not going into a store and try on 15 bikinis because Kris is thinking of going on vacation.' He said 'I understand.' So for the next three or four scripts all was well, and then I get this script in which, for no apparent reason, I was running around a hotel room in a bikini, pulling guns from God-knows-where, and chasing bad guys.

I was infuriated. But I said 'Okay.' I went to the wardrobe lady and said 'I just got a brand new bathing suit—Aaron's going to love it, so you don't have to find one for me.' During rehearsal I wore a robe over the suit the whole time. When they were ready to shoot, I dropped the robe, and I had on the tiniest bikini I could find. It was little chains connecting three peachy-pink colored triangles covering certain parts, and I was falling out of it everywhere.

The director said, 'I don't think you can wear that.' I said, 'Aaron wants bikini, he's getting bikini.' So they shot the scene, and they had to cut all around different parts of me. I got a note from him the next day through the wardrobe department, saying, 'Please tell the little rebel that this will never happen again.' From that moment on, I never had to wear a bikini without a reason."

Critics still took their shots. "The excitement of it all is underwhelming," sniffed the *Los Angeles Times'* Lee Margulies of "Angels in Paradise." Of the new Angel, Margulies wrote that "Ms. Ladd fits in nicely, which is to say she fills out a bikini nicely—that apparently being the primary qualification for joining Charlie's detective agency. She is pretty, at times vivacious and projects a lot more wholesomeness than sexiness. Her acting talent seems modest, but with something like *Charlie's Angels* it's hard to tell."

Patterns that evolved in the first season, in which Sabrina and Bosley would pursue a case from one angle, while Jill and Kelly assumed undercover roles and worked from the inside, continued with Kris. The engaging chemistry between David Doyle and Kate Jackson highlighted such episodes as "Angels on Ice" (#24), and Jaclyn Smith emerged as the sultry, honey-voiced seductress of the team (her belly dance in "Angels on Ice" is a series highlight).

Cheryl Ladd showed off her musical background in "Angels in the Wings" (#32), and shined in several comedic showcases. She played a clown in "Angels on Ice" (#24) a vacuous beauty pageant contestant in "Pretty Angels All in a Row" (#25), a naïve starlet named Taffy in "The Sammy Davis Jr. Kidnap Caper" (#34), and a hilariously thick-accented Swedish movie star in "The Jade Trap" (#44).

A time change on Wednesdays, from 10 p.m. to 9 p.m., brought more preteen and teenage viewers into the fold by the thousands. When the *Ladies Home Journal* asked 850 junior and senior high school students, "If you could exchange your mother for someone else, which famous living woman would you prefer as a parent?" Girls chose Jaclyn Smith first, followed by Cheryl Ladd; Farrah Fawcett-Majors ranked fifth, Kate Jackson sixth. Among boys, Cheryl Ladd topped the survey, followed by Cheryl Tiegs and Farrah Fawcett-Majors. Jaclyn Smith placed fourth, Kate Jackson, seventh.

Not only did Farrah now trail Cheryl as a prospective parent, her career also struggled by comparison. After losing *Foul Play* to Goldie Hawn as a result of threatened litigation, Farrah starred in the feature film *Somebody Killed Her Husband* (1978), opposite Jeff Bridges. The movie opened to dreadful reviews, and was renamed by one critic,

"Somebody Killed Her Career!". Some theaters offered free Farrah posters to the first 50 ticketholders; one Dallas moviehouse gave away just five posters—one for each member of the audience. It was the first of three straight box-office bombs for Charlie's fallen Angel. Neither *Sunburn* (1979), a romantic farce costarring Charles Grodin, nor the science-fiction adventure *Saturn 3* (1980) found an audience. "The public wants me to be the girl in *Charlie's Angels*, which is a difficult pressure to deal with," she told *Variety*.

While the press dissected her failures, Farrah also had to read about how well her former compatriots were doing. "Pinup wise, Cheryl is just as impressive," David Doyle told *People* magazine, "and she's as gifted as, if not more so than, Farrah. I think it's a stronger show now."

Said Farrah, "I was surprised I was so easy to replace."

Charlie's first four Angels. Farrah Fawcett, Kate Jackson, Jaclyn Smith and Cheryl Ladd.

CHAPTER FIVE

Jill Returns, Sabrina Departs

EASON THREE WAS A MILESTONE FOR *CHARLIE'S ANGELS*—FOR THE first and only time, the entire cast remained intact, as Kate Jackson, Cheryl Ladd and Jaclyn Smith all returned for another tour of duty.

Free from the responsibility of casting replacements, producer Ed Lakso was able to concentrate on the easiest and most enjoyable part of his job—writing stories for the new season. "I had the last great producing job in television—no associate producer, no story editor, no supervising producer," Lakso said. "I'd write over the summer, then meet with Aaron Spelling and lay out about 15 plots in an hour, and he'd say, 'Go do it.'"

Lakso also spoke with John Forsythe about the comic vignettes featuring Charlie that followed his briefing of the Angels. Forsythe didn't like the sexist double-entendres that typified these scenes, in which Charlie was often glimpsed in the company of scantily-clad bimbos. Lakso agreed that the running gag had become tiresome. "Aaron wanted to keep them in, but they stopped working," said Lakso.

"There was no need for them," said Forsythe. "Too many times on television there are things that go on that don't move the piece forward. The show succeeded on the girls. When you have three gorgeous ladies and lots of action, those scenes weren't necessary. "

Three episodes that season would be written to accommodate Farrah Fawcett-Majors' return to *Charlie's Angels*, a condition of Farrah's legal settlement with Aaron Spelling and Leonard Goldberg. "It was one of those strange things where her contract was never signed and returned by her," said Brett Garwood. "But the courts ruled that it was still a binding contract because she accepted payment for her work."

The case dragged through the courts for much of 1977, before ending in a compromise; Spelling-Goldberg agreed to drop their litigation, in exchange for Farrah appearing in three shows in each of the next two seasons. Press reports at the time proclaimed that Farrah would earn $70,000 per episode, but her actual salary was $150,000 per episode, according to her former manager, Jay Bernstein. "If she had stayed with the show, she wouldn't have made a tenth of that," he said. Of her former costars, the fallen Angel told *Us* magazine, "I hope they'll be happy about my return."

Though her film career stalled out of the gate, Farrah had become a one-woman conglomerate, and remained one of the most recognized women in the world. As a result, news of her return to Angel duty was one of the top stories of the 1978 television season. *People* magazine, in fact, called it the most celebrated return since MacArthur's.

"I didn't know how she would be—if she would hate me," said Ladd. "If I were her, part of me would be relieved that the show was doing ok, and I was out of my contract, but the ego part would say, 'you mean the show's still a hit without me?' Ladd's trepidation increased when Farrah was interviewed by Barbara Walters shortly after her return, and said of Cheryl Ladd, "I think it's inevitable that we couldn't be best friends."

When filming began on "Angel Come Home" (#48), the set on the Fox lot was closed as always, though everybody seemed to know somebody who was there when sisters Jill and Kris Munroe were "reunited."

Guest-star Dean Martin appears in the series' third season opener, "Angels in Vegas."

Reports of their first meeting filled gossip pages and entertainment columns, and no two accounts were alike.

People magazine circulated the feel-good story of a birthday party given for Cheryl on the set, during which she received a signed card from Farrah that read, "You make a terrific sister!" *TV Guide* reported that Kate Jackson and Jaclyn Smith bonded with Farrah once again, leaving Cheryl Ladd as the odd Angel out, and forced to turn to the crew for companionship.

Neither story was accurate, according to Jaclyn Smith, who reports that the truth fell somewhere down the middle. "Tense, tense, tense," was her assessment of the week's work, but there was no open warfare to speak of. "She was not warm, to anyone, because she really didn't want to be there," said Ladd of her predecessor. "But she was very professional, never rude, and she got the work done."

The ratings remained awesome. "Angels in Vegas" (#47), featuring guest star Dean Martin, opened the season with a 54 share—only a title fight between Muhammad Ali and Leon Spinks kept the episode from topping the Nielsens. "Angel Come Home" drew a 40 share, good enough for third place that week. The series finished in 12th place for the season, down from its top-ten status but still impressive.

Overall, the stories were not as inventive as they had been the previous year, but there were a few memorable shows; Jill's maternal side surfaces in Farrah's second return story, "Mother Angel," (#55), Kris loses her memory in the dramatic "Angel on My Mind" (#56), the Angels chase their criminal counterparts in the delightful caper "Counterfeit Angels" (#60), and Bosley takes a turn in the spotlight in "Angels in Waiting" (#66).

The *Washington Post* raved that *Charlie's Angels* now ranked alongside Apollo 11 in its impact on American culture. Hailed as "the granddaddy of Jiggle TV," its concept of beautiful women in jeopardy inspired several imitators that season, none of which found an audience (see sidebar). While the knock-offs faltered, the previous two seasons of *Angels* debuted in the international market, where they proved just as popular as they had been at home.

In Japan, *Charlie's Angels* somehow translated into *The Funny Women*. "When I went to Japan, it was mind-boggling. It was like being in the Beatles," recalled Cheryl Ladd. "I was this little blond chick actress, and there were thousands of people waiting in the streets to see me, and chasing my car down the street."

In the final show of season three, "Angels Remembered" (#68), Sabrina, Kelly, Kris, and Bosley celebrate their time together as a team, in between film clips featuring highlights of earlier adventures. In the closing scene, Sabrina raises a glass of champagne and says, "Here's to many, many more." It was her final act as an Angel.

Kate Jackson had had enough. Since the first season, she was unhappy with the way the series had developed out of the concept she helped create. "There was a point where you could take what was on the page and do something with it. You could try some humor. But by the third year, there was just nothing," she said. Jackson cited "Marathon Angels" (#65), comprised of one long cross-country race featuring the Angels and several comely extras running braless. "All the girls

Farrah Fawcett (middle) reunites with her former costars in "Angel Come Home."

cast had to have large breasts and wear no bras. When I heard that, I just said, 'Aw, shit.'"

Jackson, however, was already feeling hostile toward the series before the season began. During the previous summer, she was offered the role of Dustin Hoffman's estranged wife, Joanna, in the divorce drama *Kramer Vs. Kramer* (1979). She planned to film her *Angels* episodes during the week that season, and fly to New York on weekends to film the movie. But Spelling-Goldberg refused to give her the time off. Losing a role coveted by every A-list actress in Hollywood because of *Charlie's Angels* was the final indignity. "From that moment she was very unhappy," said David Doyle.

"I felt for her. When she lost *Kramer vs. Kramer*, it really tainted her enthusiasm for the show," said Ladd. "It was a heartbreaking experience—a chance to work with Dustin Hoffman on this wonderful project, and then not be able to do it. It's one thing for me to look back and think how I missed out on *Family*, but Kate could have been Meryl Streep!" It was Streep who played the role of Joanna, and for her performance she received the Academy Award for Best Supporting Actress.

Jackson's animosity toward the series was matched only by Aaron Spelling's frustration with Kate Jackson. "Last year it stopped being fun," he told *TV Guide*. "It was not a happy set, all the bitching and griping. By the middle of that season, we knew she had enough."

Kate released the statement that she met with Aaron Spelling, and worked out her departure. She described the event as "a timely, mutually amicable parting of the ways which I know will be good for everybody." Spelling, however, was not feeling as diplomatic. "Kate's being dropped for the good of the show," he told *People* magazine. "We feel it's best for Kate Jackson and *Charlie's Angels* to bring in a new Angel next year. We just didn't exercise her option. Beyond that, we have no comment."

"We all had to turn down movies. Maybe not *Kramer Vs. Kramer*, but we all had those chances," said Jaclyn Smith. There was a James

Jiggle TV

*C*harlie's Angels gets the credit (or blame, depending on your perspective) for creating a new television genre called "Jiggle TV." Loosely defined, Jiggle TV consists of any television series in which the lead roles are played by attractive young women, who wear a variety of revealing outfits in the course of each episode.

After *Charlie's Angels* became a phenomenon, other series tried to repeat the Jiggle formula. There was *Flying High* (1978-79), starring Pat Klous, Connie Selleca and Kathryn Witt as beautiful stewardesses, who brought new meaning to the term "friendly skies." *The American Girls* (1978) was an adventure series featuring Priscilla Barnes and Debra Clinger as young journalists, whose assignments for *The American Report* often required them to disrobe. In the pilot, the Girls, clad in lingerie, rescue a group of teenage prostitutes from white slavers.

Blansky's Beauties (1977) was a tenuous spinoff from *Happy Days*, in which Nancy Walker played den mother to a houseful of Las Vegas showgirls. Distraction from the mundane comedy was provided by lovely ladies Caren Kaye, Lynda Goodfriend, Taaffe O'Connell, Gerri Reddick, and Jill Owens.

Sugar Time (1977-1978) starred Barbi Benton, Marianne Black and Didi Carr as "Sugar," a trio of aspiring rock singers. Original music for the series was composed by Paul Williams. *Roller Girls* (1978) followed the adventures of an all-girl roller derby team, led by Rhonda Bates, Candy Ann Brown, Joanna Cassidy, Marcy Hanson, and Marilyn Tokuda.

Not one of these series, however, managed to capture the magic appeal of *Charlie's Angels*. Why? "Simply because *Charlie's Angels* is more than a sex show," wrote critic Frank Swertlow in the *Chicago Sun Times.* "It offers fantasy, escape and mystery. The imitations don't. They are overt in their suggestiveness and pander while the Angels merely tease." ◼

Bond movie (*Moonraker*) that I had to turn down." Now the last of the original Angels, Smith felt "very, very sad," to see her costar depart. Cheryl Ladd, however, did not share her disappointment. "It was a challenge on a daily basis," said Ladd of working with Jackson. "If people knew what really went on with her . . . they don't want to know."

"Kate hated everything I wrote," said Ed Lakso, who also shed no tears over her departure. Jackson once quipped that an *Angels* script was "so light it would take a week to get to the floor if you dropped it from the ceiling." Actually, her costars had similar feelings. "By the second year I was there, it was obvious that any of us could do any of the roles the way they were written. I could have read all of Jackie's lines, and she could have read all of mine," said Cheryl Ladd.

The cast also sympathized with her complaints about working conditions. "We were not only working 12-14 hour days, we did wardrobe fittings during our lunch breaks, five days a week, nine months a year," said Ladd. And while Cheryl had toiled for two years, Jackson's three seasons on *Charlie's Angels* were directly preceded by four seasons on *The Rookies*. Maintaining the grinding schedule of a weekly one-hour drama for seven years would daunt anyone.

While Kate Jackson's dismissal/departure can be justified for the atmosphere of calm it returned to the set, there was no justification for believing that a new actress could match the caliber of her twice-Emmy-nominated portrayal of Sabrina Duncan. Every week, Jackson demonstrated her talent for taking a standard (even sub-standard) line of dialogue and reading it in a way that sounds fresh and interesting, an ability that is both rare and invaluable in series television.

The on-screen chemistry among the first four Angels is one of the least cited reasons for the series' success, and Jackson's role as the team's field leader was crucial in that equation. She was, indeed, the only Angel who was believable as a detective. Jaclyn Smith recalled several occasions when male guest stars would try to show up the three female leads. "They want to knock the guns out of our hands. One actor did that to me and I screamed and laughed. Kate kept her gun on him, very calm and steady. She told him, 'I got this gun on you and one more move and I'll shoot.' She stayed right in the role."

Nolan's Angels

ashion was a priority on *Charlie's Angels*, and the man responsible for making certain that the Angels were always dressed to thrill was designer Nolan Miller.

In the 1950s, Miller was working part-time in a florist's shop when he first met Aaron Spelling, who was producing shows for Dick Powell at Four Star. According to Miller, Spelling was a regular customer, and the two men developed a rapport. Before long, he was designing outfits for Spelling's wife, actress Carolyn Jones. "He was just beginning his career as a producer and told me if he could ever use me, he would," Miller recalled.

Miller designed all the costumes for *Honey West* and other Spelling series, and when *Charlie's Angels* was in development, the producer requested his services again. Miller was there from the first wardrobe fitting until the final season. "Working with the girls was great," he recalled. Jaclyn Smith is such a wonderful girl. You could put her in anything—whatever it was, she looked incredible. Ten minutes after meeting her, I felt she was the kind of girl you could just put your arms around, because she was so warm.

"Farrah had a lot of style. Both she and Jaclyn loved to shop on Rodeo Drive on the weekends, and report to me on Monday to tell me which fashions they wanted for the upcoming episodes. Farrah loved going with the trends—that's why she opted not to wear a bra on the show. That's what was happening on the runways in Paris at the time, and she felt more comfortable that way."

The network, however, was not comfortable with some of Farrah's outfits. "The ABC censors were always paying close attention, to make sure a nipple wasn't protruding through her blouse to an extreme measure," he recalled.

According to Miller, Kate Jackson was not one of his more enthusiastic clients. "Kate was never interested in fashion," he said. "One season we bought fifty of the same kind of turtleneck sweaters for (Sabrina). The one time I did design a beautiful gown for her, she came onto the set wearing it with Adidas sneakers."

Cheryl Ladd was a more willing participant. "She was so easy to work with. She had a figure like Lana Turner, and was always ready to approve anything I had sketched up for her."

Famed costume designer
Nolan Miller with Jaclyn Smith

When Kate Jackson left, Nolan Miller's prayers were answered when Spelling hired Shelley Hack, a genuine super-model. "I begged Aaron to hire Shelley," he admits. "There was something about her I really liked; I was impressed with her Charlie perfume commercials, and how she could create a look just by turning her collar up, and putting her hands in her pockets. I helped her with her audition, because she knew how to wear clothes and I knew I would enjoy working with her."

But when Hack's fashion flair didn't connect with viewers, she was replaced by Tanya Roberts. "Tanya was very sweet," Miller said. "She was new to it all, and it showed." At their first meeting, the designer tried to get some idea of the new Angel's fashion sense, when her husband said, "My wife can wear anything. She has a great body!" "He turned to Tanya and said, 'Take off your clothes. Show him.'" recalled Miller. "So she stripped in front of me!" ◣

Miller gained international recognition when he created the sumptuous fashions worn by Linda Evans and Joan Collins on *Dynasty*. His designs have been worn by a who's who of Hollywood's dreamgirls, from Elizabeth Taylor and Sophia Loren to Ann-Margret and Natalie Wood. ◣

In the summer of 1979, Kate Jackson signed a $6 million contract with ABC, to make a series of television movies over the next five years, beginning with a remake of the classic film *Topper* (1937). "I guess I did cause a few problems," she confessed to *People* magazine after her departure. "What it comes down to is I got tired of them and they got tired of me." She expressed her gratitude, however, "for all the good things (*Charlie's Angels*) brought me. I think it served me well, and I think I served it well.

"There are a lot worse things to be called than an angel. And I've been called them."

Shelley Hack: The "Charlie" girl becomes a Charlie's Angel.

CHAPTER SIX

Tiffany

CHARLIE'S ANGELS ENDED ITS THIRD SEASON STILL FIRMLY ENTRENCHED among television's most popular series. Angel dolls and lunchboxes kept cash registers ringing through the summer of 1979, and concern over the task of replacing Kate Jackson seemed trivial compared to the sense of relief that her displeasure would no longer manifest itself on the set. Besides, the series had already lost the preeminent sex symbol of the decade and never looked back. Why couldn't they do it again?

"This time, unlike with Cheryl, we really went through a casting process," said Ed Lakso. Hundreds of candidates lined up outside a Fox soundstage, in a scene reminiscent of the open call that preceded the pilot. Among the hopefuls—*Flying High* star Connie Selleca, *Dallas* beauty Deborah Shelton, Dian Parkinson, the busty blond prize pointer on *The Price is Right*, and talk show host Christina Ferrare. Catherine Bach, who was turned down for being "too exotic," was later cast as Daisy Duke on the hit CBS series *The Dukes of Hazzard*.

Kathie Lee Johnson, a former gospel singer then working as one of the *Hee Haw* Honeys, saw *Charlie's Angels* as her ticket out of the cornpatch. But supervising producer Elaine Rich took her aside before

Original 1979 call sheet with eight contenders for the "Tiffany Welles" role.
Among the finalists: Michelle Pfieffer

her audition and explained that she really wasn't Angel material. Johnson, now better known as Kathie Lee Gifford, still loves to tell the story of her downfall on *Live With Regis and Kathie Lee.*

Michelle Pfeiffer tried out, as did Cher's sister, Georgette LaPierre, and Kelly Collins, the younger sister of Bo Derek. At the height of the media speculation, Aaron Spelling dropped the name of Margaret

Trudeau, the beautiful, jetsetting wife of Canada's Prime Minister, Pierre Trudeau. Some tabloids took the joke seriously.

"I didn't see anyone I particularly liked," said Ed Lakso. Though there was no shortage of hopefuls, many actresses stayed away from the audition, realizing that "Angel" status could be a double-edged sword. Instant fame was guaranteed, but the long-term prospects were more dubious, judging by the typecasting that dogged Farrah Fawcett's post-*Angels* career. "This was not, as everyone thought, a role that every actress in Hollywood coveted—it was a role that every model coveted," said Lakso. His favorite candidate was Shari Belafonte, daughter of the famed calypso singer Harry Belafonte. "She was not a great actress at the time, but there was something very engaging about her," he recalled, "and at the time we felt some political pressure to hire an African-American girl."

Two favorites finally emerged from the crowded field: Barbara Bach, a ravishing brunette who romanced James Bond in *The Spy Who Loved Me* (1977), and Shelley Hack, a cool, patrician beauty who was already among the most recognizable faces on television from her commercials for Charlie perfume. Six months after she began endorsing the product, Charlie became the most popular fragrance in the world.

"I remember there was a big Angel hunt going on, and they asked me to audition, but I wasn't particularly interested in the show," Hack said.

Newspapers announced that Barbara Bach would replace Kate Jackson, but Aaron Spelling was determined to hire Shelley Hack.

"The hunt seemed to go on for a long time. A lot of my girlfriends went in to be tested, but I wasn't involved until some time later when my agent called and said, 'It's a terrific show—you really should think about testing.' So I thought about it again and went in."

Allen Baron, one of the Angels' regular directors, handled Shelley's screen test. "I read lines and did a scene, which went very well," Hack recalled. "I remember they wanted me to wear shorts and high heels, which I thought was hilarious. I was so new to all of that, that I didn't know whether to wear stockings or not."

Aaron Spelling also wanted the finalists subjected to a personality test, so he wouldn't have to contend with another Kate Jackson. "Allen started asking questions and I answered one or two of them, and then I said out loud what I was thinking—oh my God, this is a personality test!" said Hack. "Everybody started laughing. And Allen said 'Yeah, I guess it is.' And I said, 'Allan, I left my personality at home.' It took the heat off a high pressure situation."

On April 13, 1979, the *New York Daily News* reported that Barbara Bach was the new Angel. Robin Leach confirmed her casting in the May 7, 1979 *New York Post*. "We picked Barbara after thousands of submissions," Spelling-Goldberg executive Brett Garwood told Leach. Garwood added that "scripts will be tailor-made this week to introduce the new character."

"I remember thinking Barbara Bach had it, and I started reading some stuff about her so I'd know more when she showed up," said David Doyle.

"My feeling was, no harm, no foul. She was attractive, and she could do the job," said Ed Lakso. "The problem was that she looked very much like Jaclyn." The other problem was her final screen test, which received disappointing reviews from ABC executives.

And all the while, Aaron Spelling kept coming back to Shelley Hack, whose test radiated sophistication and poise. "When it doesn't mean everything in the world to you, you can be more relaxed than anybody else," observed Shelley, who didn't even own a television in her New York apartment. Though she hoped to launch an acting career, the audition for *Charlie's Angels* meant no more to her than any other casting call, and her insouciance might have clinched her the job. "We hired her 40 percent from the screen test and 60 percent from the personality test," Spelling told *TV Guide*. "We decided she was a nice person with sparkle and intelligence."

"Aaron pictured Shelley as a young Kate Hepburn, in baggy pants and Oxfords," said Lakso. "He also liked that she was already the 'Charlie' girl, and there was a great line about the 'Charlie' girl becoming a *Charlie's Angel*. That carried a lot of weight, believe it or not."

Shelley heard the good news at her Los Angeles hotel, having just emerged from a shower. "I rushed to the phone, hyperventilating, and heard my agent also breathing heavy on the other end," she said. "Aaron wants to see you in 20 minutes!" said her agent. When she arrived, Aaron said "We'd like you to be the new Angel." Cool as ever, Shelley replied, "That's very nice."

Shelley Hack was introduced as Tiffany Welles in the fourth season opener "Love Boat Angels," but received little fanfare for her debut.

The Connecticut Yankee

orn July 6, 1947, in Greenwich Connecticut, the oldest of six children, Shelley Hack was a tomboy, though it was obvious she had inherited the willowy, cosmopolitan beauty of her mother, a former Conover model. At 14 years old she was approached by a photographer who urged her to try modeling. Figuring it was a better summer job than waitressing, Shelley agreed to a few test shots, and within months had landed on the cover of Seventeen magazine. She soon added more covers to her resumé, among them *Glamour*, *Vogue*, *Look*, and *Mademoiselle*.

After graduating from the private Greenwich Academy, Hack studied archaeology at the University of Sydney while in the midst of a trip around the world. She graduated as a history major from Smith. During her education she continued her modeling career with the Eileen Ford Agency.

Hack moved to New York's Greenwich Village to peruse an acting career. She took lessons at the Herbert Berghof Studio and landed a small role in the Woody Allen classic, *Annie Hall* (1977). She won top billing in her next endeavor, as the estranged girlfriend of a composer in the strained romance *If Ever I See You Again* (1978). On television, she appeared in an episode of the short-lived series *Married: The First Year*, and was featured in a 1979 telefilm with the memorable title *Death Car on the Freeway*.

■   ■   ■

On May 22, 1979, newspapers announced that, no, really, this time for sure, the new Angel had been cast. Shelley Hack would play Tiffany Welles, the refined, scholarly daughter of a Connecticut police chief (later changed to Boston), who happened to be an old friend of Charlie. Hack's photograph ran in almost every newspaper in America and in Europe, and her casting was mentioned on the evening news. "I couldn't believe it—what am I doing on the news?" she asked, still unaware of the impact of *Charlie's Angels*.

"We're bringing back the glamour," proclaimed Aaron Spelling, a reference to Kate Jackson's preference for blue jeans over skirts and dresses. The producers arranged for each Angel to average eight costume changes in each episode, ballooning the clothing budget to

"Bringing back the glamour" was Aaron Spelling's top priority in the Angels' fourth season.

$10,000 per week. Ed Lakso remained skeptical. "My reaction was, you guys are out of your minds. I told Aaron that I want to go on record saying that this is a big mistake."

But Jaclyn Smith and Cheryl Ladd had no such reservations. "I missed Kate a lot," said Smith, now the last of the original Angels. But she welcomed Shelley in spite of her friend's departure. Ladd, of course, was glad to see anyone else but Kate Jackson. "I was relieved at that point, that the pressure of Kate's unhappiness was being alleviated. Shelley seemed like a doll, and we were going to have a lot of fun working together."

The season premiere, "Love Boat Angels," was shot on location on the island of St. Vincent in the Caribbean. The cast of *The Love Boat* appeared in character to greet the Angels, who sail on the Pacific Princess to track down a fortune in stolen artwork. At the first read-through of the script, Shelley was seated next to guest-star Dick Sargent. He asked if she was excited about the new opportunity. "No, not really," she replied. According to Ed Lakso, he then received a bemused look from Sargent that said, "You're in trouble."

Hack's nonchalance was confirmed by a *Los Angeles Times* reporter covering the new Angel, who overheard someone ask Hack, "Aren't you nervous?" "No," said Shelley. "Why should I be?" "That wasn't arrogance," she later explained to the reporter. "It just struck me as a silly question."

Unlike Cheryl Ladd and, later, Tanya Roberts, Shelley did not feel overwhelmed by the glare of the national spotlight. "I was surprised by the amount of attention, but I had done a lot of press before. There was so much to do then, so you just deal with it."

"Shelley came in with stronger opinions than Cheryl did, which can sometimes be a mistake in an ensemble show," said Jaclyn Smith. "Cheryl really tried to fold into the groove of the show, but Shelley had her own ideas."

However Shelley Hack's deportment was viewed by the press or her costars, all that really mattered was the ease of her integration into the team. After Kris Munroe received a grand showcase in her first episode, "Angels in Paradise" (#23), a similar strategy was expected to introduce Tiffany Welles. But it didn't happen.

The official explanation from Spelling-Goldberg Productions maintained that Spelling was prepared to go with just two Angels if he didn't find the right actress, and thus wrote the third Angel's part sparingly. The truth, according to Ed Lakso, was that Tiffany's persona and Shelley's performance were not having the desired effect. "I kept pulling lines away from her, and couldn't divide them evenly because of the way the story was constructed, so they all went to Cheryl. That's why she was in the spotlight in Shelley's first episode."

Hack's fellow Angels noticed what was happening, and confronted Lakso about the changes. "Jaclyn and I were saying, 'What's going on?' recalls Ladd. It was confusing to us, because we thought they would make this big presentation for her."

"They said I was cheating Shelley," said Lakso. "I danced around it, because I didn't want to say that Shelley couldn't act, but I stuck with the revisions."

Subsequent episodes focused on one Angel, a change from the team stories of previous seasons. The decision stemmed from the casts' desire to have more time off. As a result, Hack continued to receive limited screen time, and was not featured until the tenth episode of the season, "Angels on Campus" (#78).

"Love Boat Angels" aired on September 12, 1979, and topped the Nielsen ratings. Shelley Hack appeared on the cover of *People* magazine that week; the issue ranked among the poorest-selling of 1979. Reviews of the episode were typically negative, though some critics reserved their worst barbs for the newcomer. "She is barely able to read her lines," wrote *Variety*. Spelling offered Shelley the chance to work with an acting coach, but she rejected the idea.

The next three episodes all ranked in the top ten, but then the ratings began to steadily drop, first from the top ten to the top twenty, and then down into the 30s. Even the return of Farrah Fawcett could not reverse the trend; in fact, "An Angels Trail" (#88), Farrah's final appearance on *Charlie's Angels*, finished 34th, the lowest-rated show of the season. The once unbeatable series suddenly seemed vulnerable, and when NBC moved its popular sitcom *Diff'rent Strokes* to the same time slot, the Angels sometimes finished behind Gary Coleman and company.

The Hollywood Angel Tour

*T*elevision shows usually select distinctive locations for the homes and businesses occupied by their casts of characters. Who doesn't remember the famous A-Frame home of the *Brady Bunch*, the cul-de-sac of *Knots Landing*, or the apartment complex called *Melrose Place?*

The most familiar recurring sight on *Charlie's Angels* was a two story, red brick building, with white trim and shutters, and a tall, ornate entranceway. A plaque next to the door identified the building as the offices of Townsend Investigations. The Angels gathered every week on the first floor of the building, to receive their assignments from Charlie. While the interior office scenes were shot on Sound Stage 8 at 20th Century Fox, the exterior of the agency is an actual building located at 189 N. Robertson Boulevard, in Los Angeles.

The building itself has gone through several changes and several tenants since *Charlie's Angels* left the air in 1981. It has been a dress designer studio (Herve Leger of Paris), a bridal shop, a vacuum cleaner store, and an optometrist's office. The ground level now houses the showroom for Miele (pronounced like "Sheila"), a German appliance manufacturer. The top level is occupied by Red Hour, actor Ben Stiller's production company. Cheryl Ladd may have had reason to return to "Charlie's" old office, when she appeared opposite Stiller in the 1998 film, *Permanent Midnight*.

Though the familiar red brick facade remains, gone are the two smaller first level windows, and the white shutters that lined the building evenly with the second floor. Large picture windows and red awnings have been added.

This was not the first building that appeared as Townsend Investigations. For the pilot movie, a property management firm building was used as the lavish office. Located at 8619 Sunset Boulevard, this facility, with it's high columns and unique architectural style, served well in establishing an affluent style for the never seen Charles Townsend.

During the series' five year run, establishing a back story for each Angel was not a priority. Glimpses into the personal lives of Sabrina, Jill and Kelly were a rarity in the first season, and it wasn't until Season 2 and the arrival of Kris Munroe, that one of the Angels was finally given a distinctive residence. Kris lived in a beach house, that coincidentally was also used as the home of a former client, George Anderson, in the episode "The Killing Kind" (#6).

The actual house is located in Paradise Cove, north of Malibu. With the addition of an upper level, and a Wedgwood blue paint job, the beach dwelling is today almost unrecognizable from its appearances on *Charlie's Angels*. The residence has been used numerous times in films and television series, including *Body Slam* (1986), with Tanya Roberts, and *Danielle Steele's Family Album* (1994) with Jaclyn Smith.

Kelly Garrett's home was glimpsed briefly in "Target: Angels" (#5) and in "The Seance" (#11). Despite these episodes airing only six weeks apart, different homes were used in each show. In the third season, Kelly finally received a more permanent residence. The house, nestled in Cheviot Hills, a small neighborhood in West Los Angeles, was a much easier commute for the series production staff. Just minutes from the Twentieth Century Fox lot, the home still has the same look and charm it did back in the seventies.

Most of the blame for the falling numbers was placed on Shelley Hack. "She never really had fun with her role, so I don't think she was ever comfortable," observed director Kim Manners.

The natural rhythm of conversation between Angels, something that was taken for granted in the first three seasons, was suddenly missing. David Doyle admitted, "You didn't get the feeling that these girls hung out together away from the office." Even Johnny Carson added to the onslaught; "When Hack's 'A' is put where her 'T' should be, it still doesn't jiggle," he quipped.

Cheryl Ladd felt great empathy for Shelley, having been the "new girl" just two years earlier. "There was a whole bunch of things going on that Shelley took a lot of shit for, that she didn't deserve," said Ladd. "I feel too much blame was put on her, and maybe not enough on the writers."

Ladd believes that Hack had two strikes against her from the moment she joined the series—replacing Kate Jackson, the most charismatic Angel, and being saddled with Jackson's designation of "the smart one."

"What a trap! On a show where there is very little that is truly witty, truly intelligent or terribly clever, to have to play 'the smart one'— please!" she said. "Kate pulled it off cause there was a quirkiness about her, she had the voice and an offbeat humor and a big personality. When Shelley came in, she took it too seriously. She didn't understand how kind of . . . stupid this show was. She wanted to be good in a 'I'm a good actress' kind of way, instead of concentrating on just developing a character."

David Doyle noticed the same problem, and tried to help Hack along. "(Her character) was more mature, more bookish, and that's a little hard to introduce," he said. "Shelley had a problem justifying what the part called for; she worked on the series as she would a play or a film, and I remember telling her 'you could get in big trouble, because in one episode you may do something that will seem contrary to what you'll do in the next. Don't start looking for threads that will remain constant in your character. She may have been doing that, but I think time has shown that she can act."

Despite the ratings drop, the fourth season of *Charlie's Angels* did produce several memorable episodes, including Shelley Hack's first solo outing, "Angels on Campus" (#78). "Fallen Angel" (#73) teams Farrah in her first return of the season with guest-star Timothy Dalton, who later played James Bond; the desert island adventure "Angel Hunt" (#79) is an exciting homage to *The Most Dangerous Game*, and "Harrigan's Angel" (#87) features delightful chemistry between Cheryl Ladd and guest-star Howard Duff, who plays an alcoholic detective who doesn't like "working with girls."

On Valentine's Day, 1980, Jaclyn Smith, Cheryl Ladd, David Doyle and John Forsythe all received a valentine from Spelling-Goldberg inviting them back for the fifth season. Shelley Hack undoubtedly received a lot of valentines, but nothing from her producers or ABC. Once word of her dismissal made the papers, a popular joke at the time was, "Can you imagine being fired from *Charlie's Angels* for not being a good enough actress?"

"I had a fun year," said Shelley, who left *Charlie's Angels* with the same detached air of professionalism with which she arrived. Said Ed Lakso, "As I recall, I don't think she was terribly hurt by it."

As Jaclyn Smith (left) and Cheryl Ladd await the arrival of yet another new Angel,
Spelling-Goldberg Productions had more serious issues to contend with.

CHAPTER SEVEN

Angels in Court

T HE SUMMER OF 1980 WAS NOT THE BEST OF TIMES FOR *CHARLIE'S Angels*. The unpopular casting of Shelley Hack had cut the ratings of the once unbeatable series in half. For the first time, the ABC powerhouse was vulnerable to other networks, and perhaps even to cancellation. Aaron Spelling set out upon another "Angel search," knowing that one more casting mistake might be fatal. Jaclyn Smith reiterated her intention to leave after fulfilling her five year contract, casting even more uncertainty on the series' future.

"One Love . . . Two Angels" (#92), the fourth season finale, aired on April 30 to underwhelming response. That same day, ABC attorney Jennifer Martin submitted memorandums to her superiors at the network, accusing Spelling-Goldberg Productions of perpetrating a scheme to defraud Robert Wagner and Natalie Wood of more than half a million dollars. Wagner and Wood owned 43.75 percent of *Charlie's Angels*, a result of a clause in their contract from an earlier Spelling-Goldberg TV movie, that allowed them to participate in a pilot created by the producers (see Chapter One). The story of Martin's charge broke the next day, on page one of the *New York Times*.

Martin, 32, didn't look like a disgruntled whistleblower. She was a Los Angeles native, whose lithe figure and Farrah-flipped auburn hair could have qualified her for Angel status. She was hired by ABC in 1978 to work in its contracts division, and acquired a reputation for dedication and tenacity. Promoted to associate director of contracts, she was responsible for authorizing payment to Spelling-Goldberg for certain series airing on ABC. But in reviewing the contracts, she discovered an "exclusivity provision," amounting to $30,000 per episode, that was paid to the producers, supposedly to insure that ABC would continue to have first rights to any new series they created. One invoice she found amounted to $320,000.

But Martin knew that ABC had already paid for exclusivity, which made the additional provision unnecessary. She also discovered that Wagner and Wood, who were entitled to half of all series profits, had not received 50 percent of the exclusivity payments. She first raised questions about the discrepancy in September of 1979, and received a reprimand for her efforts from ABC vice president Ronald Sunderland. One month later, she was fired, purportedly for absenteeism and sloppy work.

When Martin threatened to continue her investigation, ABC conducted a ten day internal inquiry, and issued a statement that "no improprieties were found." However, the $320,000 invoice was never paid, and the investigation resulted in a recommendation that ABC no longer honor invoices that did not reflect items "actually agreed upon and properly designated."

When the *New York Times* took up the case, they polled several television lawyers, and found that none of them had ever heard of an exclusivity provision when the show's owners and talent were already under an exclusive arrangement. Martin also produced a memo in which a Spelling-Goldberg official revealed that the provision was an artificial device, "part of a scheme to divert money from the major profit participants," the Wagners.

Martin brought her findings to the Los Angeles district attorney's office. After she passed a lie detector test, the newly-established

Julie, Julie, Julie Do You Love Me?

A aron Spelling chose the name Julie Rogers for Tanya Roberts' character, continuing a tradition of Julies in the Spelling *oeuvre*. *Twenty Dollar Bride*, the first script he sold to television in 1955, featured a character named Julie played by Jane Wyman. The name became his good luck charm; Spelling's first *Burke's Law* script was entitled "Who Killed Julie Greer," Peggy Lipton played Julie Barnes on *The Mod Squad*, Lauren Tewes played Julie McCoy on *The Love Boat*, and Wendy Schaal played Mr. Roarke's goddaughter, Julie, on *Fantasy Island*. ◼

Entertainment Industry Task Force from the D.A.'s office searched the offices of Spelling-Goldberg Productions, their lawyers, and their accountants. According to the *Times* article, the investigation focused on charges of grand theft and conspiracy.

"We are stunned and outraged by allegations that we have tried to cheat our friends, Natalie and Robert Wagner," said a spokesman for the producers. "Since we began ten years ago, Spelling-Goldberg Productions has always dealt fairly and honestly with its profit participants and we are proud of that fact. We most strongly insist that the allegations are unfounded and have been a great source of embarrassment to us and our families."

In the days before *Entertainment Tonight*, *Access Hollywood*, and *Entertainment Weekly* magazine, coverage of the entertainment industry was usually relegated to a couple of pages in a back section of the newspaper. Information about film grosses and television production deals were covered only in show business publications such as Variety. The average moviegoer and television viewer, it was believed, had little interest in what went on behind the scenes.

The *Charlie's Angels* case was the first extensive criminal fraud investigation into the finances and profit-sharing of a television series, and coverage of the investigation was the first major story in the mainstream press to analyze the way the entertainment industry functions. "Angelgate," fairly or unfairly, came to symbolize the industry's creative system of accounting.

Other entertainment bookkeeping practices came under fire. Reporters questioned figures released by Spelling-Goldberg during their lawsuit against Farrah Fawcett, which stated that *Charlie's Angels* was not financially successful. The deficit numbers were a standard network practice—successful shows did not show a profit until going into syndication. Supposedly, *Charlie's Angels* had lost more than $10 million in its first three seasons.

"After discovering the show was $10 million in the red, we were going to send Spelling-Goldberg a telegram and tell them that with one more hit show like *Charlie's Angels* , they'll soon go broke," said Ivan Goff, who with Ben Roberts owned 12.5 percent of the series. The men who wrote the series pilot filed a lawsuit to find out where the money went. They found that their financial report contained different figures from the one sent to Robert Wagner and Natalie Wood, which also varied from the one found in the Spelling-Goldberg offices.

"We welcome anyone bringing in an accounting firm and doing an audit," said Leonard Goldberg. "We have nothing to hide." The producers professed their innocence of any wrongdoing. They did not claim to have knowledge of every bookkeeping detail of every one of their series (which would have been impossible), but they insisted that the details were handled by associates in whom they had complete confidence.

Though no civil or criminal charges were filed, the story continued to make headlines throughout May and June. Spelling and Goldberg cooperated fully with the district attorney's investigation and, in a prepared statement, promised that Robert Wagner and Natalie Wood will receive "substantial" profits from the show. Ivan Goff and Ben Roberts expressed outrage that their names were not mentioned as well. "It was a shocking omission that was clearly deliberate," said Roberts. "Without our script, there wouldn't be all this money to fight over."

Warren Ettinger, an attorney for Spelling-Goldberg responded that the writers had already received $700,000 from fees, residuals, and merchandising income. "That's pretty good for two months' work," he said.

In June, a squad of investigators from the Securities and Exchange Commission arrived in Los Angeles from Washington, D.C. to join the case. The S.E.C. claimed jurisdiction to conduct a separate investigation because ABC is a publicly held company, and the commission is authorized to monitor whether the network properly disclosed information that may have impact on the investment of its stockholders.

A grand jury hearing was held on August 25. Among those who testified were David Soul and Paul Michael Glaser, the stars of another Spelling-Goldberg series, *Starsky and Hutch*. In her original claim, Jennifer Martin alleged that investment funds from *Charlie's Angels* had been diverted to *Starsky and Hutch*. After the hearing, which was closed to the press and public, David Soul was asked if he thought the allegations against the producers were true. "I don't know," he said, then added that it was "a little early in the day for him to get up."

The hearing was the lead story on ABC's *World News Tonight*, which launched its own investigation. "When the parent corporation is involved in a story, the news division does feel a greater responsibility," said ABC News vice president David Burke.

On October 1, the Federal Bureau of Investigation figured that the Securities Exchange Commission shouldn't have all the fun, and began a preliminary investigation of its own. The F.B.I. wanted to determine if information uncovered in the various other inquiries had applicability to federal white-collar criminal statutes.

One year had now passed since Jennifer Martin first asked for clarification of the exclusivity provision she found in Spelling-Goldberg's contract with ABC. While her charges were being examined by the Los Angeles District Attorney, the S.E.C. and the F.B.I., Martin applied unsuccessfully for twenty different jobs in the entertainment industry. Claiming her professional reputation had been impugned by her dismissal, she filed a $22 million lawsuit against ABC and Spelling-Goldberg Productions, listing charges of slander, conspiracy, and breach of contract.

Had all this happened in an episode of a Spelling-Goldberg tele-vision series, a story already rich in drama and tension would be resolved in an explosive finale. But such is not always the case in the real world. On December 2, 1980, District Attorney John Van De Kamp concluded that there was insufficient evidence to bring charges against Spelling-Goldberg Productions. "We cannot prove beyond a reasonable doubt that the *Charlie's Angels* profit participants were defrauded or that there was a conspiracy to defraud them in the future," said Van De Kamp. However, he also released an eighty-one-page report accusing the entertainment industry of participating in "shoddy business prac-tices" and "murky contracts."

Robert Wagner and Natalie Wood, who did not comment on the investigation while it was ongoing, expressed approval of the decision not to prosecute. Wagner, whose alleged loss of $500,000 made him the "victim" in Jennifer Martin's exposé, was then making many times that sum as the star of (and profit participant in) another Spelling series, *Hart to Hart*. "As friends of Aaron Spelling and Leonard Goldberg, we are delighted with this result, and we look forward to a continuing relationship both personally and professionally," said the Wagners in a statement.

Jennifer Martin, who first accused Spelling-Goldberg of defraud-ing the Wagners, only to have the the alleged victims support the alleged perpetrators, expressed disappointment in a statement issued through her attorney. "She is, in retrospect, confident that her actions in this matter were justified and in the long run will help ABC."

Martin may or may not have found a legitimate discrepancy, but victimless crimes rarely get prosecuted. There was so much money to go around in the TV business, that all parties involved were happy with their cut even if a half-million here or there didn't appear where it should on a profit statement. Every production company participated in the shifting of funds from one series to another, and deficit financing in lieu of syndication. Spelling-Goldberg Productions did nothing wrong by industry standards; in fact, television executives speaking off the record stated that the producers had a well-deserved reputation for integrity and generosity in their profit-sharing deals.

"It's not really that big a problem, because everybody takes care of you if you play the game and don't complain," said one writer. "A producer may not share his $20,000 in profits on a show with you, but then he'll hire you to write two pilots a year and you'll have $60,000 more. So everybody makes out. It's a friendly town."

Tanya Roberts joins the cast as streetwise Julie Rogers.

CHAPTER EIGHT

Julie

B Y 1980, "MEET CHARLIE'S NEW ANGEL!" COULD TAKE ITS PLACE alongside "Congressman Caught in Scandal!" and "Cubs Lose!" as a recyclable newspaper headline. For the third time in three years, ABC and Spelling-Goldberg embarked on a quest to fill a vacancy at the Townsend Agency, which now seemed to have more employee turnover than McDonald's.

Though *Charlie's Angels* had slipped perilously in the ratings during its fourth season, the series still had enough notoriety to generate a media event around its choice of the new Angel. The artificially-inflated number of candidates supposedly considered for the role ranged from 1,000 to 2,000, depending on which publicity person was telling the tale. Actually, only five actresses received screen-tests. Susie Coelho tried again, after being passed over for the role played by Jaclyn Smith. Jayne Kennedy, a former model now best-remembered as the scoreboard-garbling commentator on CBS's *NFL Today*, was also a leading candidate. But the stunning Kennedy, at 5'10", towered over the diminutive Cheryl Ladd, which may have cost her the role.

The final decision, as always, belonged to Aaron Spelling, and his candidate was an unknown actress named Tanya Roberts. Spelling first met Roberts in 1978, when she auditioned for a guest role as a rape victim on the Spelling-Goldberg TV movie *Waikiki* (1979). The producer liked Tanya enough to then cast her in a special two-hour episode of *VEGA$*, in which she played a police detective. At the time, Spelling was also searching for Kate Jackson's replacement on *Charlie's Angels*, and Tanya's name was briefly in the running.

The *VEGA$* appearance was intended as a pilot for the spinoff series *Ladies in Blue*, which would star Roberts and Michelle Phillips as beautiful, streetwise police officers. The pilot didn't sell, but Spelling was apparently determined to get Tanya Roberts on a series, and invited her to test for *Angel* duty. At the time, Roberts didn't comprehend the importance of the invitation. "It was just another screen test, and I tried not to get too excited about it," she recalled. "I'm not a television fan, except for *I Love Lucy* reruns. But I knew it was a big show and everyone loved it."

Roberts filmed two screen tests, one with brown hair, and a second with red hair (five years after the pilot, Spelling-Goldberg were still trying to recruit that elusive combination of a blond, brunette, and redheaded Angel). "After the second test, Aaron said he'd call me the next day, and that I'd know first thing in the morning if I had the part because a limousine would arrive at 6 a.m., to take me to an interview with Rona Barrett," said Roberts. The limo appeared on schedule, and Tanya Roberts, who still hadn't met her costars, was hired to play the tough-talking, streetwise Julie Rogers.

The Bronx Bombshell

orn within walking distance of Yankee Stadium in the Bronx, New York, on October 15, 1956, Tanya Leigh grew up enchanted by watching old movies on television. She was the daughter of a pen salesman who had no interest in that particular family business—the world of classic cinema was her passion, especially films featuring such strong-willed beauties as Bette Davis, Lana Turner, and Joan Crawford.

At the age of 15, the rebellious Tanya quit school, and hitchhiked across America. She married a fellow traveler, though her mother later had the marriage annulled. In New York, she tried to launch an acting

Julie Rogers
(Tanya Roberts) attracts
unwanted attention in
"Angel in Hiding."

career, and found an agent right away. "This agent was right out of an old movie—four secretaries with headphones, working on a switchboard with little cubicles separated by chicken wire," she recalled. Nonetheless, he found her jobs in commercials for such products as Excedrin, Aspirin, and Clairol hair products. She also had a brief but successful stint as a model with the Wilhelmina agency.

Tanya honed her acting skills in plays staged in Canada, and several off-Broadway productions, including *High Structure*, *Picnic*, *A View from the Bridge*, and *The Hydes of March*. One afternoon, while waiting in a movie theater line with her sister, Barbara, she met an aspiring screenwriter named Barry Roberts, a man she would later marry. "He's been the strongest influence in my life" she says. "I was a completely underdeveloped kid when I met him. He created me as a person."

Two weeks after the couple moved to Los Angeles, Tanya was cast in the film *The Betsy* (1978), as a groupie chasing Tommy Lee Jones at the racetrack. Her contribution was left on the cutting room floor, but it gave her the opportunity to meet costars Laurence Olivier and Robert Duvall. Her next would-be big break came from a costarring role in *Tourist Trap* (1978), a low budget thriller with Chuck Connors.

She was cast as one of the stewardesses in *Flying High* (see *Jiggle TV* sidebar) but was replaced by Connie Sellecca (who, coincidentally, once auditioned to be an Angel!) Other television and theatrical films followed, in which Tanya was usually cast as a girl in a bikini: *California Dreaming* (1979), *Pleasure Cove* (1979), and *Zuma Beach* (1980), all featured the buxom brunette cavorting in the sun and sand. Her biggest career setback was missing out on the title role in Blake Edwards' comedy *10* (1980), the film that made Bo Derek famous, when Edwards decided at the last moment to hire a blond.

■ ■ ■

Roberts' background was similar to that of Julie, who seemed more suited to *The Alley Cats* than *Charlie's Angels*. Clearly, Spelling hoped to make the refined Tiffany Welles a distant memory by replacing the debutante with a tigress. But Roberts, though she seemed a natural choice for the role, claims she has no idea why she was cast. "I didn't know why. Maybe because I was completely undemanding, and I worked really hard."

After chatting with Rona on *Good Morning America*, Tanya was finally introduced to the cast. "She had the best figure out of all of them—even the other girls said so," raved David Doyle.

"She had the most beautiful skin of anyone I had ever seen in my life," said Cheryl Ladd. "Her eyes were mesmerizing, she had an incredible body, and I thought, 'I don't want to work with this bitch!' (laughs). "She's gorgeous—they always say that you don't get everything—she got everything." Shortly after their first meeting, Ladd invited the new girl to a get-acquainted dinner. "I had never heard language like that before!" said Ladd of her sassy colleague. "She was one of the toughest chicks I ever met."

Tanya Roberts' official coming-out party was held at the Century Plaza Hotel in Los Angeles. Wearing a daring blue silk dress with thigh-high slits, the 24-year old starlet fielded questions from the media in attendance, and gamely offered the standard answers to the now-standard questions. "It's all very exciting," she said. Of her costars, she asserted, "We got along just fine." To the usual criticism of *Charlie's Angels* lack of substance, she retorted, "I don't see this show as some nothing fluff-off acting job. It's fantasy, sure, but there's nothing wrong with fantasy."

"It was ridiculous—it was crazy," she said of her instant prestige. "One minute you're struggling as an actor in New York, and then all of a sudden photographers are waiting for you outside of restaurants. It was very disconcerting, because I knew I hadn't done anything to deserve it. To this day, I've never been much for publicity, which probably isn't smart for an actress."

Plans to introduce Julie in the special two-hour episode "New Orleans Angels" were scrapped after the road trip was deemed too costly. "Aaron was spending a fortune on *Dynasty*, and everyone was losing interest in *Charlie's Angels*," said Ed Lakso. "Instead, we went to Hawaii because we had been there before, and already had production people in place." An actors strike shut down the series for four months, further plunging schedules and budgets into turmoil.

Five of the first six shows were filmed in Hawaii, boosting the bikini-count per episode to new heights; for the first time in the history of the series, all three Angels appeared in two-piece bathing suits at the same time. Even Bosley was going topless. Some critics viewed the costume-shedding as a crass attempt to win back viewers, but Kelly, Kris, and Julie were actually wearing more bathing suits because business suits would have looked funny on the beach. Plans for *Charlie's Angels* beyond the upcoming season were no longer a priority for anyone, except perhaps newcomer Tanya Roberts.

"I wasn't aware then that it would be the last year, but I knew everybody else wanted off the show. And I was making money for the first time in my life!" said Roberts, who was hired for $12,000 per episode.

Jaclyn Smith reaffirmed her decision to leave at the end of her contract, and with none of Charlie's original Angels remaining, it was assumed that the series would end, unless Tanya Roberts became a revitalizing force akin to the first wave of Farrah-mania. "I was too young and naive to put that kind of pressure on myself," Roberts said.

"I was so involved in my personal life at that time, so there was a lot of that final year that I had psychologically checked out on," remembers Cheryl Ladd. Her seven- year marriage to David Ladd ended in the winter of 1979, and she was beginning a new relationship with singer-composer Brian Russell, to whom she is still married today.

Fatigue had taken hold of the set, so much so that David Doyle mooned his costars during production of the episode "Waikiki Angels" (#97) just to break the monotony. "Everybody was tired—I'll get a reaction out of them," said Doyle. The burnout became so severe that Ed Lakso, who had written more than 40 episodes by the fifth season, had to call his wife to ask "What's the name of the brunette? Kelly?"

There remained, besides professional pride, one more incentive to keep the show going one more year. Syndication deals are more favorable for a series that runs more than 100 episodes. At the end of four years, *Charlie's Angels* had 92 episodes in the can. "We needed five years; the deficit financing then was about $25,000-$30,000 per episode, but the network could live with that awhile longer to get the syndication deal," said Lakso.

Charlie's Angels debuted its fifth season on November 30, 1980, with a two-hour introduction of Julie Rogers, followed immediately by a one-hour episode that explained the *Angels'* move to Hawaii. The three-hour *Angel* marathon finished in Neilsen's top ten. Soon after, however, the show was losing its regular time slot to the Sunday night competition of *Archie Bunker's Place* on CBS, and *CHiPs* on NBC.

A midseason move to Saturday nights at 8 p.m. did little to reverse the falling numbers. For the week of February 28, 1981, the show that had set records for viewership ranked sixty-third out of the sixty-five shows surveyed by Nielsen. Ironically, while the Angels struggled to find an audience at home, episodes from the first season premiered in France and Italy, and reignited *Angel*-mania in Europe.

Two weeks later, ABC programming chief Tony Thomopoulos announced that *Charlie's Angels* was being put on "telecast hiatus," but the euphemism wasn't fooling anyone. As *People* magazine quipped, "The jiggle was up." An official cancellation notice was handed down in March of 1981. The final four original episodes of the 109-show run aired in June, and struggled in the ratings against the summer rerun offerings of the other networks.

"It was a relief more than anything," said Cheryl Ladd of the confirmation that her *Angels* days were over. "And yet, after all those years there were a bunch of us that had really become a family. (director of photography) Richard Rawlings, (director) Kim Manners, (assistant director) Jeff Kibbee, (producer) Elaine Rich, and Jaclyn and I—it was tough to think that we weren't going to see each other as much."

"I was on the Fox lot, writing the *T.J. Hooker* pilot, when Aaron called and invited me to the wrap party for *Charlie's Angels*," recalled Rick Husky, the series first producer. "I thought that was very nice, since I hadn't had anything to do with the show since the first ten episodes. It was huge gathering, from what I recall." Kate Jackson returned to share the celebration. Farrah Fawcett and Shelley Hack did not. Tanya Roberts, who had the most to lose from the cancellation, partied with the rest of the cast, and walked away with no regrets. "Everything is a learning experience, and I learned a lot from that show. I had a lot of fun, and the people were all wonderful to work with."

It's a wrap! Cast and crew gather in Charlie's office to celebrate the final episode of *Charlie's Angels*.

The Angels today: (top left clockwise) Jaclyn Smith, Tanya Roberts, Farrah Fawcett, Cheryl Ladd, Shelley Hack and Kate Jackson.

CHAPTER NINE

Life After Charlie

FTER *CHARLIE'S ANGELS* HAD BEEN ACCUSED OF MISOGYNY, IN-competence, and everything short of the downfall of Western civilization, news of the series cancellation was received with an unexpected outpouring of sadness, even among its harshest detractors. "Oh God, I already miss it," wrote television critic Ben Brown in his mea culpa. "I'll admit, back in 1976 I was among the hordes who found something lacking in the sociological perspective of the show. I wrote long, analytical pieces about the pimp-hooker relation-ship between the body-less Charlie and the body-ful angels. I moaned at the dumb writing."

Brown claims he saw the light thanks to a friend's ten-year-old daughter, who loved the show and wasn't buying any of his arguments about exploitation. The Angels were in control, she said. They drove fast cars, and outwitted the male villains.

"*Charlie's Angels*, even in its recent decline, was bigger than the Angels themselves," he admitted. "I no longer believe the show depended exclusively on its exploitative hook for its top-ten performance."

"One of modern TV's true marvels," raved AP writer Peter Boyer. "One of the most influential shows ever to hit television," wrote the *Denver Post*. "Whether the show's long success could have been ascribed to art, fantasy, errant pop culture, pulchritude, or showbiz hype isn't important. *Charlie's Angels*—for a time, at least—was the embodiment of what people wanted to see, and that is the only yardstick of success in a flighty business."

There were mixed feelings among the cast and creative team as well. It is sad and ironic that a series now remembered so fondly by so many, as one of television's most carefree hours, was such a trial for so many of the people who worked on it. But the passage of time has softened some of the adverse memories, and amplified the good times.

"I can't say this of every show I produced, but I loved *Charlie's Angels*," said Aaron Spelling in 1986, on the occasion of its tenth anniversary. "It put us over the top and made our company financially secure and incredibly desirable."

"The show was a true phenomenon," said Barney Rosenzweig. "It had an enormous influence on the medium." Rosenzweig still praises *Charlie's Angels* as a series that empowered women, as opposed to exploiting them. "I had a long conversation with Gloria Steinem, about why this show was an important feminist document. Before *Angels*, never in the history of Hollywood had two women related to each other like Paul Newman and Robert Redford in *Butch Cassidy and the Sundance Kid* (1969), or Donald Sutherland and Elliot Gould in *MASH* (1970). That's why I did *Cagney and Lacey*. But there would never have been a *Cagney and Lacey* without the foundation laid by *Charlie's Angels*. It was a hit because it had vitality, it had chemistry, and all those ephemeral things that no one can predict."

"*Charlie's Angels*" brought so much to my life—it if weren't for the show I may never have had the success I have today." said Jaclyn Smith. "We had to prove we were more than just Barbie dolls prancing around, but I think over the years we have all overcome that. I will never be able to live down the image, but I am proud to be part of a project that so many people have enjoyed over the years!"

"I've done so many other projects, and at this point in my career enough time has passed that I can look back and feel good about it, and see why it was so popular in a way that I couldn't see then," said Cheryl Ladd. "I've also had 20 years of people telling me what the show meant to them. It was fantasy entertainment, but there was enough reality that you could project yourself into it. We really became your Wednesday night girlfriends, or pals, or babes. The little girls wanted to be us, the young women wanted to wear our clothes, and the guys wanted to do us."

Who would have guessed that a show about three detectives who couldn't find their boss would become a global phenomenon? *Charlie's Angels* has aired in more than 90 countries, from Sri Lanka to Bangladesh. In the United States, perpetual reruns have introduced the show to new generations of fans, who have made icons of the characters and the actresses who portrayed them.

Though they haven't answered to "Angel" in more than 20 years, Farrah Fawcett, Kate Jackson, Cheryl Ladd and Jaclyn Smith will forever be defined by the time they spent working for Charlie. The series is mentioned in reviews of every project they've appeared in since, and they can't appear on a talk show without answering questions about their *Angel* days. And if none of their subsequent films, television movies, or stage appearances rivaled *Charlie's Angels* in popularity, the cast have at least overcome the scourge of typecasting, and have worked steadily for the past two decades in an impressive variety of projects.

Farrah Fawcett's first post-*Angels* films did not fare well, but she has since silenced her critics with laudable performances in several roles (for complete credits, see Appendix C). Fawcett earned raves as a spoiled socialite in the telefilm *Murder in Texas* (1981), and as photographer Margaret Bourke-White in a 1989 TV biography. She was nominated for an Emmy Award as an abused wife in the wrenching made-for-TV drama *The Burning Bed* (1984), and was nominated again for her work as a modern-day Medea in *Small Sacrifices* (1989).

In 1986, Fawcett reprised her acclaimed off-Broadway performance as a rape victim in a film adaptation of *Extremities*. In 1987, she

Farrah Fawcett (pictured with Paul Le Mat) earned rave reviews and an Emmy nomination for her performance in *The Burning Bed* (1984).

joined an elite group of actresses to be nominated for a Golden Globe for a movie (*Extremities*) and a television show (*Nazi Hunter: The Beate Klarsfeld Story*) in the same year.

In 1997, Farrah posed nude for *Playboy* magazine, and for *Playboy*'s controversial pay-per-view special *Farrah Fawcett—All of Me*. Her decision to do so, coupled with a bizarre 1998 appearance on *The Late Show With David Letterman*, prompted several unflattering tabloid stories.

Farrah's relationship with actor Ryan O'Neal lasted from 1979 to 1997, and produced one son, Redmond James O'Neal (born 1985). Shortly after her separation, Fawcett made headlines after being victimized in a domestic abuse dispute with her new boyfriend, director James Orr. Her personal setbacks have not dimmed her sense of humor, or her desire to work—in 1998, she participated in the animated video *The Brave Little Toaster Goes to Mars*, in which she provided the voice to—what else—a faucet.

■　■　■

In the past two decades, Jaclyn Smith has held the unofficial title of "Queen of the Made-for-TV Movie." She has appeared in more than 25 telefilms, including *Jacqueline Bouvier Kennedy* (1981), *Rage of Angels* (1983), *Florence Nightingale* (1985), *Windmills of the Gods* (1988), and *Kaleidoscope* (1990). She received a Golden Globe nomination for *Jacqueline Bouvier Kennedy*, and is one of two ex-Angels to receive a Star on the Hollywood Walk of Fame (Farrah is the other). Smith returned to series television in 1989 as *Christine Cromwell*, an elegant investigator and financial advisor to the rich and famous. The ABC show, which featured the distinguished supporting cast of Celeste Holm and Ralph Bellamy, lasted one season.

Smith appeared—seven months pregnant—on the cover of the February 22, 1982 issue of *Time* magazine, for an article on the "new

Jaclyn Smith, the "Queen of the Miniseries," starred in *Jacqueline Bouvier Kennedy* (1981), opposite James Franciscus.

baby boom." She thus became one of a select few show business personalities to grace the cover of *Time* twice.

For three decades, Smith has been lauded as one of Hollywood's most beautiful stars. She wrote *The American Look—How it Can Be Yours* for Simon & Schuster in 1984, launched one of the most successful celebrity-endorsed fragrances, "Jaclyn Smith's California," for Max Factor in 1989, and released an exercise video, *Jaclyn Smith's Workout for Beauty and Balance*, in 1993. In 1999, Smith was named one of *People* magazine's list of "50 Most Beautiful People."

She is still among the most sought-after actresses on the small screen, and after fourteen years of promoting her Jaclyn Smith Collection of fashions, she's done more for K-Mart than the "blue light special." More than 40 million women now wear her endorsed clothing designs, hosiery, sunglasses, handbags, and jewelry. She lives with her fourth husband, heart surgeon Bradley Allen, and her two children, Gaston Anthony (born 1982) and Spencer Margaret (born 1985).

■ ■ ■

After her contentious departure from *Charlie's Angels*, Kate Jackson appeared in the feature films *Dirty Tricks* (1981), *Making Love* (1982) and *Loverboy* (1989), but like her fellow Angels she's been most conspicuous on television. Jackson is the only Angel to star in a successful series before *Angels* (*The Rookies*), and the only Angel to star in another successful series after leaving her halo behind. In 1983, she began a four year stint as housewife Amanda King in the CBS espionage adventure *Scarecrow and Mrs. King*. She earned a Golden Globe nomination, to go with the three she received for *Charlie's Angels*.

In 1987, during the series' run, Jackson was diagnosed with breast cancer. Surgery was successful, and she returned to work in a 1988 sitcom adapted from the film hit *Baby Boom* (1987), starring Diane Keaton. She played lawyer J.C. Wiatt, whose life is turned upside-down after she adopts a baby daughter. The NBC series lasted one season.

A reoccurrence of her cancer was detected in 1989. Jackson underwent a partial mastectomy, followed by six weeks of radiation.

Kate Jackson (pictured with
costar Bruce Boxleitner)
made a successful return to
series television in
Scarecrow and Mrs. King
(1983-87).

She was deluged with cards and gifts from fans. She has since passed the crucial two-year and five-year post-operative marks without any further reoccurrences.

Jackson's made-for-TV movies include *Empty Cradle* (1993), *Justice in a Small Town* (1994), *A Kidnapping in the Family* (1996), and *Satan's School for Girls* (2000), a remake of the 1973 telefilm in which she starred with Cheryl Ladd. In 1998, she received an Emmy nomination for her guest appearance on *Ally McBeal* (1998), as a television newswoman who hires Ally after she is dismissed from her job.

Now single after three unsuccessful marriages, Jackson adopted a son, Taylor, in 1995. She is currently at work on her autobiography.

■　■　■

"I look back sometimes and ask, 'Did I make the right decision?' because having *Charlie's Angels* on my resume has sometimes been a ball and chain when it comes to meeting film directors and producers," said

Cheryl Ladd and Richard Burgi
starred in the CBS drama
One West Waikiki (1994)

Cheryl Ladd. "But it has also given me a 20 year career of doing what I like to do." Ladd followed up *Charlie's Angels* with a series of specials, continuing the musical career she embarked upon during her days as Kris Munroe. Her first album, *Cheryl Ladd*, yielded a top 40 single in "Think it Over." Ladd released a second album, *Dance Forever*, and a third in Japan, *Take a Chance*, as well as two greatest hits compilations. In the Far East, her music has proven popular enough to top Elton John and Paul McCartney for the number 1 position on the Japanese charts.

Ladd's numerous TV movies include *Grace Kelly* (1983), *A Death in California* (1985), *Bluegrass* (1988), and *Michael Landon, The Father I Knew* (1999). "I have had the chance to do a variety of projects over the years, and I was always conscious of doing that because of *Charlie's Angels*. When people tuned in to watch a movie I was in, I wanted them to say, 'what's Cheryl Ladd doing now?' Not, 'Oh, there's Cheryl Ladd from *Charlie's Angels*.'" In 1994, she returned to series television in *One West Waikiki*, playing coroner Dawn "Holli" Holliday. The show returned Ladd to the beaches of Hawaii, but did not survive its first season on network television (reruns ran in syndication for another three years).

Ladd's feature film appearances run the gamut from the Vietnam War romance *Purple Hearts* (1984), to the seductive thriller *Poison Ivy*

(1992), to the wholesome family drama *A Dog of Flanders* (1999). In 1996, she wrote a children's book, *The Adventures of Little Nettie Windship*, coauthored by her husband of nineteen years, actor/singer Brian Russell. Ladd also serves as Goodwill Ambassador of Childhelp USA, a nonprofit organization for abused children.

An avid golfer, Cheryl Ladd now has a seventeen handicap and is one of the few non-professionals to have been sponsored by the Buick Corporation. Her website, www.cherylladd.com, earned an award from Yahoo for "Best Celebrity Website."

Cheryl's daughter, Jordan, appeared as a toddler in the *Charlie's Angels* episode "Angel on My Mind (#56), and has since become an actress herself, appearing most recently in the 1999 comedy *Never Been Kissed*.

■ ■ ■

Shelley Hack overcame the disastrous reviews she received after one season of sleuthing as an Angel, and has compiled an impressive resumé of credits on stage, screen, and television. She even won over her biggest

Jack and Mike starred Tom Mason and Shelley Hack as yuppies in love.

detractor, *Angels* writer Ed Lakso. "One year after the show, I saw Shelley in (the stage play) *Vanities*, and she did a wonderful job," Lakso said.

Hack earned impressive notices for her supporting roles in *The King of Comedy* (1983), opposite Jerry Lewis and Robert DeNiro, and in the horror cult classic *The Stepfather* (1987). On television she played Dr. Beth Gilbert in the hospital drama *Cutter to Houston* (1983), and starred in the sophisticated drama *Jack and Mike* (1986-87). She is now active in raising funds for several political candidates seeking election in California. Now married to director Harry Winer, she has one daughter, Rosie (born 1991).

■　■　■

Tanya Roberts joined *Charlie's Angels* when it was already sinking fast, but still experienced the benefits and the drawbacks of being associated with the show. "Once you've been typecast as a *Charlie's Angel*, you are set for life," she told *People* magazine in 1995. She traded in her sexy role as Julie Rogers for even sexier roles, beginning with *The Beastmaster* (1982), a movie that still plays on the TNT network about once a week. In 1984, she starred in the big-budget adventure film *Sheena*. But even the sight of a blond Roberts, cavorting through the jungle in a skimpy loincloth, could not make the film a hit. One year later, she played "Bond girl" Stacey Sutton opposite Roger Moore as Agent 007 in *A View to a Kill*.

She posed nude for *Playboy* in 1982, then received more exposure by appearing in a series of erotic thrillers, among them *Purgatory* (1988), *Night Eyes* (1990), and *Inner Sanctum* (1991). In 1995, she played a detective named Julie, an unofficial revival of her *Angels* character, in an episode of the series *Burke's Law*. In 1996, Roberts starred in the cable series *Hotline* as host of a kinky phone-in radio show, then returned to network television as sexy seventies mom Midge Pinciotti on FOX's *That '70s Show* (1998–). "This is the stability I've been looking for since *Charlie's Angels*," Roberts said. "It's a chance to prove I can do comedy—and something other than those crummy movies.

"I'm a better actress now, and a much happier person, and better prepared to cope with everything in the business," Roberts said. Although

Tanya Roberts goes native as the "Queen of the Jungle"in *Sheena* (1984).

she was remembered by her fellow Angels as the biggest party girl of the bunch, Tanya remains married to Barry Roberts, the same man she met prior to joining the series.

■　■　■

Twenty years after he left the role of John Bosley, David Doyle remarked that he still received 10–12 letters every week about *Charlie's Angels*. "I don't care whether I'm in Nebraska or Paris, I still get recognized from that show," he said in 1997. After *Angels* was cancelled, Doyle resumed his busy career as a character actor. He made guest appearances on such series as *General Hospital*, *Murder, She Wrote*, and *Lois & Clark*. He also lent his distinctive, gravelly voice to the animated series *Bonkers* and *Rugrats*. He died of a heart attack on February 23, 1997, at the age of 71.

■　■　■

John Forsythe still hasn't met two of his Angels, Shelley Hack and Tanya Roberts. "The first one I met was Farrah, and it was while she was still on the show. I was taking tennis lessons, and she had just finished a lesson with Nils Van Patten (Dick Van Patten's son). I was coming off the court when she came up to me and said 'Charlie! I finally met Charlie!'. Forsythe met Jaclyn Smith on the set of their TV movie *The Users* (1978), and was introduced to Kate Jackson for the first time at Santa Anita Racetrack. He now lives near Cheryl Ladd, and they remain close.

Forsythe's portrayal of Denver oil tycoon Blake Carrington on *Dynasty* (1981-1989) brought him two Golden Globes and three Emmy nominations. Created by Aaron Spelling, the series was one of television's most popular shows in the 1980s, rivaling even the mighty *Dallas* for preeminence among prime-time soap operas.

In the Norman Lear sitcom *The Powers That Be* (1992), Forsythe played a new U.S. Senator struggling to balance the responsibilities of his job with those of his oddball family. Despite glowing reviews, the series was cancelled after a dozen episodes. In 1993, he replaced Patrick Van Horn as host of *I Witness Video*, a show featuring sensational footage captured on home video.

■ ■ ■

The last foray into television by Ivan Goff and Ben Roberts was *Time Express*, a romantic drama with *Fantasy Island* overtones, about people who take a train trip into their past, to recapture a moment they wish to change. Vincent Price and his off-screen wife, Coral Browne, played the mysterious couple who escorted the passengers to their destinations. It was a provocative premise, but the series lasted only one month.

In 1981, the duo wrote *The Legend of the Lone Ranger*, an attempt to revive the popular masked Western hero. The film received scathing notices, though most were directed at the cast, particularly Klinton Spilsbury as the Lone Ranger.

Ben Roberts died on May 14, 1984, at the age of 68. Ivan Goff died September 23, 1999. Despite writing careers that span nearly 50 years, and incorporate film, television and the Broadway stage, the opening

Posed for success: Jaclyn Smith, Kate Jackson and Farrah Fawcett-Majors
suit up for their first adventure, March 21, 1976.

Charlie's original crime fighting team:
always dressed to thrill.

Farrah, Kate and Jaclyn: The show's scripts didn't always capitalize on their individual personalities.

Cheryl Ladd (right) eases into her role as Kris Munroe, replacing fictional "big sister" Farrah.

Cheryl Ladd: "If it weren't for David Doyle, I never would have survived the series."

Shelley Hack (right) displays her '70s fashion chic as Kate Jackson's replacement.

From sophisticated Shelley Hack (below)
to sultry Tanya Roberts (right)

Below: Charlie's last team of Angels—
Tanya, Jaclyn and Cheryl

Author Jack Condon with his *Charlie's Angels* collection.

line of both their obituaries identified Goff and Roberts as the men who "created *Charlie's Angels*."

■　■　■

Rick Husky created *T.J. Hooker* for Spelling-Goldberg; the series, starring William Shatner as a Los Angeles policeman, lasted five seasons. He was a supervising producer on *Walker: Texas Ranger*, and *Tour of Duty*, and currently serves as co-executive producer on the Sammo Hung—Arsenio Hall series *Martial Law*.

■　■　■

Cagney and Lacey, created by Barney Rosenzweig, ran for six years (1982-1988) on CBS, and became one of television's most successful and honored detective dramas. Tyne Daly (Mary Beth Lacey) won four Emmys as Best Actress in a Dramatic Series; her costar, Sharon Gless (Christine Cagney) won two Emmys. The series itself won Best Drama honors in 1985 and 1986. "My office has Emmys and Golden Globes, but right next to them I still have a picture of Farrah, Kate and Jackie. I'm proud to have been associated with them," said Rosenzweig. "They handed the baton to *Cagney and Lacey*, and we handed it to *Thelma and Louise*." Rosenzweig married Sharon Gless in 1991.

■　■　■

Ed Lakso knew his days at ABC had ended when the network sprayed over the name on his parking space, and reassigned his office while he was still in it. But he left with no regrets. "I knew *Charlie's Angels* was my swan song to television, but it gave me the financial independence to never have to write again." Lakso has since written novels and books to musicals, and savors his leisure time by fishing and going to the racetrack, where he wrote many of his *Angels* scripts.

■　■　■

Aaron Spelling has become a brand name in television, that signifies frothy adventures and glamorous romance. After a succession of immensely popular series in the 1970s and early 1980s, Spelling brought his formula for crowdpleasing entertainment to the big screen, and scored a hit with *Mr. Mom* (1983), starring Michael Keaton as a stay-at-home father.

He created another TV hit with *Hotel* (1983-1988), but as shows like *Hill Street Blues*, *L.A. Law* and *St. Elsewhere* brought a new, gritty reality to television drama, Spelling suddenly found his glitzy brand of entertainment out of favor with audiences. He continued to produce new shows, but *Finder of Lost Loves* (1984), *Glitter* (1984), *The Colbys* (1985), and *Nightingales* (1992), all suffered from poor reviews and low viewer turnout.

Spelling attempted to relaunch *Angel*-mania with a new series, *Angels '88*, but the show was cancelled before a single episode could be filmed (see sidebar) And then, just as he was about to be written off, Spelling bounced back with *Beverly Hills, 90210* and *Melrose Place*, two enormous hits for the FOX network. Since then, he's helped launch no less than 17 new shows. *Seventh Heaven* (1997) and *Charmed* (1998) were hits; *Models, Inc.* (1994), *Savannah* (1996), *Love Boat: The Next Wave* (1998), and many others were not.

■   ■   ■

Leonard Goldberg's partnership with Aaron Spelling was amicably dissolved in the early 1980s. In 1984, Goldberg was an executive producer of *Something About Amelia*, a harrowing look at incest that was praised as one of the finest television movies ever made. But much of Goldberg's post-Spelling work has been in feature films; he served as executive producer of *WarGames* (1983) and *Space Camp* (1986), and as producer on the Julia Roberts hit *Sleeping With the Enemy* (1991), and the Eddie Murphy comedy *The Distinguished Gentleman* (1992).

■   ■   ■

"Jiggle TV" was revived in the mid-1980s with NBC's *Codename: Foxfire*, starring Joanna Cassidy, Sheryl Lee Ralph and Robin Johnson as

Angels '88

*B*arry Diller was the Chairman of the Fox network in 1987. He had laughed at the Spelling-Goldberg concept for *Charlie's Angels* when he heard it in 1976, but with the keen sense of hindsight common to all network executives, he jumped at the chance to add a remake of the landmark series to his fledgling network's schedule.

The new version, titled *Angels '88*, would be produced by Aaron Spelling, but had little else in common with its predecessor. This time there would be four heavenly crimefighters instead of three, all former actresses who starred in a fictional detective series. When the series is canceled, they decide to stick together and become real private investigators. There was no Bosley, and no Charlie—a development promoted as emblematic of the strides made by women in the decade since the original series premiered.

The Spelling publicity machine announced a nationwide talent search to cast the four *Angel* roles. Twenty thousand hopefuls were pared down to 2,000, then 200, then fifteen. After

The cast of Angels '88: Clockwise from left: Teá Leoni, Karen Kopins, Sandra Canning and Claire Yarlett.

several screen tests and call-backs, four actresses were selected: Sandra Canning, Karen Kopins, Claire Yarlett, and Téa Leoni. Leoni was the only candidate discovered at one of the open casting calls. In April of 1988, the new Angels received a gala introduction to the Fox affiliates at a party in New York's Central Park.

The series, unlike it's predecessor, planned to provide a detailed biography of each character. "All of the women come from distinctly different backgrounds and have somewhat checkered pasts," revealed supervising producer E. Duke Vincent. Pam Ryan (Karen Kopins) was the dramatic actress in the group, having studied at the University of Minneapolis. She left for New York, fell victim to the hardships of show business, and worked as a waitress. She married, then divorced a fellow actor, prior to landing a role on the fictional detective series. Pam approached her detective work like a script, using ideas from her TV roles to solve cases.

Connie Bates (Claire Yarlett) was a free spirit who dressed radically chic and enjoyed flirting with danger. Originally from a middle class neighborhood in Queens, Connie frequented the punk discos in Manhattan, where she met a guitar player and traveled the world with him. While in Europe, she dabbled in modeling but returned to New York to begin a career in acting. She relied on her instincts and skills at improvisational storytelling for case work. Despite her wild background, Connie dated a straight-laced Yuppie lawyer on *Angels '88*.

The world of Pittsburgh native Tricia Lawrence (Sandra Canning) was shattered the night her father, a cop, was gunned down. She rebelled and became a wild teenager and a failing student. To escape her pain, Tricia entered the fantasy world of airline stewardessing, where she was "discovered" by a Hollywood agent. Though she was not a polished actress, her intensity made Tricia an instant success.

California girl Bernadette Colter (Téa Leoni) was the "jockette" who earned a college athletics scholarship to the University of Southern California. She excelled in tennis, but her all American good looks also earned her a place in the "Girls of USC" calendar. She performed stunts in student films which paved the way for stunt work in Hollywood. Producers, however thought she was better suited for the spotlight. Stardom came quickly for Bernie, but the pressures of fame were not to her liking. After becoming a real detective, she continued to moonlight as an actress, to keep her parents from worrying about her new career.

Bernadette's confidence on a playing field does not translate to social functions. She's as vulnerable to the opposite sex as a teenager discovering their first pangs of love.

The May 16, 1988 issue of *Time* magazine ran a photo of the new Angels, and misidentified each actress in the caption. That was the first sign that *Angels '88* may have been cursed from the start. The series was to begin filming in June, but a Writers Guild strike shut down Hollywood through the summer. Once the strike was settled, discrepancies between Spelling and Fox about the budget and direction of the series further delayed production.

Autumn passed, then winter, and on January 15 the title of *Angels '88* was changed to *Angels '89*. On April 15, the cast celebrated the one-year anniversary of their first screen test, still under contract but not yet at work. Finally, after countless rewrites and endless confusion, the series that never aired was officially canceled. In June, the cast assembled for a "Fallen Angel party," then moved on to other projects.

Téa Leoni fared best. She starred in the Fox series *Flying Blind*, followed by the NBC sitcom *The Naked Truth* and the feature film *Deep Impact* (1998). Leoni married *X-Files* star David Duchovny in 1998. Sandra Canning, the first African-American Angel, played Grace Jeffries on the soap opera *Days of Our Lives* from 1989-1990. Her older sister, Lisa, with whom Sandra is often confused, is a correspondent for *Entertainment Tonight*.

Karen Kopins is one of those personalities whose face is immediately familiar, but whose name is still unknown. She appears in numerous television commercials and series guest spots, and may be remembered by comic book fans as Veronica Lodge in the TV movie *Archie: Return to Riverdale* (1990). Claire Yarlett was probably the best-known of the four Angels thanks to her recurring role as "Bliss" on Aaron Spelling's *Dynasty* spinoff, *The Colbys* (1985-87). Like Sandra Canning, she also joined the cast of *Days of Our Lives*, playing Whitney Baker in 1990-91. Yarlett still turns up on various series, including *Lois and Clark* in 1995, and *ER* in 1998. ▨

three sexy government agents. But it wasn't until *Baywatch* that the formula returned to prominence. This fun-in-the-sun saga of California lifeguards, starring David Hasselhoff and a seemingly endless parade of gorgeous women (Pamela Anderson, Yasmine Bleeth, Donna D'errico, Traci Bingham, Gena Lee Nolin, etc.) debuted in 1989 and became the most popular television series in the world.

But *Charlie's Angels* remains the reference point for every series featuring female leads (*Baywatch* acknowledged its heritage with an *Angels* spoof in 1997), and it is doubtful that any show will recapture the national imagination like the one that started it all. There's still a magic attached to the name, as evidenced when the Lifetime cable network aired a marathon of movies featuring *Charlie's Angels* stars in 1996, and scored some of the highest ratings in its history.

There was talk of reunions through the years, but it never got serious. In fact, notable *Angel* gatherings have occurred only three times since the series was cancelled.

In 1992, The People's Choice Awards presented a special award to Aaron Spelling. During the salute, a turntable on stage rotated to reveal Cheryl Ladd, Jaclyn Smith, and Kate Jackson. To a tumultuous ovation from the largely celebrity audience, they paid homage to the man who gave them their wings.

In March of 1994, *People* magazine celebrated its 20th anniversary with a special double-issue, featuring several "Where are they now?" features. The original Angels gathered for a photo session, and a bull session, both of which were featured in the magazine's 11 x 25" pullout centerfold. In 1998, Farrah Fawcett, Kate Jackson and Jaclyn Smith appeared together on television for the first time since 1977 at ABC's *All-Star Party for Aaron Spelling*.

■　■　■

In the 1990s, several classic television series were adapted into feature films. Most of them (*The Avengers, Leave it to Beaver, Sgt. Bilko, The Wild, Wild West*) were disasters. Aaron Spelling revived *The Mod Squad* in 1999, with less than satisfactory results. A *Charlie's Angels* remake seemed

The new *Charlie's Angels*: (from top) Cameraon Diaz, Drew Barrymore and Lucy Liu.

inevitable and, in 1998, actress Drew Barrymore acquired the movie rights for her production company, Flower Films. Barrymore set herself up as star and coproducer, with Spelling-Goldberg.

The project suffered several delays, including the casting of Barrymore's fellow Angels, and finding a workable script. Cameron Diaz joined the cast in the summer of 1999, and Lucy Liu (*Ally McBeal*) became the third Angel just weeks before production began. Among those who passed on the halo— Halle Berry, Lauryn Hill, Angelina Jolie, Ashley Judd, Jenny McCarthy, Thandie Newton, Gwyneth Paltrow, Jada Pinkett, Liv Tyler, and Catherine Zeta-Jones. Comedian Bill Murray signed on to play Bosley, and John Forsythe reprised his series contribution as the voice of Charlie. The supporting cast includes Tim Curry, Tom Green, Matt LeBlanc, Kelly Lynch, and Sam Rockwell.

The film was directed by Joseph McGinty, better known as "McG," the director of several music videos. *Charlie's Angels* marks McGinty's feature debut. Screenwriters Ed Solomon (*Men In Black*, *The X-Men*), John August (*Go*) and Ryan Rowe penned the original draft, in which the new Angels, Dylan (Barrymore), Natalie (Diaz) and Alex (Liu), must rescue handsome billionaire Eric Knox after he is kidnapped by industrial terrorists. The script went through several revisions, including one in which genetically-engineered supermodels plot to take over the world.

Inspired perhaps by the original series' pilot, the story depicts the Angels as intelligent, multilingual detectives with a mastery of the martial arts. But history repeated itself when Sony Pictures demanded less conversation, and more jiggle.

Kate Jackson, Farrah Fawcett and Jaclyn Smith, a winning combination that
worked well for the first twenty-two episodes of the series.

Épisode Guide

PILOT

Charlie's Angels

ORIGINAL AIRDATE: **March 21, 1976**

PRODUCED BY: **Aaron Spelling and Leonard Goldberg**

WRITTEN BY: **Ivan Goff and Ben Roberts**

DIRECTED BY: **John Llewellyn Moxey**

GUEST STARS: **Bo Hopkins (Beau Creel) Diana Muldaur (Rachel), Tommy Lee Jones (Arum), David Ogden Stiers (Scott Woodville)**

Private detectives Sabrina Duncan, Kelly Garrett and Jill Munroe are summoned to the offices of the Townsend Agency by their mysterious, unseen boss. "This is a tough one, Angels—needs the feminine touch!" cautions Charlie Townsend, though a telephone loudspeaker.

Townsend's liaisons, Bosley and Scott Woodville, brief the Angels on the disappearance of Vincent La Mer, wealthy owner of the Samarra Vineyards. In the seven years since La Mer vanished, no ransom demand or farewell note has ever been found. With La Mer about to be declared legally dead, Samarra will be turned over to his second wife, Rachel. The Angels' client, whom Charlie does not name, is determined to stop Rachel and her lover, Beau Creel, from inheriting the business.

Kelly arrives at Samarra posing as Janet La Mer, Vincent's long lost daughter. After a rigorous cross-examination, her story is accepted by Rachel and Beau, who recognize the threat she poses to their acquisition of the vineyard. They attempt to poison her that night.

Posing as an attorney, Woodville shows up at Samarra to "expose" Kelly as an impostor; he tells Rachel that the "real" Janet La Mer is flying in tomorrow. When confronted, Kelly, who has already learned that Bo and Rachel killed Vincent, claims to have kidnapped Janet months earlier. After injecting the heiress with truth serum and learning her personal history, she reveals that the La Mer fortune is worth even more than Rachel suspected, and will share the information for a 50/50 split.

The next day, Sabrina turns up at Samarra as Janet, accompanied by Jill and Bosley as members of her entourage. Professing no interest at all in

Farrah Fawcett (left) and Jaclyn Smith, unaware of the success that would lie ahead of them.

the will, she offers to let Rachel and Beau keep the property, in exchange for their agreement to build a bird sanctuary on a part of the vineyard. After spotting Bosley snooping around the swampland where Sabrina suggested the sanctuary be built, Beau is certain that the treasure described by Kelly, whatever it is, must be on that spot.

Allowing himself to be captured, Bosley tells Beau that there's oil beneath the land. That night, Beau retrieves the body of Victor Le Mer, so it won't be discovered when the swamp is dredged. The Angels are one step ahead, and take Beau and Rachel into custody. Back at the office, Charlie tells them that their client was the one and only Janet La Mer, who had hoped to find proof that her father was murdered.

COMMENTARY

"It's Charlie, Angel! Time to go to work!"

With those words, five years of slick, sexy adventures begin. The clever script by Ivan Goff and Ben Roberts packs red herrings and double switches into a wonderful game of deception, and certainly reflects the type of case-work the Angels would have tackled had the two former *Mission: Impossible* writers remained with the series. Though Goff and Roberts complained of Aaron Spelling's tampering with their sophisticated style, and the sacrificing of plot for titillation, there is no shortage of skin in their pilot; Jaclyn Smith makes her first appearance as Kelly in a tiny white bikini, and emerges again a few minutes later wrapped in a towel after a shower.

"Why can't we ever see Charlie?" asks Jill in the first Angel briefing scene. Scott Woodville explains that "nobody sees Charlie but me," but offers no explanations. Jill seems to have a crush on her unseen boss in this first adventure; she confesses to laying in bed trying to put "a face . . . and a body" with the voice.

As a result of Kate Jackson's last-minute decision to play Sabrina instead of Kelly, it is Jaclyn Smith who is featured in the first 30 minutes of the 90 minute telefilm, as Kelly establishes her cover as a phony claimant to Victor La Mer's will. Sabrina, Jill, and Bosley turn up later, all playing characters in the elaborate charade to trap Beau and Rachel. Even Charlie participates in the case, something he would rarely do in the ensuing series. But since the Angels spend almost the entire film masquerading as other people, the real characters and personalities of Sabrina, Jill, and Kelly are never clearly revealed. Sadly, this would not become a priority even after the series began.

Tommy Lee Jones appears in the film as Arum, a scruffy ranchhand who sees through Kelly's role-playing, but does nothing to interfere because he's glad to watch the rich folks suffer. "He was very nervous," recalled Jaclyn Smith. "I remember taking his hand, and it was shaking." Jones would earn an Academy Award nomination four years later for *Coal Miner's Daughter* (1980), and would win the Oscar for Best Supporting Actor in *The Fugitive* (1993).

Season One
1976-1977

Kate Jackson (Sabrina Duncan)

Farrah Fawcett-Majors (Jill Munroe)

Jaclyn Smith (Kelly Garrett)

David Doyle (John Bosley)

John Forsythe (Charlie Townsend)

EPISODE 1: *Hellride*

ORIGINAL AIRDATE: September 22, 1976

PRODUCED BY: Rick Husky

WRITTEN BY: Edward J. Lakso and Rick Husky

DIRECTED BY: Richard Lang

GUEST STARS Don Gordon (Gene Wells), Mayf Nutter (Eddie Dirko), Kurt Grayson (Ted Kale), John Dennis Johnston (Jerry Adams), Jenny O'Hara ("Bloody" Mary Barrows)

Stock car driver Suzy Lemson is killed during a race, and suspicion falls on her mechanic, Jerry Adams. Adams hires the Angels to clear his name, and refute allegations he was negligent in his job. He suspects Suzy's chief track competitor, "Bloody" Mary Barrows, and her mechanic-boyfriend, Ted Kale.

Sabrina becomes Jerry's new driver, while Bosley and Jill make a grand entrance at the track as evangelist "Brother John" and his sexy daughter. They soon discover that Suzy's car was sabotaged, and that Ted Kale was responsible. Kale and Mary are part of a scheme hatched by the track promoter to steal $500,000 in diamonds.

COMMENTARY

The first episode introduces two prominent series staples: the exterior shot of the red brick building that is home to Charles Townsend Associates, and the teasing glimpses of Charlie, usually from behind, in the company of a scantily-clad beauty. He is a tall man, with black hair (gray hair in later episodes), most likely in his mid-40's, but beyond that little can be ascertained.

There is a comfortable chemistry already developing between Jaclyn Smith, Kate Jackson and Farrah Fawcett, especially in the scene when Jill and Sabrina share a laugh over the antics of Bosley as Brother John. Farrah gets the episode's best line; "What denomination are you, little lady?" Kale asks Jill, who purrs, "35-24-35."

Critics, however, were not impressed, and greeted the news series with scathing reviews. "That didn't bother me," said writer-producer Rick Husky. "This was not a show for the critics, it was a show for the audience." "Hellride" finished eighth in the weekly Neilsen ratings, with a remarkable 45 share.

The climactic race should have been more exciting, though it's use as a means to transport stolen diamonds is cleverly conceived. Sabrina's remark about becoming "the next Janet Guthrie" is a reference to the first female driver to race in the Indianapolis 500. Guthrie did not finish the race after qualifying in 1977, but placed ninth in a field of 33 in 1978.

Anne Ramsey, an Academy Award nominee in 1987 for *Throw Momma From the Train*, appears as the jealous wife of a bespectacled man who gets an unexpected embrace from Jill.

EPISODE 2: *The Mexican Connection*

ORIGINAL AIRDATE: September 29, 1976
PRODUCED BY: Rick Husky
WRITTEN BY: Jack V. Fogarty
DIRECTED BY: Allen Baron
GUEST STARS: Cesare Danova (Frank Bartone), Edward Power (Jim Taylor), Joe Burke (Nick Doyle), Arnold Soboloff (Steiner), Robert Tafur (Col. Morales)

Dan Mason, a pilot for a small Mexican airline, hires the Angels after a fortune in heroin is discovered on his plane. Sabrina joins the crew of Mason's colleague, Jim Taylor, as a stewardess, while Kelly and Jill investigate the owner of the airline, Frank Bartone. The dream of Bartone's daughter, Maria, to become a professional swimmer provides Jill, a former champion, with her cover.

The Angels locate the lab where the heroin is processed, and discover that the contraband is being transported inside bottles of 1957 vintage Burgundy. Jill finds the same bottles in Bartone's wine cellar—and Bartone finds Jill. Thinking quickly, she pretends to be in the employ of Escobar, a shadowy, rival drug kingpin, and reveals Escobar's plan to meet with several prominent clients in Los Angeles, in an attempt to take over Bartone's territory.

COMMENTARY

Sex was the most potent weapon in the Angels' crimefighting arsenal and, when deployed as it is here by Jill and Kelly, the bad guys don't stand a chance. Jill reduces Bartone's henchman to jelly with a wink and a smile. Kelly, posing as a schoolteacher on holiday in Mexico, dons a bikini ("Every time I wear it I get proposals—but not for marriage") to capture Bartone's attention.

"The Mexican Connection" is not one of the better first season episodes, but it establishes for the first time traces of an individual personality for each Angel, provided as much by the actresses as by the script. Several magazine articles about the series describe Sabrina as "multilingual" because she speaks one line of Spanish in this episode. If she knows any other languages, it is never mentioned again.

Rick Husky hoped to interest Fernando Lamas in the role of Bartone, but Lamas thought the role of a Mexican druglord was too cliché. "I offered to lighten up the character, give him more to do, but he wouldn't change his mind," Husky recalled.

Charlie, left in traction after a skiing accident, unleashes one of his most explicit double-entendrés, while describing the exotic physical therapy techniques prescribed by a voluptuous nurse. "I tackle them whenever I can rise to the occasion. As a matter of fact," he says as the blond bombshell massages his plaster-encased leg, "I'm getting the urge right now." Oh, Charlie!

EPISODE 3: *Night of the Strangler*

ORIGINAL AIRDATE: **October 13, 1976**
PRODUCED BY: **Rick Husky**
WRITTEN BY: **Pat Fiedler, based on a story by Fiedler, Glen Olson and Rod Baker**
DIRECTED BY: **Richard Lang**
GUEST STARS: **Richard Mulligan (Kevin St. Clair), Dean Santoro (Jesse Woodman), William Beckley (Alec Witt), Alex Henteloff (Heinz Brandon), Rosemary Forsyth (Michelle St. Clair)**

A fashion model working for clothing manufacturer Kevin St. Clair is murdered by the "Rag Doll Strangler." St. Clair becomes a prime suspect, as does his wife, Michelle, who makes no secret of her jealousy over St. Clair's rumored affairs with several models. Jill and Kelly pose as models, Sabrina as a photo stylist. After an altercation with Kelly, Michelle is found strangled with a rag doll. Since her husband was visible during the attack, suspicion turns to the company's photographers, Heinz Brandon and Alec Witt, and its public relations man, Jesse Woodman.

COMMENTARY

The various suspects aren't developed enough for a successful whodunit, though Richard Mulligan, who would join the cast of the bawdy sitcom *Soap* one year later, makes a convincing Lothario.

Jaclyn Smith plays a dual role as both Kelly and Dana Cameron, the model who is murdered in the opening scene. For the second time in three episodes, her undercover assignment offers little cover at all—a white bikini once again becomes the disguise of choice. "I didn't protest at all—what's wrong with a bikini?" said Smith. "I never felt exploited. I didn't think it was risque or provocative. I looked at *Charlie's Angels* as a family show!"

Jill's sudden interest in astrology ("Is he a Scorpio?" she asks of St. Clair at Charlie's briefing; "It's a bad cycle for Scorpios right now!") casts her unfairly in the California blond airhead stereotype; later, it is Jill who sees through St. Clair's attempt to frame Heinz.

Sabrina, who left the Mata Hari assignments to her cohorts in future episodes, plays the seductress here to a more than willing Alec Witt. She also

In a scene from "Night of the Strangler" Jaclyn Smith (right) was the
only Angel to wear a bikini in the first season of the series.

wraps up the case with a right cross to St. Clair's jaw that is worthy of *The
Avengers*' Emma Peel. "Kate enjoyed that," said Rick Husky.

EPISODE 4: *Angels in Chains*

ORIGINAL AIRDATE:	**October 20, 1976**
PRODUCED BY:	**Rick Husky**
WRITTEN BY:	**Robert Earll**
DIRECTED BY:	**Phil Bondelli**
GUEST STARS:	**David Huddleston (Sheriff Clint), Anthony James (Karl Stern), Christina Hart (Billie), Mary Woronov (Maxine), Kim Basinger (Linda Oliver), Neva Patterson (Warden Sorenson), Brooke Tucker (Fran), Lauren Tewis [Tewes] (Christine Hunter)**

Christine Hunter hires the Angels to find her sister, Elizabeth, who disappeared after being paroled from a rural Southern prison. Sabrina, Jill, and
Kelly allow themselves to be arrested and booked into the prison. During
the grueling work detail, they question other convicts about Elizabeth.

Jaclyn Smith, Farrah Fawcett-Majors, and Kate Jackson
in "Angels in Chains"

A few nights later, they are given cocktail dresses, taken to a party at the warden's residence, and offered the opportunity to work as prostitutes in exchange for special privileges. They learn that Elizabeth was killed after she refused to cooperate. The warden becomes suspicious after the Angels ask too many questions, and orders the sheriff to dispose of them.

COMMENTARY

Probably the most famous episode of *Charlie's Angels*, but certainly the most infamous. The November 22, 1976 *Time* magazine cover story on "TV's Super Women" opens with a recounting of the plotline in lurid detail: ". . . the matron, dressed SS style, clearly lesbian in sexual orientation, orders the girls to 'Strip down to your birthday suits;' That's only the beginning. Beatings, threats of rape and enforced prostitution follow, not to mention an imminent triple murder when they find out too much.

"What is this?" the article queries, "A report on the latest skin flick? A case study on the fantasy life of a troubled adolescent? Nope. Just a plot summary of an episode from the hottest new television show of the season." The article further described "Angels in Chains" as "raunchy" and "family-style porn." "If they were going to blast the show, they could have at least given me credit for writing it!" said Robert Earll, who wrote *Time* a letter requesting recognition. It was not published.

"The controversy came from the same people who now protest *NYPD Blue*," said Rick Husky. "Looking back, *Charlie's Angels* seems so innocent—they show more skin on *Saved By the Bell* now. However, on "Angels in Chains," I do remember a lot of the executives on the lot coming over to watch the dailies, and smiling."

Earll first approached Rick Husky with another story idea, that was later rejected. "Rick then showed me three episode titles given to him by Fred Silverman; one of them was 'Angels in Chains.' When I saw that title, I said, 'that one's mine!'" All the time-honored clichés of women-behind-bars flicks are here—the sadistic matron, played with lascivious sneer by Mary Woronov, dialogue like "I'm gonna be watchin' you, Sweetcakes!"; the fat, sleazy sheriff and his bumbling deputy, the warden who conceals her involvement in dirty business with a compassionate, June Cleaver smile, and the obligatory shower and hosedown scene. Best line—Kelly to the matron; "How long has it been since you've been sprayed?"

The sociological inferences drawn from scenes of three beautiful women, chained together, being chased through a swamp by men and bloodhounds, became the opening volley in almost every feminists' condemnation of the series as exploitative and misogynist. However, the episode also portrays the Angels as intelligent, capable professionals, and having all three work undercover together allows for more of the easy group repartee` that was among the show's greatest strengths in its first three seasons.

In addition to the teasing glimpses down Farrah's unbuttoned prison shirt, there were more girlwatching opportunities provided by Lauren Tewes, a.k.a. your cruise director, Julie McCoy, on *The Love Boat*, and guest star Kim Basinger as convict Linda Oliver. At the end of the episode, the paroled Linda is hired as the Townsend Agency's new receptionist, but is never seen again. Basinger, later an Academy Award winner for *L.A. Confidential* (1998), was a candidate for Angel status herself, after the departure of Farrah Fawcett-Majors.

EPISODE 5: *Target: Angels*

ORIGINAL AIRDATE: October 27, 1976
PRODUCED BY: David Levinson
WRITTEN BY: David Levinson
DIRECTED BY: Richard Lang
GUEST STARS: John Horn (Harry Wardlow), Tom Selleck (Dr. Alan Samuelson), Michael Bell (Bill Duncan), David Healy (Cavendish), John Agar (Col. Blaylock), Irene Tedrow (Sister Anne), Thayer David (Meeker)

After shots are fired through Kelly's bedroom window, Charlie devotes the full resources of his agency to finding the gunman. Later, when Jill narrowly escapes a similar attack, the Angels focus their investigation on recently-released criminals apprehended by Townsend & Associates.

Sabrina allows the would-be killer to believe that his attempt on her life was successful, allowing her more freedom to investigate. Kelly and Jill take refuge in Charlie's mansion, where they discover that the assassin's real target is Charlie.

The Angels compare notes in the home of their mysterious boss, in "Target: Angels."

COMMENTARY

"Target: Angels" is the only episode in the series to provide any detailed information about the backgrounds of Sabrina, Jill, and Kelly, and their lives before Charlie and away from the office. "Fred Silverman called me, (because) he didn't like the direction that the series was going, character-wise," said writer-producer David Levinson. "After talking with each girl, I got a feel for their basic natures, to incorporate their persona into their television counterparts."

Jill, we discover, is a tomboy-athlete who spends her off-hours coaching a girl's basketball team. Kelly was abandoned by her parents as an infant, and raised in an orphanage. A pre-*Magnum P.I.* Tom Selleck plays her boyfriend, Dr. Alan Samuelson. "Tom had just been fired off a pilot, and he was very upset about it," remembers Jaclyn Smith. "But I remember in the dailies, all people could talk about was 'Who's the guy?'" As originally written, the scene between Kelly and Alan implied that the good doctor had spent the night in the Angel's home; Jaclyn Smith asked that the scene be changed to a more innocent scenario, and producer David Levinson complied.

Sabrina's pre-Angel life includes an ex-husband, police detective Bill Duncan, and a father who served in the military. Col. Blaylock is played by John Agar, the former husband of child star Shirley Temple, and the star of numerous 'B' movies in the 1950s. There is more insight into Bosley as well; "We spent a great deal of time and money recruiting and training you all— you'd be very difficult to replace," he says, masking his genuine affection for the Angels with concern over the company budget.

The episode also shows the homes and apartments of all three Angels, as well as Charlie's palatial mansion at 674 Vinewood Lane. "Wow," says Jill after stepping inside, "remind me to ask for a raise!" The story that launches all this belated exposition is a well-crafted, fast-paced tale that places the Angels in the unique position of rescuing their unseen boss. In the amusing final scene, Charlie returns home by cab, sees the Angels and orders the driver to turn around before he can be spotted.

"Target: Angels" is the first of many showcases for Kate Jackson, who shows here why her portrayal of Sabrina received two Emmy nominations. Switching effortlessly from comic banter with her ex-husband to a touching scene with her father, to a no-nonsense detective grilling a tough mercenary, Jackson is never less than captivating. This episode reunites her with former *Dark Shadows* costar Thayer David, though they share only one brief scene together.

"After the episode aired, I got a call from Ivan Goff," Levinson recalled. "He said that this was exactly the type of format and direction that he and Ben Roberts wanted the series to take."

EPISODE 6: *The Killing Kind*

ORIGINAL AIRDATE: November 3, 1976
PRODUCED BY: Rick Husky
WRITTEN BY: Rick Husky
DIRECTED BY: Richard Benedict
GUEST STARS: Robert Loggia (Paul Terranova), Joseph Ruskin (Koslo), Hugh Gillin (Harvey Sunday), Frank Maxwell (Fitzgerald), Judson Pratt (Dr. Dignam), Clarke Gordon (George Anderson), Nancy Stephens (Brooke), Janis Jamison (Inga)

George Anderson, an old friend of Charlie's, hires the Townsend Agency after the body of his daughter, Brooke, is found on a beach near the Moonshadows Resort. Her death is ruled a drowning accident, but George tells the Angels that Brooke, a journalist, was investigating an explosive, "Watergate-type" story involving Moonshadows, and was frightened of the resort's developer, Paul Terranova.

The Angels establish covers at Moonshadows; Kelly poses as a fashion photographer, and Jill becomes the resort's new tennis instructor. Kelly uncovers evidence of an illegal land transaction between Terranova and the county planning commissioner.

COMMENTARY

"The Killing Kind" was the first series episode filmed, and establishes the approach used most frequently by the Angels throughout the first three seasons. Kelly and Jill (later Kris) take the undercover assignments that put them in swimwear and tennis shorts, while Sabrina, sometimes joined by Bosley, follows other leads from outside. "It was actually a second pilot, because it set the tone for everything from story structure to wardrobe, and brought into shape where the series was going to go," said writer-producer Rick Husky. The assignment of Townsend company cars (A Mustang for Kelly, a Cobra for Jill, a Pinto for Sabrina) became the first of many points of contention for Kate Jackson. "She complained about getting the dumpy, square one, while Farrah and Jaclyn got cool cars. Actually, she was right!" said Husky, laughing.

We learn that Charlie is married from his statement that the case was a request from his ex-wife, "along with a request for more alimony." Bosley, too, is said to be married, though he courts several women in future episodes.

Inga, the sadistic Swedish masseuse, is good for a laugh, but there's not much detective work necessary here, and the attempts of a land developer to expand a resort does not make for riveting drama. Even the team scenes miss this time, as Jill is once again saddled with more scatterbrained dialogue.

EPISODE 7: *To Kill An Angel*

ORIGINAL AIRDATE:	November 10, 1976
PRODUCED BY:	Aaron Spelling and Leonard Goldberg
WRITTEN BY:	Rick Husky
DIRECTED BY:	Phil Bondelli
GUEST STARS:	Robert Donner (Korbin), Craig Ludwin (Masters), John Zaremba (Dr. Stafford), Lee Bryant (Gail Francis), Skip (Dennis Dimster)

Kelly misses a meeting at the office because of a "date she couldn't break." Sabrina and Jill wonder if wedding bells are on the way, but Kelly's "date" is with Skip, a 12-year-old autistic boy. During their visit to an amusement park, Skip finds a gun that was discarded after being used in a murder. Unaware of the danger, he points the loaded weapon at Kelly and pulls the trigger.

While Kelly fights for her life in the hospital, the Angels and Bosley investigate. At the amusement park, they find a dead body in the Tunnel of Horrors, and realize that Skip, if he witnessed the murder, may be in danger. Sure enough, one of the killers recalls seeing the boy with Kelly and visits her in the hospital, pretending to be Skip's long-lost father. Under the influence of sedatives, Kelly tells him where Skip will most likely be found—the merry-go-round at the park.

COMMENTARY

Aaron Spelling and Leonard Goldberg, listed as executive producers for the entire series run, also earn a producer's credit on this episode, as a result of Rick Husky's departure. The story, a retread of one of Spelling's *Mod Squad* episodes, begins uncharacteristically with the end of a case, and Charlie congratulating the Angels on a job well done.

Husky's script provides proof that these women are really genuine detectives; a note attached to an old timecard is the only clue to the identity of Skip's parents. No one at the mental health facility has been able to track them down in three years, but Sabrina and Jill do the job in one afternoon! The show's best scene, however, features the usually-cool Sabrina losing control in the hospital waiting room, after learning that Kelly has been shot. "That (role of Skip's friend) had Farrah's name on it, and it was changed to me, because my character was more maternal," reveals Jaclyn Smith. "She didn't understand that. It's not that we were jealous of one another, but we all wanted something interesting to do."

Kelly would take another bullet to the head in the final *Angels* episode, "Let Our Angel Live."

EPISODE 8: *Lady Killer*

ORIGINAL AIRDATE: November 24, 1976
PRODUCED BY: David Levinson
WRITTEN BY: Sue Milburn
DIRECTED BY: George McCowan
GUEST STARS: Hugh O'Brian (Tony Mann), Alan Fudge (Dave Erhard), Richard Foronji (Danny Auletta), Jan Shutan (Paula), Bob Basso (Victor Burrell)

Two centerfolds for *Feline Magazine* are disfigured and killed. Publisher Tony Mann hires the Angels to save his empire from the murders and labor problems that seem to be arranged by a rival publisher. Jill sets herself up as a potential victim by posing as the next centerfold.

COMMENTARY

The Angels learn a lesson about gender assumption, when they fail to acknowledge the possibility that a woman could be killing centerfolds. "Sometimes," says Sabrina, "I think we're the biggest chauvinists of all." But even without the giveaway clue in the episode's title, viewers probably had twitchy Paula pegged from the start.

Feline Magazine and the Feline Clubs are obviously derivative of *Playboy*, right down to the ears and tails worn by the waitresses. Hugh O'Brian, who plays swinging *Feline* publisher Tony Mann, played Wyatt Earp in *The Life and Legend of Wyatt Earp* (1955-1961), one of the best television westerns.

The attempted murder of Jill with a tennis ball machine is undeniably unique, but the episode's biggest surprise is that, once the groundwork is laid for Jill to pose as a centerfold, there is no scene depicting her photo session. This is the first time the series passes on a perfect opportunity to unwrap an Angel. The "Feline" costume worn by Jill is the same outfit worn by Cheryl Ladd, when she plays a knife-thrower's assistant in the second season episode "Circus of Terror" (#27).

The killer's first victim is played by Martha Smith, who later costarred opposite Kate Jackson in *Scarecrow and Mrs. King* (1983-1987).

EPISODE 9: *Bullseye*

ORIGINAL AIRDATE: December 1, 1976
PRODUCED BY: David Levinson
WRITTEN BY: Jeff Myrow
DIRECTED BY: Daniel Haller
GUEST STARS: L.Q. Jones (Sgt. Billings), Robert Pine (Dr. Conlan), Marla Pennington (Jenny Warren), Peter Leeds (General Green), Kelly Sanders (Trainee)

A W.A.C. recruit is shot to death on the rifle range of an army base, and the base commander enlists the Angels to investigate. Jill and Kelly struggle through basic training, and look into rumors that Sergeant Billings, a medical supply officer, was having an affair with the victim.

Born three days apart in October, Kate Jackson and Jaclyn Smith
celebrate their birthdays on the set of "Bullseye."

Sabrina suits up for nursing duty at the base hospital, where she learns of long-standing animosity between Billings and her boss, Dr. Conlan. She later discovers, after a patient dies of cardiac arrest because her medicine had expired, that the two men may be co-conspirators in a plot to buy and sell outdated pharmaceuticals at a profit.

COMMENTARY

Though it's fun to see Kate Jackson back in nurse's whites, a reminder of her stint as Jill Danko on *The Rookies*, most male viewers probably weren't all that thrilled about Farrah Fawcett and Jaclyn Smith in baggy army fatigues, with their million dollar curls squashed under olive drab helmets.

"Bullseye" is the first episode to denote Kelly's reputation as a sharp-shooter, though at this point her skills are still developing. As bad guy Sgt. Billings, veteran character actor L.Q. Jones makes the first of his four series appearances. Robert Pine (Dr. Conlan) is best-known to classic TV fans as Sgt. Joe Getraer on *CHiPs* (1977-1983).

EPISODE 10: *Consenting Adults*

ORIGINAL AIRDATE: December 8, 1976
PRODUCED BY: David Levinson
WRITTEN BY: Les Carter
DIRECTED BY: George McCowan
GUEST STARS: Audrey Christie (Maggie Cunningham),
Laurette Spang (Tracy Martel), Alan Manson
(Bialy), Dick Dinman (Clifton Cunningham),
George Sperdakos (Duran), Ward Wood
(Cooley), G.W. Bailey (Mumford)

Following an afternoon tryst with a sexy college coed, antique store owner Clifton Cunningham returns to find his shop ransacked. Among the missing items is a valuable ceramic frog. Unbeknownst to Clifton or the crooks

who robbed his store, a local smuggling ring stashed a fortune in diamonds in the frog, and kidnap Clifton when it turns up missing.

The Angels, hired by Clifton's mother, Maggie, check the store's records and learn that Clifton had recently signed up with the Consenting Adults computer dating service. They find out from his "date," Tracy Martel, that Consenting Adults is actually a front for a prostitution and robbery ring. Jill and Kelly sign on as call girls, with Bosley as Bachelor #1, hoping

In "Consenting Adults," Jill Munroe (Farrah Fawcett-Majors) eludes her pursuers on a skateboard.

to set up the robbers to be filmed and followed. The trick succeeds, but when Sabrina tails the thieves too closely, the Angels end up with another missing person to locate.

COMMENTARY

One of the season's highlights, and the first of two terrific *Angels* scripts written by Les Carter, a freelance magazine writer and former Los Angeles disc jockey. "Consenting Adults," has clever twists, humor, action, and the most famous chase scene in the series' history. "Twenty years later, when I'm asked which episodes I wrote, all I have to say is 'the one with the skateboard,'" Carter said. "For some reason, that one is stuck in people's minds."

The moments of chemistry and camaraderie glimpsed in previous episodes reach a fruition, alongside scenes that allow each individual Angel to shine. Kate Jackson makes a standard kidnapping scene memorable at the smugglers' hideout; Jaclyn Smith's depiction as the toughest Angel begins here, when the soft-spoken Kelly shakes down a burly bartender. "I was very proud of how I wrote for Jaclyn in that episode," Carter said. "She is so sweet and so beautiful, I thought it would be fun to write her against type. There was such a contrast between the way she looked and the way she delivered some very tough dialogue." Bosley introduces a loud Texas millionaire character that would be revived in such future episodes as "The Vegas Connection" and "The Big Tap-Out." And no television series from the 1970s is complete until it features a guest appearance by Laurette Spang.

But this episode belongs to Farrah Fawcett, first for her subdued but sexy turn as a prostitute, but primarily for her escape via skateboard from a gang of gun-toting thugs. The scene was originally scripted as a motorcycle chase, but producer David Levinson, concerned about the cost, asked Carter to come up with something different. "Skateboards were just starting to become a phenomenon on the west coast, so I thought it would be fun to have Farrah on a skateboard, being chased by an ice cream truck," Carter said.

Levinson loved the idea, until another problem surfaced—there were no women in the stunt union qualified to handle the scene. Carter picked up an issue of *Skateboard* magazine, hoping to find someone who could pass for Farrah from a distance. "I found a girl named Desireé, got her address from the magazine, and offered her the job. She was fantastic." Desireé subsequently joined the stunt union and *Charlie's Angels* became the first job of her new career.

After watching Jill execute a series of daring maneuvers on her sidewalk surfboard, teenage boys who already knew Farrah was beautiful certainly became convinced that she was the perfect woman. Watching the chase now, the use of the stunt double is obvious—another childhood fantasy crushed. However, that didn't stop one magazine from releasing a pullout poster of Farrah striking a pose on a skateboard.

EPISODE 11: *The Seance*

ORIGINAL AIRDATE:	December 15, 1976
PRODUCED BY:	Barney Rosenzweig
WRITTEN BY:	Robert C. Dennis and Edward J. Lakso
DIRECTED BY:	George Brooks
GUEST STARS:	René Auberjonois (Terrence), Carole Cook (Madame Dorian), George Wyner (La Plante), Kathryn Fuller (Putty), Nancy Cameron (Miss Ohio), Gertrude Flynn (Grace Rodeheaver), Tonya Crowe (Young Kelly)

The Angels are hired to investigate a jewel theft at the mansion of Grace Rodeheaver, a wealthy but eccentric widow. Suspecting an inside job, they conduct background checks on Grace's inner circle, including her "spiritual advisor," Madame Dorian.

Kelly, posing as an heiress in need of Madame's counsel, is hypnotized by her assistant, Terrence. At a seance that night, she recalls in the voice of a little girl the painful memories of her childhood spent in an orphanage. Still under Terrence's post-hypnotic suggestion, she is unable to resist revealing her true identity.

COMMENTARY

"The Seance" contains more details on Kelly's unhappy upbringing as an orphan, but not much else. Jaclyn Smith plays the hypnosis scenes as gamely as possible. "I loved that episode," said Smith. "It's one of my favorites."

This is the first Angels episode to be produced by Barney Rosenzweig, who would later win two Emmy Awards for producing *Cagney and Lacey*, another action series with female protagonists. "We were influenced by *The*

Exorcist on that one," Rosenzweig recalls of the episode. "I remember talking to Ed Lakso about doing a seance, during which Jaclyn starts talking in another voice. 'Now, you tell me how we get there and what's going on,' I told him. And in about three days or less, he'd have the script. He was the fastest writer I'd ever seen in my life."

René Auberjonois (*Benson, Star Trek: Deep Space Nine*) makes the first of two series appearances here. The little girl who plays Kelly as a child is not credited in the episode, but *Knots Landing* fans will recognize her as Tonya Crowe, who played Olivia Dyer from 1980-1990.

EPISODE 12 *Angels on Wheels*

ORIGINAL AIRDATE:	December 22, 1976
PRODUCED BY:	Rick Husky
WRITTEN BY:	Charles Sailor, teleplay by Charles Sailor, Jack V. Fogarty and Rick Husky
DIRECTED BY:	Richard Benedict
GUEST STARS:	Andra Akers (Jessica Farmer), Dick Sargent (Hugh Morris), Nate Esformes (Toby Rizzo), Kres Mersky ("Bad Betty" King), Taylor Larcher (Jeremy Carr), Steve Sandor (Red Loomis)

Karen Jason, a beautiful roller-derby skater, is killed during a match by "Bad Betty" King, one of her teammates. Karen's sister believes that the incident was murder, not a freak accident, and hires the Angels to prove it. The detectives' suspicions are raised when they discover that Karen's team, the Los Angeles Tornadoes, is heavily insured, and that the owner of the team, Hugh Morris, also owns the insurance company.

Jill, masquerading as Karen's sister, joins the team. Sabrina poses as an insurance investigator, but Kelly breaks the case after finding a key to a bus station luggage locker in Karen's apartment. Inside the locker, she finds a suitcase full of money and fake drivers' licenses, each with a picture of Bad Betty above a different name. The Angels learn that Betty is in league with the team's coach and the head of Morris's insurance division, all of whom are getting rich off of phony accident claims.

COMMENTARY

Another episode everyone remembers, though insurance fraud is not exactly a dynamic subject. Roller-derby seems part of a bygone era now, but the Los Angeles Thunderbirds were still drawing huge crowds in the 1970s, and the sport's gritty exhibition of sex and violence must have seemed a natural for an *Angels* script. Most of the action was shot at the Thunderbirds' rink, and members of the team were used as extras. Jill wears wheels as she did in "Consenting Adults," and Farrah actually does some skating this time, though a double is still used for the tough stuff.

Kelly's car is sabotaged twice in the same episode; for the attempt that worked, someone should have explained exactly how Charlie knew there was a bomb on board. The same car, or one just like it, was blown up again in the fourth season episode "Toni's Boys" (#91). Poor Kelly must have very high auto insurance premiums.

Dick Sargent, best known as the replacement Darrin Stevens on *Bewitched*, makes the first of his three series appearances.

EPISODE 13: *Angel Trap*

ORIGINAL AIRDATE: **January 5, 1977**
PRODUCED BY: **Barney Rosenzweig**
WRITTEN BY: **Edward J. Lakso**
DIRECTED BY: **George McCowan**
GUEST STARS: **Fernando Lamas (Jericho), Phyllis Avery (Janine), John Larch (Kamden), James Jansen (Desk Clerk), Ken Del Conte (Bartender), Roy West (Officer Cohen)**

The members of an elite O.S.S. Intelligence unit formed during World War II are being murdered 30 years later. The last two survivors are Charlie Townsend and George Camden, the official client on the case. The Angels consult a former operative for the French government, who now owns a Los Angeles boutique. From the method used in the murders, she speculates that they may be the work of a master assassin known only as Jericho.

Camden agrees to be Jericho's next target, at a public park that is staked out on all sides by the Angels and Bosley. Their quarry shows up on schedule, but does not make any attempt on Camden's life. Jill follows Jericho back to his hotel and arranges a chance meeting that night, which leads to a lunch date the next day. Warned by his client that someone has made inquiries into his whereabouts, Jericho suspects Jill and lines her up in the crosshairs of his rifle.

COMMENTARY

Thus far, the Angels have been getting by on bravery, luck and basic detective work, but in "Angel Trap" they are faced with an adversary that is their equal in cleverness. Jericho, played by the suave Fernando Lamas, is a cool, debonair James Bond-type villain (he even strokes a kitten in one scene), approaching the end of his career. Lamas brings a poignancy to Jericho's reflections on the life he chose for himself, and on what might have been.

Throughout the first three seasons, the screen time allotted to each Angel was usually commensurate, but here the spotlight is on Jill's conflict between the demands of her assignment and her unexpected affection for a professional killer. "There's no question that I was partial to Farrah," said producer Barney Rosenzweig. "She was not single at the time, and I was not attractive or interesting enough to interest her, but we liked each other. I thought she was just terrific, and I probably had a tendency to give her more to do."

That Jill would take pity on Jericho after a five-minute encounter in a hotel bar indicates that she's still being written as Charlie's most airheaded Angel. But Farrah Fawcett's Malibu dazzle plays well opposite Lamas's European refinement, and their May-December infatuation makes "Angel Trap" another fine episode.

EPISODE 14: *The Big Tap-Out*

ORIGINAL AIRDATE: January 12, 1977
PRODUCED BY: Barney Rosenzweig
WRITTEN BY: Brian McKay
DIRECTED BY: George Stanford Brown
GUEST STARS: Richard Romanus (Roy David), John J. Fox (McMasters), Tony Giorgio (Blackjack Dealer), Bert Remsen (Pinky Tibbs), Norman Bartold (Mr. Platt)

Police detective Ben McMasters apprehends Roy David, an expert safe-cracker, but the case is dismissed on a technicality. The frustrated McMasters asks the Angels to recover $40,000 still missing from David's last job, and to bring the arrogant thief to justice.

Since David only steals to finance his compulsive gambling habit, their first assignment is to empty his bankroll. A two-part sting operation does the trick; first, Sabrina pretends to have a foolproof horserace handicapping system, that fails after David bets $20,000 with her bookmaker, played by Bosley. Jill gets the rest of his stake in a fixed blackjack game. To coax David into attempting another heist, Jill "loses" a set of blueprints to a private casino, during a staged hit-and-run accident.

COMMENTARY

Several of the most entertaining *Charlie's Angels* episodes involve an elaborate con scheme engineered by the Angels on a hapless male victim. After subjecting their mark to a dizzying medley of manufactured dilemmas, often casting themselves as helpless females and playing on his ego, they lower the boom and then gather to gloat en masse as he is led away. Perhaps Ivan Goff and Ben Roberts were right all along.

"The Big Tap-Out" is the first of these Angel-cons, and one of the best, thanks to Richard Romanus's performance as the fidgety, temperamental Roy David. Roy's bravado at blackmailing Sabrina into sharing her handicapping system, his surrender to the distraction provided by Jill at a rigged blackjack table, and his desperation at being impeded in his getaway by Kelly as a typical frazzled "woman driver" are so well-played by Romanus that you almost feel sorry for the guy. The payoff scene, in which David realizes he's been had, is a gem.

"The episode was an homage to *The Sting*," said Rosenzweig, whose brother appears as a policeman in the episode's final scene. The script was written by Brian McKay, who in 1971 cowrote the screenplay for Robert Altman's famed revisionist western *McCabe and Mrs. Miller*. "He was a friend who had fallen on hard times, and wanted a job," Rosenzweig said.

EPISODE 15: *Angels On a String*

ORIGINAL AIRDATE: **January 19, 1977**
PRODUCED BY: **Barney Rosenzweig**
WRITTEN BY: **Edward J. Lakso**
DIRECTED BY: **Larry Doheny**
GUEST STARS: **Theodore Bikel (Professor Peter Wycinski), Gary Wood (Paul), Charles Cyphers (Haller), Jude Farese (Karl), Albert Paulsen (Rabitch)**

The Angels take a well-deserved vacation at a luxurious resort. Sabrina discovers to her delight that Professor Peter Wycinski, the distinguished author and diplomat, will also be there, to deliver an important speech on stability in eastern Europe. Though she is chided by her coworkers for having a crush on a 60-year-old teacher, she yearns to meet him during the trip.

As luck would have it, Wycinski is booked into a room near Sabrina's. Their eyes meet across a courtyard, and to Sabrina's surprise the smitten professor spryly vaults over his balcony railing with a bottle of slivovitz. Later, while she boasts of the encounter to Jill and Kelly, the professor passes by, surrounded by F.B.I. agents. When he fails to recognize Sabrina, she suspects that something is amiss.

COMMENTARY

Trouble follows the Angels on holiday, in this diverting change-of-pace episode without an official case or client. The villains are typical TV Communists, but there's a beneficial extra twist in the Angels having to outwit both the bad guys and the F.B.I., who are unaware of the plot against Wycinski. "Angels On a String," described by Rosenzweig as "Foreign Correspondent with Henry Kissinger," provides another fine showcase for Kate Jackson, who plays against the classy self-control she projects naturally with an unexpected giddiness in Sabrina's first meeting with the professor.

Theodore Bikel, who appeared opposite Audrey Hepburn in *My Fair Lady* and Mary Martin in Broadway's original production of *The Sound of Music*, plays the unlikely object of Sabrina's crush. "The dual role was fun to play, and it was interesting to participate in what was then one of the top series on TV," Bikel said. "What struck me odd was that I got on so well with Kate Jackson, (who) had a reputation of being difficult and moody. With me she wasn't—it was a good working experience."

The resort the Angels visit was the same one used in "The Killing Kind" (#6), and will be seen again in "Angel in a Box" (#63).

EPISODE 16: *Dirty Business*

ORIGINAL AIRDATE: February 2, 1977
PRODUCED BY: Barney Rosenzweig
WRITTEN BY: Edward J. Lakso
DIRECTED BY: Bill Bixby
GUEST STARS: Alan Feinstein (Baylor), John Calvin (Danner), Sidney Clute (Lembeck), Eda Reiss Merin (Esther Goldman), Warren Berlinger (Marvin Goldman)

Arsonists hit a movie film lab and escape in a black, late model Ford, leaving the beaten and burned owner, Marvin Goodman, to put out the fire. Goodman's mother, despite his objections, hires the Angels to discover who is trying the put their company out of business.

Assuming the arsonists had planned to destroy one of the cannisters of film, Kelly starts viewing every reel in the lab, and finds that Marvin has been blackmailing investors by filming their indiscretions in a motel room. Unbeknownst to Marvin, one of the figures walking through the background of the frame is Baylor, a deputy district attorney, who was filmed while planting evidence to augment his conviction rate.

COMMENTARY

The Angels are better than their material here, though the rescue scene featuring Jill is sharply executed and shot by director Bill Bixby, best known for his work in front of the camera in *The Courtship of Eddie's Father* and *The Incredible Hulk*. "We had fun coming up with the jokes in that one—Little Bo Peep and her sheep in a porno movie," said Rosenzweig. "There was also a bit of (Orson Welles') *Touch of Evil* in there." Any regular viewer of one-hour detective dramas will know that Baylor is the bad guy right away, simply by how the character is introduced, and by how he acts during a dinner date with Jill. Sitting across the table from the handsome but deadly D.A., Farrah is beyond breathtaking; twenty years later, it is no mystery at all why she became so omnipresent in America's pop culture.

EPISODE 17: *The Vegas Connection*

ORIGINAL AIRDATE:	February 9, 1977
PRODUCED BY:	Barney Rosenzweig
WRITTEN BY:	John D.F. Black
DIRECTED BY:	George McCowan
GUEST STARS:	Michael Callan (Cass Harper), Brooke Bundy (Elsbeth), Ned Wilson (George Mallin), Walter Mathews (Max), Carla Borelli (Tina)

Wealthy businessman George Mallin hires the Angels to find a motive for the bizarre behavior of his wife, Tina. Sabrina follows Mrs. Mallin, and observes her stealing money from her husband's safe, selling valuables at a pawn shop, and then playing cards at a poker club and losing on purpose!

A background check on the other players at the table turns up one common denominator—a connection to the Versailles Hotel and Casino in Las Vegas. When confronted, Tina admits that she is being blackmailed into losing at poker; the money is returned to the Versailles where, five years before her marriage, Tina performed as a dancer. Faced with a financial crisis, she was persuaded to "entertain" a high roller by Cass Harper, producer of the hotel's stage show. Incriminating photos of that tryst now threaten to destroy her marriage.

COMMENTARY

Although Cass Harper's blackmail scheme is almost exactly the same as Marvin Goldman's in the previous episode, "The Vegas Connection" is a fun show with a terrific closing scene, in which the Angels gather to gloat at the hospital bed of the soundly beaten Cass Harper. This is the first of three series episodes set in Las Vegas, though for this case the cast and crew never left California. Stock interior and exterior footage of Caesars Palace was used to represent the fictional Versailles Hotel.

Writer John D. F. Black qualified for living legend status after serving as producer for the first season of *Star Trek*, and writing several of the series' best episodes. "I was not a (*Charlie's Angels*) viewer, but Aaron was pretty upfront about what he wanted—Vegas, razzle-dazzle, car chases, slick bad guys—that's more than any writer needed to come up with the story." Black kept a fan club photo of the three Angels on his desk, "so I could remember who was who."

As Elsbeth, a tough girl with a soft heart who helps the Angels trap Harper, Brooke Bundy contributes one of the most memorable single-episode guest appearances of the series' run. Her introduction as a potential love interest for Bosley could have been explored further, perhaps in a subsequent episode.

EPISODE 18: *Terror on Ward One*

ORIGINAL AIRDATE: **February 16, 1977**
PRODUCED BY: **Barney Rosenzweig**
WRITTEN BY: **Edward J. Lakso**
DIRECTED BY: **Bob Kelljan**
GUEST STARS: **Sally Carter Hunt (Nurse Farragut), Jack Bannon (Dr. Danworth), Michael McGreevey (Ted Blain), Fran Ryan (Nurse Fager), Arch Johnson (Halvorsen)**

Student nurses in a hospital ward are attacked by a would-be rapist wearing surgical garb. Jill and Kelly pose as nurses and start compiling a list of suspects. Among the prime contenders are the doctor on duty at the time, Tom Danworth, a gruff patient named Halvorsen, and the "Kissing Intern,"

Kelly (Jaclyn Smith) and Sabrina (Kate Jackson) investigate the "Terror on Ward One."

whose advances toward every nurse in the ward have been rejected.

Danworth is found dead next to a confession note, but the Angels see through the attempted frame and confront intern Ted Blaine, the son of a man who died on Danworth's operating table. He confesses to framing Danworth, but not to the attacks.

COMMENTARY

One of the better first-season shows for David Doyle, whose character finally gets a first name—John—and whose field assignment as a patient leads to unexpected and amusing consequences. "Without Ed Lakso, I wouldn't have got as many interesting things to do, especially as comic relief," Doyle said. By now, the relationship between Bosley and the Angels has softened and become more affectionate, though it would always remain platonic.

Shot in slasher-movie style but without the graphic violence and body count, "Terror on Ward One" is an average outing notable only for Doyle's contribution. As in "Dirty Business" and many others, the nicest guy in the vicinity turns out to be the nutcase.

EPISODE 19: *Dancing In The Dark*

ORIGINAL AIRDATE: **February 23, 1977**
PRODUCED BY: **Barney Rosenzweig**
WRITTEN BY: **Les Carter**
DIRECTED BY: **Cliff Bole**
GUEST STARS: **John Van Dreelen (Alexander Cruz), Logan Ramsey (Schaffer Goodhew), Jean Allison (Laura Clusak), Benny Baker (Murphy Myrphy), Dennis Cole (Tony Bordinay)**

When Laura Clusak, the widow of a famous baseball player, attempts to break off an affair with gigolo dance teacher Tony Bordinay, she is blackmailed with planted drugs and photographs of their tryst. She pays $10,000 to avoid a scandal that could keep her husband out of the Baseball Hall of Fame. After his induction, she hires the Angels to exact revenge.

Jill becomes the new disco dancing teacher at the studio where Tony works. Sabrina waltzes into Tony's class as a neurotic rich girl looking for private lessons. Tony and his partner-in-crime jump at the opportunity for another set-up. Schaffer Goodhew, a detective of dubious morals who takes the dirty pictures, is lured out of town by Bosley, allowing Kelly to step in as the photographer.

COMMENTARY

As he did on "Consenting Adults," writer Les Carter once again elevates the standard of storytelling on *Charlie's Angels*, and the result is the highlight of the first season, and one of the best episodes of the entire series.

Kate Jackson, wearing an ill-fitting fedora and thick glasses, is hilarious as the nerdy dance student; "I wrote that role of a lonely, neurotic woman, who is taken advantage of by a gigolo, partially out of revenge for Kate's cruel words about my first script," said Les Carter with a laugh. "It really disturbed her, and (director) Cliff Bole told me, years later, the she took all her anger out on him. I thought if she objected that much she would sabotage the scene, and not make it funny, but I was surprised and delighted that she did a terrific job."

Farrah shows off her moves doing the hustle and the bump (ah, the good old days) in Jill's audition at the studio. Okay, she's not Karen Lynn Gorney from *Saturday Night Fever*, but she looks more than proficient in a brief adagio with guest star Dennis Cole, who later married Jaclyn Smith. Charlie makes a rare appearance in the field, as a chauffeur for Bosley during his cover as Sabrina's father.

Les Carter would later write scripts for *Baretta* and *Cagney and Lacey*. "I was grateful for getting the break on *Charlie's Angels*, and learned a lot of lessons about story and structure. But I felt if I remained with that one show, I could get stuck in a particular style of writing that I didn't want to continue," he said.

EPISODE 20: *I Will Be Remembered*

ORIGINAL AIRDATE: **March 9, 1977**
PRODUCED BY: **Barney Rosenzweig**
WRITTEN BY: **Melvin Levy, story by: Richard Powell**
DIRECTED BY: **Nicholas Sgarro**
GUEST STARS: **Ida Lupino (Gloria Gibson), Peter MacLean (Frank Ross), Alfred Ryder (Barkley), Jan Peters (Galbraith), Wynn Irwin (Barney), Louis Guss (Lunchie)**

Gloria Gibson, legendary movie star of a bygone era, is haunted by images from her films. Still grieving over the death of her husband, Nicky, a gambler who left Gloria in debt, her attempt at a career comeback is threatened by rumors that she is losing her sanity. She calls upon her old friend Charlie for help.

COMMENTARY

When Ida Lupino reads her lines, she has . . . an . . . annoying . . . habit . . . of . . . pausing . . . between . . . every . . . word . . . she . . . says. "Ida could not remember two words in succession," recalled Barney Rosenzweig. "This was beyond a memory problem. The editor and I struggled in the cutting room to make that picture work. It was very, very sad." The character, a knock-off of Norma Desmond from the 1950 film classic *Sunset Boulevard*, wasn't much to begin with anyway. No surprises at all in this one.

Farrah Fawcett gets one of her last assignments as a series regular.

EPISODE 21: *Angels At Sea*

ORIGINAL AIRDATE: **March 23, 1977**
PRODUCED BY: **Barney Rosenzweig**
WRITTEN BY: **John D.F. Black**
DIRECTED BY: **Allen Baron**
GUEST STARS: **Frank Gorshin (Harry Dana), David Watson (Tom Lavin), Harold J. Stone (John Strauss), Katie Hopkins Zerby (Jerian), Michael Irving (Jack Armetage)**

The Townsend Agency is hired to find out who is trying to drive a popular cruise line out of business. Before they leave the office, they find a mannequin pinned to the door warning against any interference. Their covers blown before they've even been established, the Angels and Bosley set sail into a sea of possible suspects.

During the voyage, Sabrina, Kelly and Bosley all escape deathtraps, and another passenger is murdered. They discover that entertainer Harry

Dana is behind the attacks, but his capture does not mean the danger has passed. Dana reveals that there are bombs planted throughout the ship, set to detonate before any help can arrive.

COMMENTARY

The shortage of escape routes in the middle of the Pacific Ocean heightens the tension in this above-average outing, the first of three Angels adventures set on a cruise ship. "Aaron already had the set built for *The Love Boat,* and wanted to use it for an *Angels* story—he said it would save him $100,000," writer John D. F. Black said. Some of the exteriors where shot in Long Beach, California on the Queen Mary. In a setting where everyone wears a swimsuit, the fact that no bikinis were used in the making of this episode indicates a recognition that the necessity to play the skin card is no longer as considerable.

The standard whodunit pattern is shaken up when the guilty party is captured halfway into the episode. The interrogation scene that follows allows veteran comedian/impressionist Frank Gorshin, who plays Dana, the opportunity to perform half of his nightclub act, including dead-on impressions of James Cagney, Kirk Douglas and Ed Sullivan. His over-the-top portrayal of a psychotic who leaves cryptic clues to his scheme is reminiscent of Gorshin's Emmy-nominated performance as The Riddler on *Batman*.

Kelly, in finding her way out of a locked room filled with poison gas, demonstrates her ingenuity as the escape artist of the team, as she would again in "Angels on Ice" and "Avenging Angel."

EPISODE 22: *The Blue Angels*

ORIGINAL AIRDATE: May 4, 1977
PRODUCED BY: Barney Rosenzweig
WRITTEN BY: Edward J. Lakso and Laurie Lakso
DIRECTED BY: George Stanford Brown
GUEST STARS: Dirk Benedict (Barton), Tom Ligon (Miller), Timothy Carey (Burt), Michael Bell (Bill Duncan), Ed Lauter (Lt. Howard Fine), Joanne Kerns (Natalie)

A murder at the Paradise Massage Parlor exposes rumors of corruption in the police department's vice division. Chief Fenton, who helped train the Angels at the police academy, hires his former pupils to find out if a rogue cop is tipping off the parlors before they are raided. Sabrina and Kelly rejoin the force; Jill and Bosley take over ownership of the Paradise.

Sabrina is assigned to assist Detective Howard Fine, the vice division's top investigator. She finds out that academy cadets, under Fine's supervision, are taking protection money from potential vice targets.

COMMENTARY

The final episode of the first season has the Angels coming full-circle, and returning to the police academy where Charlie rescued them from their "hazardous duties." Chief Fenton, their former boss, is referred to but never seen. Michael Bell makes his second and final appearance as Sabrina's ex-husband, Bill Duncan. Kelly's reputation as a sharpshooter, first revealed in "Bullseye," is utilized again in her scenes at the police academy.

Though writer Edward J. Lakso claims he was not inspired by *The Three Stooges*, the use of the codename "Doc" for a character named Howard Fine does seem suspicious ("Calling Dr. Howard, Dr. Fine, Dr. Howard!").

Dirk Benedict, a good guy on *Battlestar: Galactica* and *The A-Team*, plays one of the corrupt cadets. *Growing Pains* star Joanne Kerns plays one brief scene from a hospital bed as a beaten-up prostitute. "That one I don't remember at all," said Barney Rosenzweig. "By then, I was packing my bags."

Season Two
1977-1978

Kate Jackson (Sabrina Duncan)

Jaclyn Smith (Kelly Garrett)

Cheryl Ladd (Kris Munroe)

David Doyle (John Bosley)

John Forsythe (Charlie Townsend)

EPISODE 23: *Angels in Paradise*

ORIGINAL AIRDATE: **September 14, 1977**
PRODUCED BY: **Ronald Austin and James Buchanan**
WRITTEN BY: **John D.F. Black**
DIRECTED BY: **Charles S. Dubin**
GUEST STARS: **France Nuyen (Leilani Sako), Al Harrington (Ned), Tom Fujiwara (Billy Sako), Lei Kayahara (Ewa Sako), Jake Hoopai (Apa)**

Sabrina and Kelly voice their displeasure at Charlie's hiring of a new Angel, after Jill leaves the team to become a professional race car driver. "Maybe we'll work with her, maybe we won't," warns Sabrina. Seconds later, Kris Munroe bursts through the office doors of the Townsend Agency, having been plucked from the police academy in San Francisco by Charlie. All of the Angels' concerns dissolve at first sight of Jill's younger sister, who is welcomed to the fold.

The new team's first assignment—find Charlie, who has been kidnapped during his vacation in Hawaii. Sabrina, Kelly and Kris follow the kidnapper's instructions and meet their "client," Leilani Sako, a smuggler who orders the Angels to break her husband, Billy, out of jail in exchange for Charlie's release. They do the job as directed, but by then Charlie is taken from Leilani's clutches by a rival smuggling gang led by the crude Mr. Blue.

Sabrina (Kate Jackson), Kris (Cheryl Ladd) and Kelly (Jaclyn Smith) in "Angels in Paradise."

COMMENTARY

This lavish introduction of Cheryl Ladd offered sumptuous travelogue footage of Hawaii, beaches full of beauties in bikinis, and plenty of action on land and sea, all to distract viewers from the absence of megastar Farrah Fawcett-Majors. Ladd's easy smile and beguiling kid-sister spunk have a girl-next-door appeal different from that of the unapproachably beautiful Farrah but, in sheer sex appeal, Ladd more than meets the standard. Taking no chances, however, Aaron Spelling and Leonard Goldberg made certain that her entire wardrobe for this two-part adventure could fit in her change purse.

"What I remember most was the crowds on the beach, and how difficult it was to film," said Ladd, who learned to surf during the trip. "We were in Honolulu, where everybody was on vacation, and they all knew the Angels were there."

"I had worked a lot of shows in my day, but I never saw the pandemonium this show brought," said producer Ronald Austin. On the eve of Ladd's first day of filming, Austin had dinner with Cheryl and her husband, David. "We were dining outside the restaurant, and I recall saying to Cheryl, 'Enjoy the serenity while you can, because it won't last for long.' Boy, was I right!"

Ladd's official Angel rite of passage, "the wearin' o' the thong," occurs in an amusing moment when a high school breaks class because "Surf's up!" Kris, who had been questioning a teacher connected to the case, rides the Pacific waves (though, like Farrah, her actual stuntwork is limited). She apparently wears even less in a modest but amusing nude scene opposite Norman Fell. Yes, Mr. Roper himself.

Throughout the first season, the three Angels functioned as equals; beginning with "Angels in Paradise," Sabrina clearly emerges as the field leader of the team. After Charlie's briefing, it is Sabrina who instructs Kelly and Kris on which leads to pursue, and who takes charge of the negotiations with Leilani.

France Nuyen, later a regular on the hospital series *St. Elsewhere*, makes her first entrance in a bikini even briefer than Cheryl Ladd's. Unlike the cookie cutter villains of many previous and subsequent episodes, Leilani is a charming but deadly adversary—a woman of breeding and iron will who would kill without compunction if she doesn't get her way. Her reference to the team as "Angels" indicates that the expression is not just a term of endearment bestowed by Charlie. "It's a pleasure to meet you, Charlie's Angels!" she exclaims after emerging from the surf, suggesting that the Townsend team have attained a certain degree of acclaim.

The jailbreak scene is one of the most clever and well-executed action sequences in the series, and there's a cameo from Don Ho, who must be contractually obligated to appear in every television show that takes a Hawaii road trip. But ultimately, "Angels in Paradise" is a showcase for Cheryl Ladd, who is featured in every prominent scene. By the time she wiggles her grass skirt during a hula performance, at the luau that closes the episode, the producers hoped she would be accepted by viewers as she was by Kelly and Sabrina. The ratings of the next few weeks would tell the story.

EPISODE 24: *Angels on Ice*

ORIGINAL AIRDATE:	September 21, 1977
PRODUCED BY:	Edward J. Lakso
WRITTEN BY:	Rick Edelstein
DIRECTED BY:	Robert Kelljan
GUEST STARS:	Phil Silvers (Max), Jim Backus (Iggy), James Gammon (Billy), Geoffrey Binney (Jack Ward), James Oliver (Paul), Vicky Perry (Shirley Ward), Inga Schilling (Olga), Tom Lawler (Luisi)

Ice show stars Jack Ward and Helene Robinson are kidnapped six days before opening night, and suspicion falls on Billy, a mentally ill handyman with a crush on Helene. The Angels, however, suspect there's more to this case, especially after two foreign skaters, Olga and Luisi, offer their services to the show, having already memorized the routines of the missing stars.

Next to disappear is Iggy, the show's prop man, along with a floor plan of the auditorium. Iggy is soon replaced by a relative of Olga's. A promising lead is provided to Sabrina by a homeless man living in the parking lot, who links the series of crimes with a limousine sporting diplomatic license plates. Kelly follows the limo to an Arabian restaurant, but she is captured and locked in an abandoned warehouse with Iggy and the missing skaters.

COMMENTARY

The second consecutive two-part episode, and one of the unqualified highlights of the Sabrina-Kelly-Kris era. Cheryl Ladd, playing Farrah's role with few alterations in the script, fits comfortably nonetheless into her undercover tasks alongside Jaclyn Smith. "I liked that one because I got to play the clown," Ladd said. Oddly enough, even when "Angels on Ice" was meant for Jill Munroe, a scene was written in which she was to have trouble learning to ice skate, when Jill had roller-skated like a pro in the previous season's roller derby show, "Angels on Wheels" (#12).

While Kris and Kelly take to the ice, Sabrina and Bosley demonstrate their now finely-honed comedic rapport in scenes opposite Jim Backus and Phil Silvers. Silvers died a few months after this performance; as the beleaguered owner of the ice show, he launches into several Sgt. Bilko-style tirades, mostly directed at Charlie— "I call you for help and what do I get? Three cheerleaders!"

"He had vertigo and couldn't get on the escalator in the last scene," said Jaclyn Smith. "I had them restage the scene, and he was so appreciative that he sent me a bottle of perfume the next day."

The assassination attempt at the climax is ingeniously conceived and staged, as is Kelly's airborne escape from a locked storeroom. The scene in which an attractive female figure skater is attacked probably gave Tonya Harding ideas, but the episode's most memorable moment on most viewers' scorecards is Jaclyn Smith's stint as a sultry, veiled belly dancer.

EPISODE 25: *Pretty Angels All in a Row*

ORIGINAL AIRDATE: September 28, 1977
PRODUCED BY: Edward J. Lakso
WRITTEN BY: John D.F. Black
DIRECTED BY: John D.F. Black
GUEST STARS: Burton Gilliam (Ulmer), Richard Kelton (Hubie), Jack Knight (Ben Pawl), Steve Franken (Fred), Millicent (Patricia Barry), Billie Jolene (Doney Oatman), Bobbie Mitchell (Grace Cooley)

Someone is sabotaging the "Miss Chrysanthemum" beauty pageant in Freebairn, Iowa. Before all the contestants are scared away by mysterious accidents, pageant producer Ben Pawl begs the Angels for help. Kelly and Kris go undercover as contestants, while Sabrina and Bosley play reporters covering the event for television. The two competing Angels have fun with the assignment, especially when it comes time to impress the judges, but the case becomes serious when shots are fired through Kris's hotel room window.

COMMENTARY

Who could have guessed that, so soon after the departure of Farrah Fawcett-Majors threatened to become a death-knell for the series, *Charlie's Angels* would respond with another contender for its best episode ever? This hilarious send-up of beauty pageants, written by John D. F. Black, contains memorable comedic moments from all three Angels and David Doyle.

Kris (Cheryl Ladd, left) and Kelly (Jaclyn Smith, far right) go undercover
as beauty pageant contestants in "Pretty Angels All in a Row."

At first, Kelly and Kris express a patronizing bemusement toward the Miss Chrysanthemum Pageant, and play their parts accordingly; "I'd like to study brain surgery," Kelly tells the judges with the appropriate sing-song delivery. Asked to name her favorite color, Kris solemnly replies, "My favorite colors are red, white and blue, because they're the colors of our flag of freedom." Another beauty participates in the talent competition by reciting a soliloquy from Shakespeare's *The Merchant of Venice* while twirling batons.

Gradually, however, Kris and Kelly actually start taking the competition seriously, much to the amusement of Sabrina, who is having her own fun indulging the secret agent fantasies of producer Ben Pawl.

"I really loved that show," said Black. "The only reason to do a beauty pageant story is to send it up. Nobody else was writing *Charlie's Angels* like a comedy, and I thought that's what it should be."

"Farrah was still there when that one came together, and I wrote a magic act for her," he recalled. "She wanted it to be funny, so I included a scene where she would take her top hat off and there would be a pigeon on her head. When Farrah left and Cheryl came in, she thought the magic act would be fun, except for the pigeon. 'I don't think Aaron's gonna want me walking around with pigeon droppings on my head,' she told me."

Jaclyn Smith rehearsed an elaborate dance number for Kelly's talent competition, the first time she could utilize her talents as a dancer on the series. Before the scene was shot, however, she pulled a hamstring and could not perform the routine, which explains why she is seated on a stool for much of the performance. "I was really into the dance in rehearsal—I thought I was Juliet Prowse, then I kicked too high and hurt myself," she recalls. "It really put a damper on what I could do. My big moment—what a shame."

The Miss Chrysanthemum theme, written by Ed Lakso, has all the annoying jingle catchiness of an old Cowsills record, and stays in the mind for days. "John (D. F. Black) said we needed a theme," Lakso said, "and I ad-libbed something really corny on the piano, just kidding around, and he said, 'Yeah! That's perfect!'" The pageant, held in Iowa according to the script, was actually shot in the Santa Monica City College auditorium. The bikini worn by Debbie, the contestant from London, is the same bikini worn by Kelly in the *Charlie's Angels* pilot. The stock footage of an applauding audience was the same footage used for the ice show in the previous week's episode, "Angels on Ice." It would be used a third time in the fifth season episode, "Mr. Galaxy" (#107).

EPISODE 26: *Angel Flight*

ORIGINAL AIRDATE: October 5, 1977
PRODUCED BY: Edward J. Lakso
WRITTEN BY: Brian McKay
DIRECTED BY: Dennis Donnelly
GUEST STARS: Fawne Harriman (Angela Hart), Robert Gentry (Gene Knox), Marshall Thompson (Meadows), Phil Roth (Eddie), Ben Hayes (Bill Glover), Lisa Moore (Mai Ling), Lee Travis (Paula)

Flight attendant Angela Hart is harassed by a stalker who leaves black roses in her car and apartment. She calls upon her old college roommate, Sabrina, for help. Kris and Kelly enroll in stewardess school, and Sabrina moves in with Angela, but that doesn't stop the stalker from depositing his calling card in the kitchen coffee pot, and leaving undetected.

Suspicion falls upon Angela's ex-boyfriend, Gene Knox, until another flight attendant is killed by a karate chop to the throat, and a black rose is found by the body. Angela is contacted again by the stalker, who orders her to assist in hijacking a stewardess training flight. When the entire flight crew all wind up unconscious in the cockpit, it's up to Kelly to land the plane safely.

COMMENTARY

Even *Flying High* offered a better take on stewardesses than this uninspired episode. Jaclyn Smith plays the famous Karen Black scene from *Airport '76* but, unlike the crosseyed Karen, she gets no help at all from Charleton Heston. "You may have to land the plane," warns a grave voice from the Los Angeles Airport, and of course Kelly brings it down. Even though her success is never in doubt, the moment should have been more suspenseful.

It was during the casting of "Angel Flight" that producer Ed Lakso met his wife, actress Lee Travis. "I needed a girl named Too-tall Paula, and saw Lee at an ABC affiliates luncheon. I was blitzed, but still went up to her and said, 'You're Paula! You're Paula! I've got a part for you—call me!'"

"I thought he was kidding," recalls Lee Travis, "until my agent told me he produced *Charlie's Angels*." Travis reported to work, thrilled to be starting her first job on a prime time TV series, and soon discovered that Ed hired many people he met socially. "We had just started to date, and then I found myself in a dressing room with his ex-girlfriend, Fawne Harriman, with whom he had just broken up!"

Had the episode been built entirely around the hijacking scheme gone awry, rather than wasting the first half-hour on all that black rose nonsense, it might have had a chance. Fawne Harriman's Angela is an uncooperative, hysterical drip of a client, who is so unsympathetic that viewers may have rooted for the stalker.

EPISODE 27: *Circus of Terror*

ORIGINAL AIRDATE: **October 19, 1977**
PRODUCED BY: **Edward J. Lakso**
WRITTEN BY: **Robert Janes**
DIRECTED BY: **Allen Baron**
GUEST STARS: **James Darren (David Barzak), Charles Tyner (Anton Tarloff), Denny Miller (Helmut Klaus), Patty Maloney (Tinkle Belle), Ramon Bieri (Yanos Barzak)**

The Barzak Circus is driven to the brink of bankruptcy by malfunctioning equipment and attacks on its performers, culminating in the sniper shooting of a trapeze artist. The owner's gypsy code of honor forbids him from contacting the police, but his modern-thinking son, David, hires the Angels to investigate.

Cover stories in place—Sabrina plays a clown, Kris the assistant to the knife-thrower, Kelly as motorcycle daredevil "Go-Go Garrett," they set out to learn who is trying to drive the circus out of business, and immediately become targets of Anton Tarloff. A genteel mime from a long tradition of circus performers, Tarloff blames Barzak for the accidental death of his daughter during a performance, and cannot rest until the gypsy circus has been destroyed.

COMMENTARY

Mission: Impossible did the circus-themed story best, even with Mary Ann Mobley as a guest star. The Angels cover is not exactly the *Greatest Show on Earth,* or even of the season, but the guest roles are proficiently filled by James Darren, Ramon Bieri as Barzak, and Charles Tyner as Tarloff. As suave gypsy David Barzak, James Darren becomes Sabrina's second client-romance—quite a departure from Theodore Bikel in "Angels On a String." The circus scenes were shot on location at California State University at Northridge.

"Circus of Terror" was the first episode shot for the second season, and the first episode to be produced by Edward Lakso. "I was very nervous about the scene with the motorcycle wipeout," he recalls. "I thought the stunt coordinator had set the camera up too close, so if the stuntman lost control of the bike, someone could get hurt." After a long argument, the coordinator agreed to back up the camera about 20 feet. "As it happened, the guy blew the stunt, and came sliding right into the cameraman's lap. Nobody got hurt, but if we hadn't moved it could have been bad."

EPISODE 28: *Angel in Love*

ORIGINAL AIRDATE:	October 26, 1977
PRODUCED BY:	Ronald Austin and James Buchanan
WRITTEN BY:	Skip Webster and Jack Mackelvie
DIRECTED BY:	Paul Stanley
GUEST STARS:	Peter Haskell (Doug O'Neal), Carole Cook (Hildy Slater), Charles Picerni (Frank Slater), Tom Simcox (Lon Molton), Amanda McBroom (Lorraine Fielding)

Hildy Slater, the owner of the trendy singles resort Utopia West, hires the Angels when the understaffed and overburdened local sheriff fails to find the killer of her nephew, Frank. Kelly and Kris replace the employees who hastily departed after Frank's body was found in his cabin, and Sabrina plays a journalist.

Sabrina becomes infatuated with Doug O'Neal, a guest at the resort. Kelly has him investigated and learns that Doug is actually B.J. Smith, an extortionist who escaped from an airborne plane with $2 million in cash.

COMMENTARY

Sabrina Duncan, the least cupcake-like of the three Angels, is now falling in love as often as Marcia Brady (see last episode). Doug O'Neal is the most serious of her one-episode flings, though it is not at all convincing that the smart Angel would fall for this guy's transparent line, even when uttered with old western charm by guest star Peter Haskell.

The character of B.J. Smith, who steals money on an airplane and escapes via parachute, is obviously inspired by D.B. Cooper, a real-life hijacker who absconded from Northwest Airlines Flight 305 with $200,000 in 1971, and was never found, probably because the Angels never looked for him. His exploits were the subject of the 1981 film *The Pursuit of D.B. Cooper*.

A mid-episode scene featuring all three Angels in a hot tub is one of scant few moments in which Kate Jackson goes anywhere near the cheesecake aspects of the series. According to producer Ronald Austin, the scene was added at the request of Aaron Spelling, to "spice up the episode." "Angel in Love" also allows Bosley to go shirtless, so at least it's equal-opportunity exploitation.

EPISODE 29: *Unidentified Flying Angels*

ORIGINAL AIRDATE: November 2, 1977
PRODUCED BY: Edward J. Lakso
WRITTEN BY: Ronald Austin and James Buchanan
DIRECTED BY: Allen Baron
GUEST STARS: Dennis Cole (James Britten), Ross Martin (Dr. Perine), Bill Striglos (Teddy), Ken Olfson (Seth), Ernestine Barrier (Mrs. Sheridan)

Missionary Joyce Sheridan returns from Africa after learning that her rich, eccentric Aunt Charlotte has been reported missing. Charlotte Sheridan was last seen spending time and money at the Celestial Research Foundation, a facility that promises its members the chance to meet alien races and travel through outer space.

Dr. Perine, the administrator of the foundation, contends that he is in regular contact with "space people," and his assertions are substantiated by a respected former astronaut, James Britten. Kris and Bosley pose as a married couple who wish to join the foundation, but they can't find anyone willing to answer questions. Kelly has better luck, masquerading as a sexy spacegirl to get information on the Foundation from a nebbishy member.

COMMENTARY

Perine's scam is so blatantly see-through that it doesn't make for much of a case, but the lighter tone of the episode allows for some broader comedic moments, expertly played by the cast. It's a toss-up for the highlight between Kelly's stint in an aluminum-foil spacesuit, in which she resembles one of Captain Kirk's conquests on *Star Trek*, and Sabrina's portrayal of a crass, gum-snapping private eye with a thick New York accent, one of the few characters she would revive in future episodes. Cheryl Ladd, still stuck in Jill's role, plays a spoiled California doll opposite sugardaddy Bosley, just as Farrah did in "The Big Tap Out."

Ross Martin, who played Artemus Gordon on the classic series *The Wild, Wild West*, exchanges one fast-talking con man role for another. Dennis Cole makes his second *Angels* appearance, once again playing a rat, and shares several romantic scenes with his then-girlfriend, Jaclyn Smith. Kelly's exposure as a detective makes one wonder why the Angels often used their real names on cases.

EPISODE 30: *Angels On the Air*

ORIGINAL AIRDATE:	November 9, 1977
PRODUCED BY:	Ronald Austin and James Buchanan
WRITTEN BY:	William Froug
DIRECTED BY:	George Brooks
GUEST STARS:	Nicolas Coster (Professor Croyden), Linda Dano (Joy Vance), Larry Golden (Dwayne), Taylor Lacher (Buck Willis), Larry Gilman (Gary)

KBEX radio reporter Joy Vance has her life threatened, and the list of suspects is a long one. The Angels follow up on the many criminals that were prosecuted on the strength of Joy's investigative reports, but the prime suspect is Buck Willis, a helicopter pilot and Vietnam veteran, who was replaced by Joy as the station's traffic reporter. Sabrina rides with Buck, now only hired as the pilot, while Kelly replaces Joy at the radio station.

COMMENTARY

A by-the-book plot, featuring a mysterious stalker, a female victim, and a grab bag of suspects, that works best in those moments that deviate from the pattern. Cheryl Ladd's amusingly unconvincing portrayal of a tough biker chick is a hoot, especially opposite Larry Golden as an *Easy Rider* wannabe. Two popular soap opera stars played featured roles; Linda Dano plays the victimized Joy, and Nicolas Coster, usually up to no good in daytime as well, plays the guilty Professor Croydon. Jaclyn Smith convincingly chases down the bad guys in a memorable action scene—a few months before, her running skills would help ABC win the annual *Battle of the Network Stars*.

EPISODE 31: *Angel Baby*

ORIGINAL AIRDATE: November 16, 1977
PRODUCED BY: Ronald Austin and James Buchanan
WRITTEN BY: George R. Hodges and John D.F.Black;
STORY BY: George Hodges
DIRECTED BY: Paul Stanley
GUEST STARS: Edward Winter (Hugh Tomlinson), Scott
Colomby (Tommy), Sunny Johnson
(Marie), John Karlen (Chaffey), Bruce
Fairbairn (Jayce), Mrs. Morris (Jean Allison)

Tommy goes AWOL from the Air Force when letters from his girlfriend, Marie, stop arriving. He returns from the Far East to Los Angeles, but cannot find Marie at her home, and her roommates refuse to reveal her whereabouts. After being arrested for causing a public disturbance, Tommy uses his one phone call to ask Kelly for help. During her time as a policewoman, Kelly convinced Tommy, then a cocky streetfighter, to join the military and turn his life around.

Kelly agrees to help, and with Charlie's blessing hires the agency to take the case. They find out from Marie's roommates that Marie was pregnant with Tommy's child, and didn't want him to learn the truth. She sought help and protection from a non-profit home for girls under the auspices of philanthropist Hugh Tomlinson, that is actually a front for a baby brokerage operation.

Posing as a pregnant woman desperate for money, Kelly infiltrates the home and informs Marie of Tommy's return. Bosley and Sabrina visit the home as a childless couple interested in buying Kelly's baby. The plan proceeds on schedule, until emotion clouds the judgment of Tommy and Marie, and they are captured by Chaffey, a vicious bodyguard in Tomlinson's employ.

COMMENTARY

One of the series' most powerful episodes; George R. Hodges' one and only script for the show is a serious, unflinching treatment of the grim subject of baby brokers. Only the epilogue scene set in the Townsend offices contains any of the smiles and breezy interplay of most *Angels* stories. The cast responds admirably to the depth and intensity of the material, and shatters the bimbo clichés and critics' accusations of skin- peddling. "Angel Baby" is laudable drama, without bikinis or even a modicum of prurient enticement.

Sabrina, Kelly and Kris all excel in their undercover assignments, but this time there is no sense of fun in the play-acting of the roles. For the first time, Cheryl Ladd is able to break free from parts designed for her predecessor, and put her own spin on the blond Angel. As a downtrodden, amoral gold digger, she uses desperation, not flirtation, to tempt Tomlinson into revealing his secret business. Had Farrah still been around, her interpretation would inevitably have been much different. Kate Jackson, as a harridan of an adoptive mother, loses herself completely in the brittle voice and clipped mannerisms of her character-within-a-character.

John Karlen, an Emmy-winner for *Cagney and Lacey*, shared many scenes with Jackson on *Dark Shadows*, but they only exchange gunfire here. As Chaffey, one of the Angels' most cold-blooded adversaries, Karlen is the first villain to be felled with an Angel's bullet. The on-camera shooting, a series first, is not treated lightly—after Kris fires the fatal shot, she stands frozen, on the verge of a breakdown, until she is comforted by Sabrina. "Instead of making it a light, 'Angel' moment, they made it a real moment," said Ladd.

EPISODE 32: *Angels in the Wings*

ORIGINAL AIRDATE:	November 23, 1977
PRODUCED BY:	Edward J. Lakso
WRITTEN BY:	Edward J. Lakso
DIRECTED BY:	Dennis Donnelly
GUEST STARS:	Shani Wallis (Ellen Jason), Gene Barry (Frank Jason), Nicolas Beauvy (Larry Jason), Michael Fox (Austin Wells), Nehemiah Persoff (Anton), Lew Palter (Mancino), Michael Fairman (Cal Stone), Hal Needham (Julio), Tony Epper (Canty), Tammy Greenough (Norma)

Singing star Ellen Jason asks for Charlie's help after she is nearly killed by a falling stagelight, during rehearsals for a new show. The soundstage where the alleged accident happened is rumored to be haunted, but the Angels focus their investigation on non-supernatural suspects, such as Ellen's embittered ex-husband, Frank, and the show's suspicious producer.

COMMENTARY

"Angels in the Wings" provides a musical showcase for Cheryl Ladd, who performs a cute song and dance number with Gene Barry when Kris joins the cast of the beleaguered musical production. Writer Ed Lakso also penned the music and lyrics for four original songs used in the episode. "We wanted to give Cheryl a spotlight, since she still hadn't been completely accepted by the cast," said Lakso.

"I loved doing it, but at the same time it was an enormous amount of work, with all that singing and dancing plus learning lines." said Ladd.

The sets and backdrops for two of the musical numbers were borrowed from old MGM musicals. "Everybody knocked themselves out on that one to make it look great, and they were all jazzed when they saw the results," recalls Lakso. However, Leonard Goldberg didn't seem impressed when he first screened the episode. "Aaron was out sick, so Leonard came in to watch it, and he just glowered through the whole thing. At the end, he just got up and walked out. But when it ran, it got a huge rating, and to Leonard's credit, he called the next morning and apologized," said Lakso. "We became friends after that."

Shani Wallis, who plays Ellen Jason, is best known for her portrayal of Nancy in the stage and screen versions of the musical *Oliver!*. Her ex-husband is played by Gene Barry, whose professional relationship with Aaron Spelling dates back to *Burke's Law*. Hal Needham, a former stuntman who directed *Smokey and the Bandit* (1977), and *Cannonball Run* (1981), has a bit part in the episode as a loan shark's henchman.

EPISODE 33: *Magic Fire*

ORIGINAL AIRDATE:	November 30, 1977
PRODUCED BY:	Ronald Austin and James Buchanan
WRITTEN BY:	Lee Sheldon
DIRECTED BY:	Leon Carrere
GUEST STARS:	Rudy Solari (Danzini), Victoria Carroll (Mary Ann), Howard Witt (Joseph Watson). E.J. Andre (Wendell Muse)

When several fires are mysteriously started at Fashion City warehouses, a legendary arsonist called the "Magic Man" is suspected. Wendell Muse, a magician who uses fire in his act, asks the Angels to clear his name after he is questioned by the police.

Sabrina masquerades as a French fashion designer, at a warehouse that may be the Magic Man's next target. That night, the warehouse goes up in flames, with Sabrina inside. Before making her escape, she discovers that the fire was set by loading phosphorous into a telephone receiver, which is later ignited by a phone call. Using this knowledge, the Angels set a trap for the Magic Man.

COMMENTARY

The Magic Castle, a real Los Angeles magic club, provides the backdrop for this average outing. Comic relief is provided by Bosley's turn as the telepath Zoltan, and by Sabrina hamming it up as a flighty French designer.

The shower has been a dangerous place for blondes since Alfred Hitchcock's *Psycho* (1960), and Kris nearly becomes its latest victim. She turns on the water, and narrowly avoids a blast of fire shot from the nozzle.

EPISODE 34: *The Sammy Davis Jr. Kidnap Caper*

ORIGINAL AIRDATE:	December 7, 1977
PRODUCED BY:	Ronald Austin and James Buchanan
WRITTEN BY:	Ron Friedman
DIRECTED BY:	Ronald Austin
GUEST STARS:	Sammy Davis Jr. (Himself/Herbert Brubaker III), Altovise Davis (Herself), Norman Alden (Louis Fluellen), Robert Pine (Andy Price), Martin Kove (Georgie), Harry Rhodes (Ben Brody)

After two attempts are made to kidnap Sammy Davis Jr., the entertainer's manager, Ben Brody, hires the Angels to provide security. A third attempt is made at Davis's home, that mistakenly nets Herbert Brubaker III, the winner of a Sammy Davis Jr. lookalike contest. A ransom note demanding $375,000 in eight hours prompts Sabrina to wonder about the unusual choices in dollar amount and delivery time.

COMMENTARY

A fun show with a feather-light plot built around special guest star Sammy Davis Jr., who plays both himself and celebrity look alike Herbie Brubaker. "Sammy was a friend of Aaron Spelling's, and wanted to do the show," said writer Ron Friedman, who was recruited by Spelling from writing the detective series *Starsky and Hutch* to contribute the script. "I don't recall if the dual role was my idea or Aaron's, but Sammy loved it," Friedman said. Davis seems to be having a ball costarring with his wife and three beautiful Angels. "I think I'm gonna love danger!" he says after being introduced to his new bodyguards.

The investigation inspires one of Kris's more amusing undercover jobs, as a naive would-be starlet looking for work. "Hi! I'm Taffy!" she announces with a cheerleader smile to an agent's secretary. "I loved working with Sammy," Ladd said. " I had always been a fan of his, and he couldn't have been kinder. That one was special."

EPISODE 35: *Angels on Horseback*

ORIGINAL AIRDATE: December 21, 1977
PRODUCED BY: Edward J. Lakso
WRITTEN BY: Edward J. Lakso
DIRECTED BY: George W. Brooks
GUEST STARS: Angel Tompkins (Jean Trevor), Woodrow Parfrey (Sheriff Hayden), William Phipps (George Jackson), James Sikking (Frisch), Ted Markland (Ed Cole)

During an overnight bus ride to the Sunwest Dude Ranch, a passenger identified as Joseph Frisch is murdered. The sheriff questions everyone on the bus to no avail, so the Angels and Bosley are booked onto the next bus to Sunwest, to get better acquainted with the suspects.

Frisch, it turns out, was on the run from the mob with a bankroll amassed from a bogus real estate deal. A coroner's report later reveals that the dead man was an innocent victim forced to change identities with Frisch, to give the fleeing mobster a head start on his getaway.

COMMENTARY

It's possible this whole episode was conceived to set up the climactic chase on horseback, with the Angels in full cowgirl regalia. Kate Jackson, riding a supposedly runaway horse at full gallop, actually gets to do a little stunt-work this time.

"Angels on Horseback" contains the first Angel swimsuit shots in quite awhile, which seem all the more gratuitous considering the episode is set on a dude ranch. In an early scene that has nothing to do with the plot, Kelly and Kris try on sexy new suits, to prepare for a possible case in the Caribbean.

EPISODE 36: *Game, Set, Death*

ORIGINAL AIRDATE:	January 4, 1978
PRODUCED BY:	Edward J. Lakso
WRITTEN BY:	Worley Thorne
DIRECTED BY:	George Stanford Brown
GUEST STARS:	Bibi Besch (Carrie Jo Evans), Larry Block (Arlos Spinner), Seth Foster (Kyle), Tiffany Bolling (Helga), George Caldwell (Fisk), Lynda Beattie (Sandy)

Kris joins the professional women's tennis tour after three players fall victim to various deliberate accidents. Several competitors drop off the tour, and those that remain are all potential suspects. . .and potential victims.

Sabrina and Kelly go undercover as a fashion designer and model. They focus their investigation on a boorish sportscaster who once lost a "Battle of the Sexes" match to player Carrie Jo Evans.

COMMENTARY

The second episode of the season to use a shower as a deathtrap (see "Magic Fire")—and it doesn't work this time, either. The tennis theme seems to be a giveaway that "Game, Set, Death" was written with Farrah Fawcett in mind, but the script was actually completed after Ladd was cast. Cheryl Ladd's inexperience with a racquet, however, prompted numerous severe and awkward edits in Kris's challenge match with the sportscaster.

Still, even Farrah's court skills couldn't save this turkey, in which all three Angels actually end up held at gunpoint by one of the lamest villains they've ever faced.

EPISODE 37: *Hours of Desperation*

ORIGINAL AIRDATE: January 11, 1978
PRODUCED BY: Edward J. Lakso
WRITTEN BY: Ray Brenner
DIRECTED BY: Cliff Bole
GUEST STARS: Stanley Kamel (Dinsmore), Peter Palmer (Fred Michaels), John Quade (Brown), Edward Power (Clint Murdock), Taurean Blacque (Dr. Stevens)

After stealing $1 million in diamonds, Clint Murdock tries to flee from his two accomplices, and gets away despite being shot. Dinsmore, the brains behind the heist, hires the Townsend Agency to get the diamonds back. To make certain they cooperate, he ties a belt of explosives around Sabrina's waist, that will be detonated by remote control in ten hours.

Kelly and Kris check the hospitals for gunshot victims. They just miss Murdock, but trace a phone call he made to Earl Jackson, a fence. The trail eventually leads to Murdock, who is found dead, and without the diamonds. After learning that Jackson has been arrested in the south of France, and the gems confiscated by the authorities, the Angels realize they will have to find another way to save Sabrina.

COMMENTARY

An interesting variation on the "race against time" theme, buoyed by Stanley Kamel's performance as Dinsmore, a psycho with an itchy detonation finger. Taurean Blacque, later a costar of *Hill Street Blues*, plays the doctor who treats Clint Murdock.

EPISODE 38: *Diamond in the Rough*

ORIGINAL AIRDATE: January 18, 1978
PRODUCED BY: Ronald Austin and James Buchanan
WRITTEN BY Brian McKay, Ronald Austin and
James Buchanan; story by Brian McKay
DIRECTED BY: Ronald Austin
GUEST STARS: Dan O'Herlihy (Freddie Brander), Bert
Remsen (Brewster McFarland), Sid Haig
(Reza), Robert Perault (Ali), René Enriquez
(Faris Salim)

Freddie "The Fox" Brander, a legendary cat burglar, is falsely accused of stealing the famous Light of Arabia diamond. Freddie tells the Angels that the diamond is actually in a Caribbean mansion belonging to Faris Salim, an Arab businessman of questionable character. He suggests they help him steal it back, so the Light of Arabia can be displayed in a museum, and Freddie will have a great last chapter in his autobiography.

COMMENTARY

Charlie's Angels does *Rififi* (1954), an always-reliable plot when it's done right. The Angels, assisted by Freddie the Fox, figure out a method to pull the impossible jewel heist, despite dozens of guards, security cameras, an electronically-wired floor, and a poisonous snake inside the glass case that houses the Light of Arabia. As a secretary working for Salim, Kelly, on her first day, actually asks another employee where the boss keeps the rare jewels—not exactly subtle detective work. The heist scene, played mostly in silence as it should be, is well-conceived and executed.

The parade of *Hill Street Blues* stars continues with the appearance here of René Enriquez as Salim. Bert Remsen, last seen as the lovable horse-player in "The Big Tap-Out," returns as rival cat burglar Brewster McFarland.

EPISODE 39: *Angels in the Backfield*

ORIGINAL AIRDATE: **January 25, 1978**
PRODUCED BY: **Edward J. Lakso**
WRITTEN BY: **Edward J. Lakso**
DIRECTED BY: **George Stanford Brown**
GUEST STARS: **Gary Wood (Joe Phillips), Nancy Fox (Amy Jarvis), Patch Mackenzie (Julia Smyth), Garn Stephens (Pokey), L. Q. Jones (Dan Jarvis), Heidi Von Beltz (Grinelda), Saundra Sharp (Hilda)**

Someone is trying to prevent the Ducks, a woman's football team, from suiting up for their season opener. After a rash of threatening phone calls and attacks on players by two masked motorcyclists, Ducks coach Amy Jarvis asks the Angels to join the team.

The ownership of the motorcycles is traced to Joe Phillips, an ex-football star left crippled by a career-ending injury. A search of his office uncovers blueprints to the Los Angeles Coliseum, where the Ducks will play their first game. The Angels deduce Phillips' plan to rob the stadium safe, containing the proceeds from a rock concert the previous night.

COMMENTARY

The Angels don very un-sexy helmets and shoulder pads for this one, which also contains a few locker room scenes for the voyeurs. "That was my least favorite episode," said Cheryl Ladd. "I didn't see myself, because I didn't even look in the mirror, but I took one look at Jaclyn in that football uniform, and she looked at me, and we

Kelly (Jaclyn Smith) suits up for a women's football team in "Angels in the Backfield."

just started laughing. Jaclyn is about as feminine and ladylike as they come, and to see her in that uniform, it was a scream."

Kate Jackson throws some of her own passes as the team quarterback, but she'll never be confused with Dan Marino. It's interesting to note that Sabrina, as quarterback, is once again cast as the field leader, as she would be on any other assignment. Kelly returns to her role as the enforcer, teaching the team bully a lesson when she taunts Kris, who now seems like a little sister to everyone at the Townsend Agency. Nancy Fox, who plays coach Amy Jarvis, is one of Jaclyn Smith's closest childhood friends, and would return for three more series appearances.

While Kelly and Kris hope to wrap up the case before the game, Sabrina's competitive juices won't let her walk away after Phillips is captured, especially after finding out that the Ducks' archrivals, the Panthers, have planted a spy in the huddle. In a rousing finale reminiscent of the Burt Reynolds film *The Longest Yard* (1974), the Angels return to the field and win the game.

Writer Ed Lakso knew someone with dyslexia, and incorporated the condition in the plot of this episode, long before the condition and its causes were familiar to the general public, or examined by the major media.

EPISODE 40: *The Sandcastle Murders*

ORIGINAL AIRDATE: February 1, 1978
PRODUCED BY: Ronald Austin and James Buchanan
WRITTEN BY: Skip Webster, Jack Mackelvie, Robert Dennis, Ronald Austin and James Buchanan;
STORY BY: Robert Dennis
DIRECTED BY: George McCowan
GUEST STARS: Alan Feinstein (Dave Christopher), Melissa Converse (Melissa Rossiter), John Crawford (Lt. Francona), Bibi Osterwald (Mabel), Hunter Von Leer (Hank), Melody Thomas (Betsy), Jason Evers (Larry Fallon)

Betsy, a friend of Kris's, hints that she may know something about the Sandcastle Murders, a series of Malibu beach killings in which the victims are found buried beneath a sandcastle. The Angels postpone a pending case to investigate, but Betsy become the killer's latest victim before she can reveal her information.

Kris learns that Betsy spent time in the home of Melissa Rossiter, a cosmetics magnate. After eliminating Melissa's fiance` as a suspect, the Angels concentrate on her estranged husband, Dave Christopher.

COMMENTARY

The first "non-official" case in several episodes, "The Sandcastle Murders" opens with a rare look at the Angels off-duty. At Kris's incredible Malibu beach house, which would indicate that Charlie pays one heck of a salary, they talk of planning a party, and hope that some of the L.A. Rams will stop by. The house was first seen on the series in the first season episode "The Killing Kind," (#6) when it was owned by Charlie's old friend, George Anderson.

Five writers are credited on this ambitious story, that takes several lurid twists before the final act. Alan Feinstein is terrific is Dave Christopher, one of the Angels' most clever and vicious adversaries. For a change, it is Bosley who fires the the shot that buries the bad guy.

Melody Thomas, who plays Betsy, is best known for her two decades on *The Young and the Restless* as Nikki Newman.

EPISODE 41: *Angel Blues*

ORIGINAL AIRDATE: February 8, 1978
PRODUCED BY: Edward J. Lakso
WRITTEN BY: Edward J. Lakso
DIRECTED BY: George Stanford Brown
GUEST STARS: Bess Gatewood (Amy Waters), Gary Bisig (Lenny), Bill Quinn (Ted Waters), Andy Jarrell (Eban Stone), Vincent Schiavelli (Freddie), Steve Gravers (Cooperman), Herb Braha (Hank), Lou Picetti (Doneger), Tim Rossovich (Taylor)

Amy Waters, a famous country singer with a drug addiction, is found dead from an apparent heroin overdose. The Angels are hired by Amy's father to investigate the circumstances of her death, and discover that the fatal drug was administered against her will.

COMMENTARY

The use of a cocaine-dispensing soap machine in a laundomat is a good gimmick, but "Angel Blues" is a dull episode with the predictable *Charlie's Angels* twist of the nicest guy in the area turning out to be rotten. The budget was apparently lower than average, as the Angels wear the same outfits throughout the entire adventure.

The middle act is sustained somewhat by Sabrina's revival of her gum-snapping, tough-talking New York detective guise, first used in "Unidentified Flying Angels." Writer Ed Lakso also composed the original song heard throughout the episode, "Trippin' to the Mornin,'" performed by Lynn Marta, then the girlfriend of *Starsky and Hutch* star David Soul.

EPISODE 42: *Mother Goose is Running for His Life*

ORIGINAL AIRDATE: February 15, 1978
PRODUCED BY: Ronald Austin and James Buchanan
WRITTEN BY: Del Reisman, Ronald Austin and James Buchanan
DIRECTED BY: George McCowan
GUEST STARS: Murray Matheson (Leland Swinnerton), Gilbert Green (Tony Phelan), Clifford David (Gordon Roclair), Don Knight (Jack Orwell), Bobbi Jordan (Donna), Holly Irving (Mrs. Cooley)

Leland Swinnerton, owner of the Mother Goose Toy Company, turns to the Angels for help after a rival toymaker tries to run him out of business. After an ex-con wiretapper is found dead in the company headquarters, and bugs are discovered throughout the building, the Angels learn from the dead man's fiancé that he was hired by Tony Phalen, a wealthy businessman with mob ties.

COMMENTARY

A colorful batch of guest stars: elevate this smart espionage tale, with a famous final scene, in which Kris dresses up as a doll mannequin, and pops her bubblegum when the object of her surveillance isn't looking. Sabrina goes undercover as "Jennifer Collins," the same last name she had on *Dark Shadows*.

In the epilogue scene at the Townsend office, Leland Swinnerton presents the Angels with a gift—a set of dolls in their likeness, the same ones that were actually marketed by Hasbro at the time. "Can I have a set for my niece?" asks Kelly, a strange request considering she's supposed to be an orphan.

"You'll get a share of the royalties," Swinnerton promises the Angels. But did they really? "I don't think we even got a free doll!" said Cheryl Ladd. "I don't think they wanted us to know how much merchandise was out there—millions and millions of dollars, and we got nothing. Eventually, we all got together, and got some puny little settlement— maybe $20,000."

EPISODE 43: *Little Angels of the Night*

ORIGINAL AIRDATE:	February 22, 1978
PRODUCED BY:	Edward J. Lakso
WRITTEN BY:	Mickey Rose
DIRECTED BY:	George Stanford Brown
GUEST STARS:	Paul Cavonis (Roman Vail), Jeffrey Druce (Freddie), Denise Galik (Bonnie), Tara Tyson (Mary Thomas), Grayce Spence (Mrs. Dolly Smith), Michael Warren (Lt. Mathews), James Mitchell (Jim Walker)

Two women—both prostitutes—are murdered in the same apartment building. The building's owner, Dolly Smith, calls on her old friend Charlie for help. Posing as working girls, the Angels move in and get acquainted with the frightened tenants. Jim Walker, a "client" of one of the murdered girls, calls for another date with a blonde. Kris answers the call, which turns out to be a false alarm.

Some of the tenants think the killer is Freddie, a pizza delivery man who works for a restaurant across the street from the building. The Angels follow that lead and discover that the real killer is Roman Vail, the restaurant's owner, whose displaced aggression toward his ex-wife has compelled him to desperate lengths.

Kris (Cheryl Ladd), Kelly (Jaclyn Smith) and Sabrina (Kate Jackson)
discuss a case in "Little Angels of the Night."

COMMENTARY

Freddie, the creepy pizza delivery guy with the Doug Henning haircut, is
one of those one-shot characters that most Angels fans still remember. The
viewers were most likely one step ahead of the plot on this one, though, so
the climax is not a surprise.

The *Hill Street Blues* parade of cast members continues here with
Michael Warren, who is referred to by Kris as "Sergeant" in one scene and
later as "Lieutenant" by Roman Vail (quick promotion!), before being busted
back to Sergeant in the next scene. James Mitchell, who portrayed Palmer
Cortlandt on *All My Children* for more than two decades, guest stars as
Kris's client. Their scene is made memorable by Cheryl Ladd wearing what
may be the tiniest bikini ever worn on *Charlie's Angels*. Kate Jackson's blue,
strapless, terrycloth jumpsuit was as risque as her wardrobe got; she'd wear
the outfit again in "Angels in Vegas" (#47).

EPISODE 44: *The Jade Trap*

ORIGINAL AIRDATE: March 1, 1978
PRODUCED BY: Ronald Austin and James Buchanan
WRITTEN BY: Lee Sheldon; story by Tom Lazarus
DIRECTED BY: George McCowan
GUEST STARS: Barry Bostwick (Ted Machlin), Victoria Shaw (Julie), Irené Hervey (Samantha), Dirk Benedict (Denny Railsback), Lurene Tuttle (Mrs. Machlin), Joan Leslie (Catherine)

The murder of a woman by her gigolo lover, Denny Railsback, is unintentionally witnessed by Ted Machlin, a cat burglar in the process of robbing her apartment. The Angels are hired to catch the burglar, who is blamed for the murder as well.

Sabrina and Bosley try to ascertain how the burglar gained access to the high rise building, and figure out that he was not the only person in the woman's apartment on that fateful night. They learn of her romance with Railsback, and that he is now living on a yacht that is about to be repossessed. Kelly, posing as a new tenant in the building, is courted by Machlin, unaware that he is the burglar.

COMMENTARY

This terrific episode offers conclusive proof that *Charlie's Angels* was at its very best when played with tongue planted firmly in cheek. As Swedish film star Anneke Bjornbar, owner of a priceless collection of jade, Cheryl Ladd adopts a hilarious Nordic accent, that sounds as if she's auditioning for the band ABBA— "I yust love that yade." "She wasn't written with that accent," said Ladd of her contribution to that script. "I liked those shows, the ones where we could be funny and goofy and not take it all too seriously."

The comedy continues in an auction sequence, supposedly rigged so that Kelly, in her now-familiar Southern belle guise, will be the high bidder for the jade at $150,000. Bosley, the auctioneer, gets carried away in the moment, and every time the Angels try to catch his attention, he raises the bid another $10,000. Bosley ends up selling the collection for $300,000, and must then explain his actions to Charlie.

Barry Bostwick and Lurene Tuttle, the mother of singer Jack Jones, are wonderful as a mother-son burglary ring. "I loved working with Barry," said Jaclyn Smith, who would later play Sally Fairfax to his George Washington in the 1984 miniseries *George Washington*. Dirk Benedict makes his second series appearance as a handsome sleazeball.

EPISODE 45: *Angel on the Run*

ORIGINAL AIRDATE:	May 30, 1978
PRODUCED BY:	Edward J. Lakso
WRITTEN BY:	Edward J. Lakso; story by Laurie Lakso
DIRECTED BY:	Robert Kelljan
GUEST STARS:	Don Reid (Larry Kantrelle), Carole Mallory (Rosie), Belinda Balaski (Sue Kantrelle), Bill Duke (David Pearl), Alex Courtney (Taylor), Elaine Joyce (Nancy), Judy Landers (Mrs. Chicken), Craig T. Nelson (Stone)

A car full of jewel thieves is rear-ended by Larry Kantrelle's dump truck. Before the police arrive, one of the thieves tosses a bag containing $5 million in diamonds into the back of the truck. Later, they kidnap Larry but discover that the diamonds are missing.

Sue Kantrelle hires the Angels to find her husband. Kelly takes Sue's place as the star of a nightclub act, in case the thieves come after her. Sure enough, she is mistaken for Mrs. Kantrelle and brought to join her husband. Meanwhile, Sabrina and Kris retrace Larry's route on the day of the accident.

COMMENTARY

An unusual story that does not follow the pattern of most *Angels* episodes. Fifteen minutes in, and the viewer still has no idea who's doing what to whom, which makes a refreshing change from the formula scripts that telegraph every surprise twist. The story was suggested by Edward Lakso's daughter, Laurie, prompting a sign outside the nightclub where Sue performs promoting "The Lakso Trio."

Sabrina and Kris are paired up to investigate Larry's background, which didn't happen very often in their two years together. Kelly continues to play the tough Angel, showing nerves of steel with her kidnappers. Charlie, who is almost always limited to handing out assignments in the show's opening moments, plays a mid-episode scene with David Doyle that seems inspired by an old Abbott and Costello routine. Considering that John Forsythe taped all his voiceovers in advance, their confused verbal exchange about the Mrs. Chicken delivery girl in the office sounds convincingly unpremeditated.

Viewers will recognize not only Judy Landers, who plays Mrs. Chicken, but *Coach*'s Craig T. Nelson as one of the thieves, and game show veteran Elaine Joyce as Larry Kantrelle's tractor-driving mistress.

EPISODE 46: *Antique Angels*

ORIGINAL AIRDATE:	May 10, 1978
PRODUCED BY:	Edward J. Lakso
WRITTEN BY:	Lee Travis and Edward J. Lakso
DIRECTED BY:	Leon Carrere
GUEST STARS:	Edward Bell (Greeves), Joseph Hacker (Nichols), Kenneth Tigar (Danner), Chuck Winters (Jeffers), Ken Scott (Slade), Sandy Ward (Stone), Mala Powers (Martha)

Two cannisters of libidrium, a new space-age solid fuel, are stolen from a desert manufacturing facility. The Angels are hired to find the thieves before the fuel can be sold to a hostile foreign power.

By examining tire tracks outside the facility, the Angels trace the thieves to an antique car rally in the nearby town of Termo. Charlie sends down a classic roadster so the Angels can enter the rally, and take a closer look at the other cars without raising suspicion.

COMMENTARY

Lee Travis, Ed Lakso's wife, earned her first writing credit on the season's final episode. "I read every script Ed wrote, and checked them over for continuity. In doing so, I learned the rhythm of the show, so I wrote one."

The plot is similar to "Hellride," in which criminals also use an auto race as a cover to avoid police blockades and transport stolen merchandise out of the country. The colorful period costumes and ragtime music score give this version the edge in atmosphere.

Season Three
1978-1979

Kate Jackson (Sabrina Duncan)

Jaclyn Smith (Kelly Garrett)

Cheryl Ladd (Kris Munroe)

David Doyle (John Bosley)

John Forsythe (Charlie Townsend)

EPISODE 47: *Angels in Vegas*

ORIGINAL AIRDATE:	September 13, 1978
PRODUCED BY:	Edward J. Lakso
WRITTEN BY:	Edward J. Lakso
DIRECTED BY:	Bob Kelljan
GUEST STARS:	Dean Martin (Frank Howell), Scatman Crothers (Gyb Baker), Vic Morrow (Mark Haynes), Dick Sargent (Marty Cole), Michael Conrad (Ed Slocum), Lee Travis (Joan Wells), Herb Edelman (Joey January), Robert Urich (Dan Tanna), James Hong (Professor Perkins)

After showgirl Mary Phillips becomes the second employee of the Tropicana Hotel and Casino to perish in a deadly auto accident, Tropicana owner Frank Howell hires the Angels to establish a motive for the killings. Kelly joins the hotel's show as a dancer, while Kris is hired as the new backup singer for lounge star Marty Cole. Suspicion for the attacks falls on rival casino owner Mark Haynes, who is in cahoots with Cole to put Frank out of business. Haynes is unaware, however, that Cole has taken their plan one step further.

COMMENTARY

The third season opens as the second season did, with a two-hour special, and a road trip. It was Aaron Spelling's idea to take the show to Las Vegas, to cast Dean Martin as world-weary high roller Frank Howell, and to use

Kelly (Jaclyn Smith) and Joan Wells (Lee Travis) play showgirls in "Angels in Vegas."

Robert Urich in a cameo as detective Dan Tanna from the *VEGA$* series. The Angels "return" to Las Vegas is actually their first visit, as the casino scenes in "The Vegas Connection" (#17) were shot on a 20th Century-Fox soundstage. This time, there is extensive location footage in the Tropicana and

Dunes Hotels, as well as at Hoover Dam and Lake Mead. Jaclyn Smith even gets to twirl her skirts in the Tropicana's famous Folies Bergere revue. "I was sick on that one," she remembers. "I had a fever of 102 and had to keep working."

"That was an emotional show for me," said Ed Lakso, who still remembers the limousine ride he shared with Spelling, on the way to meet Dean Martin. "I was a huge fan, so for me this was fantastic. I'm not easily impressed, but when Dean said 'I love your script,' that was a big moment." Lakso's elation turned to dismay, however, after viewing the results of Martin's first day of shooting. "He was frightened, and it showed. I called Aaron, who looked at the dailies and agreed that it was a problem.

"I had an idea—I called Dean and told him that everybody was just blown away at how great he was. 'I'm so old, and they're so young,' he said. "But I fabricated a huge lie, and told him he was wonderful. He said, 'I'm so glad you called.' It broke my heart. I hung up and cried for twenty minutes. But he was great after that."

Martin and the Angels received fine support from Vic Morrow, Scatman Crothers, and Michael Conrad, continuing the *Hill Street Blues* parade, as Slocum, Haynes' hired muscle. According to Lakso, Martin received support when the cameras stopped from Kate Jackson's stand-in, Camille Hagan. "Security was very tight while we were on location, but we found out later that Dean would sneak out at night with Camille," said Lakso's wife, Lee Travis, who appears in the episode. Hagan later married *Fantasy Island* star Herve Villechaize.

Kelly again shows off her toughness by threatening to kill Slocum if he doesn't betray Marty Cole. Dick Sargent, who is not a singer but plays one on TV, has his vocals dubbed, but Cheryl Ladd makes the most of her second musical moment on the series. The song "One For the Dealer," played over the opening credits, was written and performed by Ed Lakso, though most viewers assumed that the voice belonged to Dino.

"*Charlie's Angels* are still charging around overdosing on banalities and inexorably solving the predictably fathomable," wrote *Variety* in its review of season premiere. "Watching the three incumbent Angels go through their standard caper, it is not difficult to understand why they frequently cry out in pain over the flimsiness of the series."

EPISODE 48: *Angel Come Home*

ORIGINAL AIRDATE: September 20, 1978
PRODUCED BY: Ronald Austin and James Buchanan
WRITTEN BY: Stephen Kandell
DIRECTED BY: Paul Stanley
GUEST STARS: Farrah Fawcett-Majors (Jill Munroe), Stephen Collins (Steve Carmody), Bill Vint (Danny Bligh), Jackie Stewart (Himself), Dolly Martin (Andrea Lassiter), Horst Bucholz (Paul Ferrino), Martin Azarow (George Danforth)

Jill Munroe returns to Los Angeles from Europe, in response to an urgent cablegram supposedly sent by her sister, Kris. The message proves to be a hoax, but Jill was on her way back anyway to tell Kris of her engagement to race car driver Steve Carmody.

Jill Munroe (Farrah Fawcett, center), rejoins her former teammates in "Angel Come Home."

At the racetrack, Jill is reunited with fellow driver Paul Ferrino, who shows off his new, top-secret turbo-charged engine. One day after he voices his concern that someone may try to sabotage his new invention, the engine is blown up. The Angels, joined by Jill, offer to investigate.

COMMENTARY

"Angel Come Home," the first of Farrah Fawcett's contractually-obligated returns, is the best of the four-Angel stories, and contains the most interaction between big sister Jill and little sis Kris. "It was tough for (Farrah) to deal with the fact that after she left, the show did fine without her," said Cheryl Ladd. "She was not warm, to anyone, because she really didn't want to be there. But she was very professional, never rude, and she got the work done."

At first Steve Carmody (well-played by Stephen Collins) seems to be the latest in a series of Angel romances with the villain of the week. By this time, you have to wonder how four trained detectives could be such lousy judges of character in their personal lives. However, writer Stephen Kandell pulls a switch in the formula, and Carmody turns out to be a solid citizen. The real bad guy, Paul Ferrino, is played by Horst Bucholz, best-remembered as one of the guns-for-hire in *The Magnificent Seven* (1960). Stephen Collins is still playing one of the nice guys on the series *Seventh Heaven*. Dolly Martin, a former Playboy playmate, is the wife of comedian Dick Martin.

EPISODE 49: *Angel on High*

ORIGINAL AIRDATE:	September 27, 1978
PRODUCED BY:	Edward J. Lakso
WRITTEN BY:	Edward J. Lakso
DIRECTED BY:	Larry Doheny
GUEST STARS:	Bert Freed (Stambler), Don Reid (Harmon), Johnny Seven (Fenton), Michael Goodwin (Bill Freeman), Lee Terri (Evelyn Wales), Ben Hammer (George Faylon)

An elderly business tycoon, in failing health, recognizes a news photo of a woman killed in an auto accident as Joan Cabelli, an old flame. He reads that she is survived by a son, and hires the Angels to find out if William

Freeman, now 35 and a handsome but hardly wealthy stunt flyer, is his son, and the heir to his fortune.

The hall of records in the small town where the woman died is, suspiciously, destroyed by fire just four days after the Freeman funeral. Another man prowling around her residence is murdered. The killer escapes unseen, but a trace of the dead man's license identifies his employer as a New York corporation with underworld ties. Sabrina flies to New York to follow up on the lead, while Kelly gets to know William, a free spirit with no interest in his paternity.

COMMENTARY

An atypical storyline but a dull story, except for Cheryl Ladd's strut across the screen in a microscopic bikini and high heels, in a scene that had nothing to do with the storyline. "The crew almost fainted," recalled Ed Lakso's wife, Lee.

Don Reid, who played the truck-driving Lothario in "Angel on the Run," makes his second series appearance.

EPISODE 50: *Angels in Springtime*

ORIGINAL AIRDATE: October 11, 1978
PRODUCED BY: Ronald Austin and James Buchanan
WRITTEN BY: William Froug
DIRECTED BY: Larry Stewart
GUEST STARS: Joan Hotchkis (Dr. Slavin), Nancy Parsons (Zora), Pat Delany (Miss Ingrid), Amy Stryker (Eve Perkins), Mercedes McCambridge (Norma), Marie Windsor (Eve Le Deux)

Eve Le Deux, a grande dame of the Broadway stage, is electrocuted in a hydro massage tank at the elite Springtime Spa. Foul play is suspected when both the aging actress's memoirs and the last person to see her alive mysteriously disappear.

Hired by Eve's niece, Kris and Sabrina pose as new Springtime employees, and are greeted with cold disapproval by the managing director, Miss Ingrid. Zora, the physical therapist, tries to break Kris's neck when she is found searching the equipment room. Kelly, undercover as a rich guest, is subjected to hypnosis by the staff doctor, who uses the information she gains in these special sessions for blackmail.

COMMENTARY

A basic undercover scenario, enhanced by Mercedes McCambridge, an Academy Award winner in 1949 for *All the King's Men*, and veteran heavy Nancy Parsons, best-known as Miss Balbricker in the *Porky's* film series. Marie Windsor appeared in such classic films as *The Hucksters* (1947), *The Narrow Margin* (1952), and *Freaky Friday* (1976). She would return to the series in the episode "Angels at the Altar" (#72)

When Kelly and Sabrina compare notes, Kelly makes reference to her hypnosis in "The Seance" (#11), a rare series moment in which a previous case is mentioned. When Kris breaks into Zora's quarters, her pink athletic shorts ride up several inches, resulting in the series' most cheeky scene.

The "twist" of the friendliest face in the vicinity being led off as the killer in the final scene is a plot device that has already been overused on *Charlie's Angels*, but it actually works here, because McCambridge makes the charismatic Norma so genuinely likable. Parsons, who could read a line like "A pretty little neck—I bet it would break easy" as well as anyone, is an imposing adversary for Kris. Her attempted murder by herbal wrap joins the killer tennis ball machine in "Lady Killer" as one of the more unique methods of clipping an Angel's wings.

EPISODE 51: *Winning Is For Losers*

ORIGINAL AIRDATE: **October 18, 1978**
PRODUCED BY: **Edward J. Lakso**
WRITTEN BY: **Ray Brenner**
DIRECTED BY: **Cliff Bole**
GUEST STARS: **Jamie Lee Curtis (Linda Frye), Gary Bisig (Bill Montclair), Casey Kasem (Tom Rogers), Ray Wise (Evan Wilcox), George Pentecost (George Ritlin)**

Professional golfer Linda Frye, a longtime friend of Kris's, has her bid for a tournament leadership impeded by hate mail and a sniper's rifle. With twenty-four hours before the final round and Linda determined to play, Kris asks her fellow Angels for help.

Despite plenty of suspects, including a stalking marksman peculiarly attired in army fatigues and expensive Italian shoes, and the defending tournament champion who would sell her soul to win, the Angels are unable to gather enough evidence to form any theories.

Bill Montclair, Linda's manager, confesses to an attempt to drive Linda out of the tourney, in exchange for payment of a $100,000 debt owed from a shady land deal. He refuses to cooperate with his "associates" who want her dead, and is murdered after threatening to blow the whistle.

COMMENTARY

"Winning Is For Losers" transfers the tennis-themed story of the previous season, "Game, Set, Death" (#36), onto the golf links with little change in detail. Once again, the bitter, desperate veteran player is a suspect in a series of attacks on an attractive, talented newcomer. Also back—the manager with the hidden agenda, and the sportscaster with a sinister secret, played here by record-spinner Casey Kasem.

One of the series' most outlandish scenes takes place in this episode, in the wilderness area surrounding Linda's home. A sabotaged bridge collapses, dropping Linda and Kris into a river full of alligators. In true Tarzan tradition, Kris wrestles one of the ferocious beasts into submission. "That's one I'll love showing to my grandchildren—look, there's grandma wrestling an alligator!" said Cheryl Ladd.

As Linda, Jamie Lee Curtis actually bears a passing resemblance to future Angel Shelley Hack. Edward Lakso remembers Curtis as "a real flirt, very likable, with a great sense of humor. We knew she was destined."

EPISODE 52: *Haunted Angels*

ORIGINAL AIRDATE: October 25, 1978
PRODUCED BY: Ronald Austin and James Buchanan
WRITTEN BY: Lee Sheldon
DIRECTED BY: Ronald Austin
GUEST STARS: Lindon Chiles (Dr. Holden), Joseph Hacker (Eric Knight), Roger Bowen (Reverend Green), Jeanne Lange (Kathy Wade)

Sabrina plays a clairvoyant, in an attempt to outwit phony psychic researcher Douglas Holden, who has been swindling Claire Rossmore, a friend of Bosley's, out of a small fortune. He claims to be able to contact Claire's nephew, who died in a tragic motorcycle accident. When his associate, psychic Kathy Wade, is found dead, the Angels are convinced that Holden had her killed to cover up his scheme. They arrange another seance to contact Rossmore's nephew, with Sabrina as the medium, in an attempt to uncover the ruse.

COMMENTARY

There were several attempts at supernatural-themed stories during five years of *Charlie's Angels*; "Haunted Angels" is the best of a weak field. The methods used to convince Holden of Sabrina's psychic powers comprise the episode's best scene. The murder of Kathy Wade, committed while the victim is in a locked room with all the suspects in plain sight, is a sequence worthy of Agatha Christie, and Lee Sheldon's script offers an ingenious solution to the puzzle that doesn't cheat.

The teaming of Sabrina and Kris was a series rarity, but their scenes contained a chemistry that belied the often strained relationship between Kate Jackson and Cheryl Ladd.

EPISODE **53**: *Pom Pom Angels*

ORIGINAL AIRDATE: **November 1, 1978**
PRODUCED BY: **Edward J. Lakso**
WRITTEN BY: **Richard Carr**
DIRECTED BY: **Cliff Bole**
GUEST STARS: **Lonny Chapman (Eddie Cobb), Stephanie Blackmore (Beverly Carey), Rick Casorla (Tim Asher), Ben Davidson (Tasker), Fran Ryan (Belle Asher), Anne Francis (Margo)**

Dan Abner, owner of the Bulldogs football team, starts receiving threatening letters from religious fanatics after sprucing up the sidelines with "The Bow-wows," a squad of eight sexy cheerleaders. He ignores their threats, until one of the cheerleaders and the squad's manager disappear. After Abner hires the Angels, Sabrina takes over as manager of The Bow-wows, while Kelly and Kris join the squad.

COMMENTARY

When Kelly and Kris join a troupe of beautiful women called "The Bow-Wows," "Pom Pom Angels" begins promisingly as an opportunity to send up cheerleaders, in the same way that "Pretty Angels All In a Row" (#25) skewered beauty pageants. Instead, however, the episode takes a bizarre twist with the introduction of a religious cult led by a character listed as "Eddie Cobb" in the credits, though he's called "Andy" in one scene. By any name, he is certainly one of the more bombastic of the Angels' many psychotic adversaries. A far more intriguing mystery than Eddie's motive for cheerleader-stalking is the appearance of Anne Francis in a tiny, thankless role as Eddie's high priestess. Ten years earlier, Francis played *Honey West*, one of television's first sexy female detectives. Perhaps Francis was there as a favor to Aaron Spelling, who produced the Honey West series.

"That episode was one of the real disasters," said Lakso. "Somebody called and said we should do something with cheerleaders. It was a half-assed script, and I couldn't come up with anything better." Cheryl Ladd agrees— "I thought it was just ghastly."

Ladd and Jaclyn Smith look smashing in their undercover costumes, which are almost lawsuit-close to those worn by the Los Angeles Rams cheerleaders, but their pom pom swinging is kept to a minimum. Former football star Ben Davidson plays the Neanderthal boyfriend of the kidnapped cheerleader, and a false alarm suspect in her abduction. His dialogue consists of repeated bellowings of the line "Where's Mary Ann?" which makes him sound like a guest star on *Gilligan's Island*.

Cis Rundle, a former professional cheerleader and one of Cheryl Ladd's closest friends, received her first speaking role on the series in this episode. "Cheryl and I had been friends for years, and we made a pact that if one of us ever made it, we would take the other along with us," said Rundle. "So Cheryl helped me get a lot of roles on *Charlie's Angels*."

During the first four seasons, Rundle can often be glimpsed as Ladd's stand-in. She also played Casey Jones, the woman in a railroad engineer's hat and tube top, who entertains Charlie in "Circus of Terror" (#27), a waitress in "Angels in the Backfield" (#39), the girl throwing a football in the opening scene of "The Sandcastle Murders" (#40), and a cruise passenger in "Love Boat Angels" (#69).

EPISODE 54: *Angels Ahoy!*

ORIGINAL AIRDATE: November 8, 1978
PRODUCED BY: Ronald Austin and James Buchanan
WRITTEN BY: Lee Sheldon
DIRECTED BY: Allen Baron
GUEST STARS: Peter Brown (Mark Correll), Jack Murdock (Doc Harris), Hector Elias (Sanchez), Doug Sheehan (Ben Anderson), Parley Baer (Captain Jack McGuire), Janis Paige (Joan)

A woman is found dead on the Southern Queen cruise ship, after she reports seeing an escaped murderer aboard. The Angels are hired by the ship's captain, James Brunner, and discover that someone working on board is using the Southern Queen to transport wanted criminals to Brazil.

Kelly comes aboard as the new activities director, and Kris poses as a passenger. Once they learn that a steward, Hector Sanchez, is the inside operative, Sabrina poses as an embezzler looking to escape custody. After Kelly's cover is blown at a masquerade party, she realizes that several crewmembers, led by the ship's doctor, are also involved in the operation.

COMMENTARY

Having already saved one cruise ship from destruction in "Angels At Sea" (#21), the Angels' second ocean voyage proves just as dangerous. After the recent VEGA$ crossover, viewers may have wondered why they just didn't sail on the Love Boat; the reason is that the ship's captain, doctor and purser are all murder suspects in the script, and who'd believe Gopher as a bad guy?

Kate Jackson breaks out her Brooklynese again (see "Unidentified Flying Angels"—#29), this time as a crook on the lam. Bosley has some long-overdue time in the spotlight, after launching a shipboard romance with guest star Janis Paige. "I had worked with Janis on Broadway in a play called *Here's Love*, so that show was a reunion with an old pal," recalled David Doyle. As usual, anytime a Townsend employee falls in love it's with someone who goes to jail, but Doyle brings an unexpected emotional depth to the story.

Watch Kris's "Little Bo Peep" staff when she hides in a closet—the staff faces in opposite directions with every cut from mid-shot to close-up.

Guest star Doug Sheehan played Ben Gibson from 1983-87 on *Knots Landing*.

EPISODE 55: *Mother Angel*

ORIGINAL AIRDATE: **November 15, 1978**
PRODUCED BY: **Ronald Austin and James Buchanan**
WRITTEN BY: **Rift Fournier**
DIRECTED BY: **Don Chaffey**
GUEST STARS: **Farrah Fawcett (Jill Munroe), Olivia Barash (Samantha), Gary Collins (Victor Buckley), Roy Jenson (Max), Hermione Baddeley (Mrs. McNaughton), Robert Davi (Richie), Peggy Rea (Bridget)**

When Samantha, an imaginative and mischievous 11-year-old, claims to have witnessed a murder in the penthouse apartment of horticulturist Victor Buckley, Samantha's aunt, a former client, hires the Angels as babysitters. Jill Munroe, back in Los Angeles for a visit, joins her former partners on the case.

After speaking with the girl's nanny, Kris is ready to dismiss Samantha's story as a fantasy, but Jill remains suspicious. Angry that no one will take her seriously, Sam escapes Jill's watchful eye and returns to Buckley's penthouse. After the Angels discover that Buckley is an escaped fugitive, and the murdered man was a bail bondsman, they realize that Samantha is in grave danger.

COMMENTARY

One of the better episodes of the season, though it doesn't have the "special event" status one might expect for Farrah Fawcett's second return to action. The former Angel, after "taking third at LeMans," fits easily and comfortably back into the fold, but it's disappointing that there are not more scenes between the Munroe sisters.

The guest cast is fine, though Gary Collins is something of a tough sell as a hard-boiled killer. Robert Davi would later take on James Bond in *License to Kill* (1989), and Olivia Barash is charming as the precocious

Kelly (Jaclyn Smith), Sabrina (Kate Jackson) and Kris (Cheryl Ladd) in "Mother Angel."

Samantha. She would later play a music student named Maxie in the final two seasons of the series *Fame* (1982-87).

Kate Jackson is now in full Meryl Streep-mode—after reviving her New York street character in the previous episode, she adopts a lilting Irish brogue here to play Victor's new maid, Katie McGuire.

EPISODE 56: *Angel On My Mind*

ORIGINAL AIRDATE:	November 22, 1978
PRODUCED BY:	Edward J. Lakso
WRITTEN BY:	Edward J. Lakso
DIRECTED BY:	Curtis Harrington
GUEST STARS:	Michael Whitney (Burton), Tom Spratley (Jimmy), Billy Barty (News Vendor), Jonathan Frakes (Brad), Neil Elliot (Mel), Jenny Sherman (Jeni)

Kris attempts to intervene after she witnesses the robbery and murder of a beachfront restaurateur, but she is struck by the killer's car during his escape. She survives, bruised but disoriented. When Kris doesn't show up for work the next day, the Angels begin to investigate. The killer returns to the scene and discovers that Kris is still alive. Unaware that she has amnesia, he tries to throw her friends off the trail, so he can eliminate the only witness to his murder.

COMMENTARY

Amnesia stories are a staple of series television, probably because they usually work if done right, as demonstrated by this refreshing departure from the regular episode format. "That one I remember as being pretty good," writer Ed Lakso said.

After Farrah's departure, most of the series' best action sequences were allocated to Jaclyn Smith. But in "Angel On My Mind," Cheryl Ladd performs a greatest hits medley worthy of the Bionic Woman. When the disoriented Kris is attacked by three beach bums, she fights them off in a well-choreographed scene; later, her survival skills are tested again when she is cornered by her original assailant, and manages to hold him off until help arrives.

Fans of *Star Trek: The Next Generation* might—or might not—recognize Jonathan Frakes (Commander Ryker), as a friendly beachcomber who helps Kris during her wanderings. The little girl seen in Kris's flashbacks was played by Cheryl Ladd's daughter, Jordan. Michael Whitney, a friend of Lakso's who played the thug that stalks Kris throughout the episode, was then married to actress-model Twiggy.

EPISODE 57: *Angels Belong in Heaven*

ORIGINAL AIRDATE:	December 6, 1978
PRODUCED BY:	Edward J. Lakso
WRITTEN BY:	Edward J. Lakso
DIRECTED BY:	Paul Stanley
GUEST STARS:	Lloyd Bochner (Jellek), Eddie Firestone (Norton), Barry Quinn (Ed Jarvis), John Voldstad (Stashu)

The Angels receive word that one of their lives is in danger in "Angels Belong in Heaven."

A friend of Charlie's phones in a warning to the Townsend offices that one of the Angels has become the target of a paid assassin. Before he can name the intended victim, he is gunned down by the assassin at no extra charge. From the taped message on the answering machine, the Angels are able to find the informant's body. An address book in his pocket leads them to the discovery that Kelly is the target.

COMMENTARY

A routine adventure, described by Lakso as "a one-trick show we tried to stretch to an hour," featuring veteran bad guy Lloyd Bochner, who later played Cecil Colby for Spelling/Goldberg on *Dynasty*.

Kelly's house is different here than the one glimpsed in the earlier episodes "Target: Angels" (#5) and "The Seance" (#11).

EPISODE 58: *Angels In the Stretch*

ORIGINAL AIRDATE: **December 20, 1978**
PRODUCED BY: **Edward J. Lakso**
WRITTEN BY: **Bob and Esther Mitchell**
DIRECTED BY: **Larry Doheny**
GUEST STARS: **John David Carson (Kevin Ryan), Deirdre Berthrong (Valerie), James Gammon (Gates), Dick Bakalyan (Thad Roper), Sidney Clute (Les Ferrar), Joyce Jameson (Gini)**

Les Ferrar's winning system for betting the horses costs him his life, after he notices that a losing colt, Perdition, is minus her markings. The horse's groom and trainer kill Ferrar, after he announces his plan to contact the racing commission. They dump his body in a stall, and make it look as if he was trampled to death by a runaway stallion.

Sabrina gets hired on by the track as an exerciser, under Perdition's handsome Irish trainer, Kevin Ryan. Her investigation of Ferrar's discovery reveals that Perdition is one of a set of twins; the other horse was sold at birth to a ranch in Mexico. Now, Ryan and the groom, Gates, have brought the untrained twin back, and are alternating the two horses into races, and cleaning up by betting with their inside information.

COMMENTARY

Writers Bob and Esther Mitchell met Edward Lakso when both were turning out scripts for the military drama *Combat*. "We were aware of the criticism *Charlie's Angels* got for being strictly T & A, but Bob and I didn't think that was fair," said Esther Mitchell. "I felt it was a high-class detective show with rich characters. I'm sorry we didn't get involved with it earlier."

With the Angels back at the racetrack again ("The Big Tap-Out"— #14), Sabrina back in the saddle ("Angels on Horseback"—#35), Kelly using her magazine reporter cover (several episodes) and guest star James Gammon as a suspect ("Angels on Ice"—#24), "Angels In the Stretch" might seem like a rerun to regular viewers. Still, the twin horse gimmick works well, and Kate Jackson develops an engaging rapport with the rakish John David Carson.

"Bob came up with the idea of the switch between two horses, and Ed was a horseplayer so he liked it," Esther Mitchell recalls. "The deadline forced me to miss a high school reunion, so I named some of the horses in the final race after my old classmates."

EPISODE 59: *Angels on Vacation*

ORIGINAL AIRDATE: January 10, 1979
PRODUCED BY: Edward J. Lakso
WRITTEN BY: Edward J. Lakso
DIRECTED BY: Don Weiss
GUEST STARS: Denny Miller (Ed Fellows), Lyle Talbot (Mills), Rob Soble (Slade), Lee Delano (Dressler), John McIntire (Paul Danvers), Jeanette Nolan (Lydia Danvers)

While visiting her Aunt Lydia and Uncle Paul Danvers in the small town of Paylon, Kris, the Angels and Bosley are baffled by the cold reception they receive, and the strange disappearance of all the town's women, with the exception of Aunt Lydia. The bewildered vacationing detectives try to get answers from Lydia; after shots are fired into her home, she tells them that the town is being held hostage.

A well-known syndicate strongman is being transported to prison by forest rangers, and some of his men have prepared an escape plan. Two of them are holding a busload of women and Kris's uncle, the sheriff, to make certain the remaining townsfolk cooperate with the plan.

COMMENTARY

"There's something very strange going on here," says Sabrina, as yet another Angel vacation hits the skids. There's an ominous tone to the early scenes, as the Angels wander into a tense situation, surrounded by potential threats with no information to draw upon. This is one of the more violent episodes—the Angels shoot and kill two syndicate henchmen—but also one of the season's best.

To locate her missing uncle, Kris uses a citizen's band (CB) radio, a popular 1970s fad. "10-4, good buddy, catch you on the flip-flop."

EPISODE 60: *Counterfeit Angels*

ORIGINAL AIRDATE: **January 24, 1979**
PRODUCED BY: **Edward J. Lakso**
WRITTEN BY: **Richard Carr**
DIRECTED BY: **George Stanford Brown**
GUEST STARS: **Hilary Thompson (Carol), Linda Scruggs Bogart (Annie), Robin Eisenman (Janet), Wynn Irwin (Sam Punch), Paul Cavonis (Asher), Holly Irving (Edna Hatter), Bubba Smith (Toby)**

Three lookalike Angels steal $25,000 from a sports arena, while ostensibly performing an authorized security check. A myopic secretary identifies the genuine Angels from a photo, forcing Sabrina, Kelly and Kris to go underground to escape arrest, while attempting to track down their criminal counterparts.

The phony Angels are recruited by a nightclub entertainer in debt to a loan shark. By imitating Charlie's voice on the phone, he arranges for his Angels to gain access to a jewelry store, hoping the proceeds of the heist will save him from the consequences of a late payment. The ruse works again, but the Sabrina impostor is captured. The real Sabrina offers herself as a replacement, after the entertainer is forced to pull one more job.

COMMENTARY

At last, someone was smart enough to use Charlie's unique method of office communication against him. "That was Aaron's idea," recalls Lakso. "He just said, do one where three girls pretend to be Angels and commit crimes." "Counterfeit Angels" is great fun, primarily as a result of the convincing impressions by the lookalikes. Robin Eisenman replicates Kris's hair toss, nervous giggle and apple pie smile; Linda Scruggs Bogart does not bear a strong physical resemblance to Jaclyn Smith, but she's a near flawless soundalike of Kelly's low, sultry voice; and Hilary Thompson uncannily nails Sabrina's vocal inflections.

I had just shot a *Starsky and Hutch*, so I guess that's where they saw me, and figured I could pass for a criminal Kate Jackson," said Thompson,

"I had an absolute ball doing it." Like the other copycats, Thompson did not receive any tips from the cast. "One day Kate came to the set looking for the person that was playing her. She looked at me, said 'Oh,' and walked away. That was my entire contact with the three Angels."

A mistake was made, however, in not scripting a direct confrontation between the Angels and their doppelgangers, which would certainly have been the highlight of a delightful episode. "The girls couldn't stand it," said Thompson, laughing. "They knew we'd show 'em up!"

EPISODE 61: *Disco Angels*

ORIGINAL AIRDATE:	January 31, 1979
PRODUCED BY:	Edward J. Lakso
WRITTEN BY:	George Slavin
DIRECTED BY:	George Stanford Brown
GUEST STARS:	Zalman King (Harry Owens), Peter MacLean (Fred Heston), Shera Danese (Connie), Robert Symonds (Simon), Diane McBain (Marian), Gregory Rozakis (Mario)

The Committee for Concerned Elder Citizens hires the Angels after three elderly derelicts are found strangled on a late night bus to the beach. The only common denominator in the murders is their proximity in location to a disco called Freddie's. Kris takes to the dancefloor to meet the regulars, while Sabrina plays a writer covering the disco craze. Kelly goes undercover as a record promoter, hoping to gain the confidence of the club's popular disc jockey, Harry Owens.

COMMENTARY

One of the first episodes to put in a 1970s time capsule, "Disco Angels" is propelled by a soundtrack that was celebrated 20 years ago, ostracized ten years ago, and now sounds pretty good again. Copycat versions of "Dance, Dance, Dance" and "Disco Inferno" play over scenes rife with gold chains, wide collars, strobe lights and mirror balls; the scene in which Cheryl Ladd, partnered by Gregory Rozakis, shows off some polished and very provocative disco moves, is directly out of *Saturday Night Fever* (1977).

A pair of over-the-top performances impair the story—Diane McBain as Heston's hysterical, alcoholic wife, and Zalman King as the super-cool Harry with the Coke bottle glasses. Instead of the usual wrap-up scene at the office, the episode fades out on Harry's pre-taped incitements to the crowd in the disco—an effective ending. King is now the producer of Showtime's *Red Shoe Diaries* series, as well as several other erotic dramas.

EPISODE 62: *Terror on Skis*

ORIGINAL AIRDATE: February 7, 1979
PRODUCED BY: Edward J. Lakso
WRITTEN BY: Edward J. Lakso
DIRECTED BY: Don Chaffey
GUEST STARS: Rossano Brazzi (Vincenti Donatelli), Cesare Danova (Paolo Donatelli), Dennis Cole (Carl Hansworth), Chris George (Phil Chadway)

A U.S. government agent is killed on the slopes of Vail, Colorado, while investigating a rumor that someone will kidnap Carl Hansworth, a special aide to the President. Fearing that the identity of all federal agents has been compromised, the government turns to outside help—the Angels—to provide protection.

During a check of the guests at Hansworth's hotel, the Angels encounter Vincenti Donatelli and his son, Paolo, both members of an Italian radical group called the Patriots for a Free Society. Their suspicions of the group are confirmed when Sabrina is kidnapped, and offered in exchange for the voluntary surrender of Hansworth.

COMMENTARY

"Terror on Skis" is the only two-hour *Angels* episode that seems stretched. Writer Ed Lakso admits that the story came about only because his wife, Lee, wanted to go skiing in Colorado, so he wrote a script to bring the show there, which had to be a two-parter to justify the road trip to the city of Vail. Recurring shots of skiers shooshing down snow covered hills, freestyle jumping and nighttime candle lit shows are liberally inserted to pad the action.

Before the cast and crew even left California, however, "Terror on Skis" had begun to earn its reputation as the most trouble-plagued episode ever shot. "The logistics were horrendous. By the time we were ready to go, we had already spent more than $250,000," Lakso said. After a small fleet of trucks departed with the necessary equipment, Lakso flew to Vail, and was shocked to discover that the ground was dry. The shooting schedule required all location work to be completed in the next 14 days, and ski chases are tough to shoot without snow. "The head of the ski lodge suggested that I hire an Indian tribe from Utah to come in and do a 'snow dance.' At that point, I was ready to try anything," Lakso said.

"The tribe wanted to be paid $5,000 in advance. When Aaron got the bill, he called and said, 'I'm going through the script, and I don't see anything about dancing Indians. I told him the story, and he hung up on me." Lakso called off the deal, but the snow fell anyway, just in time.

In the opening scene, a man is shot and killed while skiing down a hill. The stuntman never arrived, so Lakso was forced to play the role himself. "Replacing an actor with a producer is totally illegal, and Kathleen Nolan, who was then president of the Screen Actors Guild, had a role in the show and was on the set. We had someone keep her busy while we shot it," said Lakso. "When she saw the show on TV, she probably realized that she was snookered."

Rossano Brazzi, best-known for his starring role in the film adaptation of the musical *South Pacific* (1958), plays the would-be revolutionary Vincenti Donatelli. "I asked him if he skied before we hired him, and he said, 'I was in the 1932 Olympics!' That was good enough for me," Lakso recalled. "So we get to Vail, and I find out he's never been on skis in his life, and he's terrified. I said to him, 'You told me you were in the Olympics!' He said, 'I was a volleyball player!'"

EPISODE 63: *Angel In a Box*

ORIGINAL AIRDATE:	February 14, 1979
PRODUCED BY:	Edward J. Lakso
WRITTEN BY:	Edward J. Lakso
DIRECTED BY:	Curtis Harrington
GUEST STARS:	Farrah Fawcett (Jill Munroe), John Colicos (Anton Karazna), Bill Fletcher (Stratton), Ed Bakey (Ed Jackson), Perry Lopez (Ruiz)

Kris is kidnapped in broad daylight, and stuffed into a car bearing the name of a resort called Georgian Acres. A note arrives at the Townsend offices that leads the Angels to believe that the kidnapper's real target is Jill Munroe. Charlie calls Jill, who rejoins the team to find her sister.

The Angels check in to Georgian Acres, where Jill is soon abducted by its wealthy owner, Anton Karazna. He is convinced that his son, Dino, who recently perished in an auto racing accident, actually killed himself because of a heart broken by Jill's rejection. Driven insane by grief, he now plans to kill Kris, so Jill will feel the pain of his loss.

COMMENTARY

For an episode that features Farrah Fawcett as a guest star, it is surprising that the most interesting scene is Kate Jackson's trying out yet another accent in her undercover guise as a French maid. The proficient but hardly exceptional "Angel In a Box" makes no apparent effort to take advantage of the opportunities offered by Farrah's return.

Ed Lakso volunteered the use of his own plane for the scene in which Jill arrives to rejoin the team, which resulted in a quintessential *Charlie's Angels* moment; "I couldn't turn the engines off, because the plane was having trouble and I wasn't sure I could turn them on again. But Farrah wanted them off for her entrance, cause they messed up her hair!" said Lakso. "We got into a beef about it, and I compromised by just turning the left engine off."

EPISODE 64: *Teen Angel*

ORIGINAL AIRDATE:	February 28, 1979
PRODUCED BY:	Edward J. Lakso
WRITTEN BY:	Bob and Esther Mitchell; story by: Laurie Lakso
DIRECTED BY:	Allen Baron
GUEST STARS:	Audrey Landers (Donna), Jane Alice Brandon (Liz), Debi Richter (Patty), Lori Lethin (Bo), Jack Fletcher (Mr. Blackmoor). Elissa Leeds (Cissy), Hal Englund (Victor)

Student Patty Cantwell is strangled at Blackmoor College, prompting the Dean to hire the Angels. Kris goes undercover as a new student, while Kelly and Sabrina join the faculty. They discover that Patty was threatened shortly before her death by Donna, a bored rich girl who runs a liquor and drug racket out of her dorm. Suspicious of all the new faces on campus, Donna resorts to intimidation, then blackmail, before locking Kris, Sabrina and Bosley into a tackroom and setting the school stable ablaze.

COMMENTARY

As in the memorable "Angels in Chains" (#4), "Teen Angel" deftly adapts elements from a popular exploitation film genre, resulting in a stand-out episode. The "Sorority from Hell," controlled by girls with fashion model looks and delinquent behavior, was a popular drive-in movie subject in the 1950s. Here, Audrey Landers inherits the Mamie Van Doren role as the ring-leader-vixen. Both Kate Jackson and Cheryl Ladd had been on the Blackmoor campus before, when it was used as the backdrop for their TV movie *Satan's School for Girls* (1973).

The second script written for the series by Bob and Esther Mitchell began as a one-page treatment suggested by Ed Lakso's daughter, Laurie. "We added to it, but the story was all there," Esther Mitchell said. They later wrote a third script for the series, about a boy genius conducting dangerous experiments with solar energy. "We used something similar on a *Land of the Giants* episode, in which Ron Howard played the boy. Ed liked the idea, but Aaron Spelling didn't want the problems working with children, so it was never made."

EPISODE 65: *Marathon Angels*

ORIGINAL AIRDATE:	March 7, 1979
PRODUCED BY:	Edward J. Lakso
WRITTEN BY:	Edward J. Lakso
DIRECTED BY:	Bob Kelljan
GUEST STARS:	Sarah Purcell (Millicent Krail), Danuta Wesley (Helga), Ronnie Schell (Ernie Flack), Edward Walsh (Tolan), Eric Mason (Castor), Walter Brooke (Twilliger)

Helga Johnson hires the Angels after her friend and running partner is kidnapped by two masked men, on the eve of her competing in Twilliger's Marathon. After a second girl is abducted, Kris and Kelly try to take the place of the missing runners, only to find that two more entrants have miraculously appeared at the last minute. The Angels crash the race mid-course, and find themselves surrounded by suspects, including a girl with a gun stashed in her waistbag, and another carrying a six-foot live python!

COMMENTARY

In a season comparatively light on T & A, "Marathon Angels" unleashes a cavalcade of jogging shorts and tight T-shirts; not surprisingly, none of the runners wear the athletic support bra recommended by fitness trainers.

Representing the viewpoint of any feminists who still care to complain about *Charlie's Angels*, Sarah Purcell plays Millicent Krail, a tough TV reporter who interviews the contestants to find out why they allow themselves to be "exploited" by Twilliger's Marathon. The twist is that most of them are actually using the race to further their own agendas; when Millicent turns the camera on three girls running together, they suddenly break into a song and dance routine as their agent looks on; another girl uses her camera time to promote a restaurant.

It's interesting to find such an insightful debate over who's exploiting who in an otherwise lightweight episode. "(Director) Bob Kelljan hated the script, and I didn't blame him—it was a stupid idea," Lakso said. "Marathon Angels" was also one of the cheapest shows in the run— the big race is routed through the backlot of 20th Century-Fox, saving money on locations.

"Marathon Angels" was one of Kate Jackson's least favorite episodes, though Jaclyn Smith enjoyed the exercise from her scenes in the marathon competition. "It was good to get out and run. I always preferred doing the physical things to sitting in the office and chit-chatting about the case."

The story's Arab characters are depicted in broad stereotypes. Their antics—"Did I buy Rodeo Drive? Son of a Camel!" are too cartoonish to really be offensive, but they probably wouldn't get by the guardians of political correctness anymore.

EPISODE 66: *Angels in Waiting*

ORIGINAL AIRDATE: March 21, 1979
PRODUCED BY: Edward J. Lakso
WRITTEN BY: Edward J. Lakso
DIRECTED BY: Allen Baron
GUEST STARS: Pat Crowley (Ellen), James B. Sikking (Wellman), Ed Ruffalo (Bartender), Jeff Eagle (Waiter), Tad Tadlock (Waitress)

Bosley, fed up with being the Townsend Agency's paper-pusher, challenges the Angels to a game of hide-and-seek. He disappears, promising to call every two hours with a clue to his whereabouts. The game takes a dangerous turn when Bosley and his lovely female companion are shot at by Lawrence Wellman, recently paroled after serving eight years in prison for murder. The case against him was developed by Bosley, who has now become a target for revenge.

COMMENTARY

David Doyle takes a long-overdue turn in the spotlight, as "good old, dependable Bosley" yearns for more action out in the field. "David kept asking, 'Why can't I have a lead (role)?'" recalled Ed Lakso, "I told Aaron it wouldn't hurt, though he was against it, and came up with the premise that Bosley felt taken for granted." As with the Angels, when Bosley falls in love it's usually with the perpetrator-of-the-week, though Pat Crowley seems as unlikely a co-conspirator in a murder as Mother Teresa.

"Letting the character blossom that way was a present from Ed," said David Doyle. "That was a fun episode for Bosley." However, he disagrees with Lakso's recollection that he had pushed for a featured role. "I wasn't crying about having enough to do, though I did spend a lot of time in my trailer waiting. I made enough money waiting for those girls' hair to dry to send my daughter to Vassar."

James B. Sikking makes his second series appearance, up to no good once again. Also back is the Santa Monica Pier, a popular Southern California location that figures prominently in several episodes.

EPISODE 67: *Rosemary, for Remembrance*

ORIGINAL AIRDATE: May 2, 1979
PRODUCED BY: Ronald Austin and James Buchanan
WRITTEN BY: Lee Sheldon
DIRECTED BY: Ronald Austin
GUEST STARS: Ramon Bieri (Jake Garfield), Gilbert Green (Renaldi), Robert Karnes (Gordon Sanders), Barbara Starbuck (Frau Himbere), Michael Shannon (Tim Stone), Ron Lombard (Belding)

Jake Garfield, a Prohibition-era gangster recently released from prison, tries to reopen the investigation into the 44-year-old murder of his wife, Rosemary. Jake is certain that the killer is Lawrence Renaldi, a rival gang-leader still alive and working in the bottling business. He hires the Angels after two attempts are made on his life.

Sabrina approaches Renaldi, posing as the author of a book on prohibition. He denies any vendetta, and accuses Jake of killing Rosemary. Kris is given bodyguard-duty in Jake's mansion, while Kelly tracks down the police detective who originally worked the murder case. He also blames Jake for the death of his wife. Astonished at Kris's resemblance to his beloved Rosemary, Jake becomes delusional, and begins to relive the events of Rosemary's final night. Kris dresses in one of Rosemary's gowns to encourage the fantasy, hoping to solve the decades-old mystery at last.

COMMENTARY

In nearly every episode to this point, the assignments allocated to all three Angels have been roughly equal in size. But "Rosemary, for Remembrance" is practically a solo outing for Kris, with Sabrina, Kelly and Bosley providing little more than back-up. Cheryl Ladd also plays the ill-fated flapper, Rosemary, in flashback. "I loved playing dress-up," said Ladd. "In South Dakota during many a blizzard, our whole entertainment was this box of clothes in the basement; we'd spend hours being other people. For me, anytime I got to do any of that stuff on the show, it was great. I especially liked that episode because it was very different."

Bosley's mention of "the Sheldon case" is a reference to the episode's writer, Lee Sheldon, whose script is rich in Gothic atmosphere. As soon as

Kris is warned, "Don't go in the room above the garage!" by the stern German housekeeper, you begin counting the minutes until she does.

EPISODE 68: *Angels Remembered*

ORIGINAL AIRDATE: **May 16, 1979**
PRODUCED BY: **Edward J. Lakso**
WRITTEN BY: **Edward J. Lakso**
DIRECTED BY: **Kim Manners**
GUEST STARS: **None**

Charlie arranges a surprise party for his Angels, to celebrate their three years together. Before they leave for vacation, the Angels reminisce about their most dangerous, puzzling, and exciting cases.

COMMENTARY

Very few television series attain the level of prominence necessary to be allowed the self-indulgence of a "Greatest Hits" show, but by this time *Charlie's Angels* certainly qualified. The final episode of the third season, in which the series was still firmly entrenched among TV's top twenty shows, features highlights from the past two years and a larger-than-usual contribution from John Forsythe. "It's called a short-budget show, done at the end of the season when we were out of money," Lakso said. "I loved that episode, because all I had to do was come up with a premise and a few lines of dialogue, then cut to the tapes. We shot the whole thing in one day." One of those lines, "Mother always said, 'Pretty is as pretty does,'" was uttered by Kelly, who again seems to have forgotten that she was an orphan.

The clips, especially a montage of undercover disguises and accents, are superbly-chosen. Also recalled: Kris's first appearance in "Angels in Paradise" (#23) and her disoriented adventures on the beach from "Angel On My Mind (#56);" Kelly's belly-dance from "Angels on Ice" (#24), and Sabrina's romances with Dean Martin from "Angels in Vegas" (#47) and Doug O' Neil from "Angel in Love (#28)." Notable by their absence are any clips featuring Farrah Fawcett, an indication that the animosity over her departure had still not subsided.

In the final scene, Kate Jackson raises her glass to toast their birthday as a team, and says, "Here's to many, many more." She was never seen on the show again. "We knew at the time that she was unhappy, and probably would not be back next season," said director Kim Manners. "It was an emotionally-charged atmosphere."

Season Four
1979-1980

Jaclyn Smith (Kelly Garrett)

Cheryl Ladd (Kris Munroe)

Shelley Hack (Tiffany Welles)

David Doyle (John Bosley)

John Forsythe (Charlie Townsend)

EPISODE 69: *Love Boat Angels*

ORIGINAL AIRDATE: September 12, 1979
PRODUCED BY: Edward J. Lakso
WRITTEN BY: Edward J. Lakso
DIRECTED BY: Allen Baron
GUEST STARS: Bert Convy (Paul Hollister), Bo Hopkins (Wes Anderson), Lee Travis (Eleanor Case), Dick Sargent (James Avery), Gavin MacLeod (Captain Stubing), Bernie Kopell (Doc), Fred Grandy (Gopher), Ted Lange (Isaac), Lauren Tewes (Julie McCoy), Judy Landers (Blonde girl)

Five million dollars worth of gold and bronze artwork is stolen in spectacular fashion from the Los Angeles Harbor. The insurance company that covered the artwork sends an agent to brief the Angels, and Charlie sends them on a Caribbean cruise to intercept the dashing thief, Paul Hollister, and his accomplice, Wes Anderson. With Sabrina now married and retired from detective work, Kelly and Kris are joined by a new recruit, Tiffany Welles. Bosley stays in Los Angeles to trail Eleanor Case, the fence for the merchandise.

Hollister is attracted to Kris, and the feeling becomes uncomfortably mutual, especially after Kris learns that all the money from his crime will be used to smuggle distressed people out of Vietnam. As a result of the Angels' intervention, the thieves are able to work out a deal with the insurance company that satisfies all parties.

COMMENTARY

Kate Jackson is written out of the series in the same manner as Farrah Fawcett—a brief exchange of dialogue in the episode's opening moments. Sabrina, we are told, is now married and expecting her first child, so it's time to meet a new Angel.

Tiffany Welles, graduate at the top of her class from the police academy in Boston, is the daughter of one of Charlie's best friends. As with Cheryl Ladd, a special two-hour season premiere is used to introduce the tall, cool, chic Shelley Hack in memorable style. Instead of the Hawaii backdrop of "Angels in Paradise," the team is off to the Virgin Islands on the Love Boat. The appearances of stars Gavin McLeod, Bernie Kopell, Fred Grandy, Ted Lange and Lauren Tewes amount to little more than cameos, but the crossover between two signature shows of the 1970s is still fun, perhaps even moreso now than at the time.

Unlike Ladd's debut, however, a decision was made to gradually introduce Hack into the fold and, as a result, her contribution in the episode's first half is almost nil.

The tiny white bikini worn by Kris Munroe was featured in the pages of *Us* magazine, and resulted in Sears pulling their sponsorship of the series.

Bo Hopkins, who appeared in the series pilot, returns in another important episode. Dick Sargent makes his third *Angels* appearance, and Lauren Tewes, before becoming your cruise director, played the client in "Angels in Chains" (#4) But the episode's best scene did not feature Hack or Ladd or any of the guest stars, but an armored truck that is robbed via helicopter, in the most spectacular stunt ever seen on *Charlie's Angels*. "Love Boat Angels" topped the Nielsens the week it was aired, the last time that a series episode finished at number one.

EPISODE 70: *Angels Go Truckin'*

ORIGINAL AIRDATE: September 19, 1979
PRODUCED BY: Robert Janes
WRITTEN BY: Lawrence Dobkin
DIRECTED BY: Richard Carr
GUEST STARS: Joanne Linville (Maggie Brill), Royce D. Applegate (Bingo), James Carrington (Sam Willis), John Chappell (Cafe Manager), James Crittenden (Bobby Lee), Mickey Jones (Bo Mackey)

A cargo of pharmaceuticals is abducted en route from a truck by a method that is inexplicable even to the driver. Maggie Brill, owner of the trucking company, hires the Angels to solve the mystery. Kris and Tiffany join the company after a week in trucking school, and prepare to run a replacement shipment, hoping the thieves will try again. Kelly poses as a waitress at a truck stop along the route.

The same series of events leading up to the first heist is repeated— brake trouble along the highway, and a fight outside the truck stop. The shipment is stolen by switching the trailers in less than one minute, while the staged fight commences. The Angels figure out that Maggie master-minded the operation, hoping to make money by stealing her own cargo.

COMMENTARY

A formula undercover story, elevated by a clever mystery and two memorable guest stars—Joanne Linville as plain-speaking Maggie Brill, and Royce D. Applegate as a hulking truck driver dropped to his knees by Kelly after an attempted sexual harassment.

The CB radio craze, mentioned in the previous season's "Angels On Vacation" (#59), plays a major role in the resolution of this case; Kris, using the handle "Angeleyes," sweet talks the truckers on Highway 4 into lending a hand. Later, back at the office, Charlie tells Kris that traffic is still slowing down on that stretch of highway, a result of truckers frantically searching for her frequency!

EPISODE 71: *Avenging Angel*

ORIGINAL AIRDATE: September 26, 1979
PRODUCED BY: Edward J. Lakso
WRITTEN BY: Edward J. Lakso, story by: Laurie Lakso
DIRECTED BY: Allen Baron
GUEST STARS: Cameron Mitchell (Frank Desmond),
Stephen McNally (Joseph Thurgood),
Dick Bakalyan (Eddie Feducci),
Steve Kanaly (Harold Sims)

Kelly's past as a police officer comes back to haunt her when Frank Desmond, a heroin smuggler sent to prison with her help, is released from prison and out for vengeance. Desmond slips uncut heroin in Kelly's coffee at a neighborhood diner. While under its influence, she is abducted by Desmond's former partner, Joseph Thurgood, who is certain that Kelly and Desmond still have possession of confiscated drugs that "disappeared" after the trial. When Kelly cannot offer any answers, Thurgood abducts Desmond as well. While Kris, Tiffany and Bosley try to track down their partner, Kelly and Desmond join forces to escape.

COMMENTARY

This is the first of several fourth season episodes written to feature one Angel, relegating the rest of the team and Bosley to supporting roles. The reason for this shift away from one of the series' greatest strengths, the teamwork and camaraderie displayed by its three stars, was requests from the cast for more time off, and an inability to recycle existing scripts written for Kate Jackson with Shelley Hack.

Kelly is in the spotlight for "Avenging Angel," and Jaclyn Smith responds with her best performance as an Angel. Though she remains surprisingly lucid for someone strung out on heroin, Smith delivers a dramatic portrayal of involuntary drug addiction. Kelly's calm, cool demeanor is shattered by the heroin, her subsequent abduction, and the necessity to collaborate with the smuggler responsible for her dementia. Struggling to maintain control of her senses, she proves once again that no locked room can hold Kelly Garrett. "It was a meatier role than usual—more challenging," said Smith.

Steve Kanaly, taking a break from the goings-on at Southfork on *Dallas*, plays one of Thurgood's associates. "Avenging Angel" is the only series episode to feature no input from Charlie.

EPISODE 72: *Angels At the Altar*

ORIGINAL AIRDATE: October 3, 1979
PRODUCED BY: Robert Janes
WRITTEN BY: Larry Alexander
DIRECTED BY: Lawrence Dobkin
GUEST STARS: Kim Cattrall (Sharon), John David Carson (Scott Miller), Adrienne Larussa (Claudia), Joseph Hacker (Randy), Robert Walker (Burt Marshall), Parley Baer (Grandpa)

A handsome skiing champion, Scott Miller, is engaged to marry Sharon Kellerman, a beautiful young heiress, and one of Kelly's best friends. After the groom has three near-fatal accidents in the week preceding the ceremony, the Angels are engaged to uncover the reason why.

After Scott barely survives a fourth accident, suspicion falls on Sharon's jilted boyfriend, a Vietnam veteran with trouble adjusting to civilian life. However, Kris turns up a connection between Scott and Sharon's sexy cousin, Claudia; the accidents were only a ruse, perpetrated by Scott, to deflect suspicion from a plot to kill Sharon.

COMMENTARY

Okay, here's an episode that opens with the friend of an Angel in the throes of bliss over her upcoming wedding—what have we learned, students? Yes, keep your eye on the groom, especially considering the bride-to-be is wealthy. Sure enough, John David Carson, who romanced Sabrina in "Angels In the Stretch" (#58), is back to cause trouble once more as the two-timing, fortune-hunting Scott Miller.

For the second week in a row, the spotlight stays on Jaclyn Smith, and *Charlie's Angels* becomes *The Kelly Garrett Show*. Meanwhile, Shelley Hack is kept so far in the background that even Charlie now has a more significant role. Kim Cattrall, a favorite movie sexpot of the 1980s after performances in *Porky's*, *Police Academy* and *Mannequin*, plays the ill-fated bride.

EPISODE 73: *Fallen Angel*

ORIGINAL AIRDATE: October 24, 1979
PRODUCED BY: Robert Janes
WRITTEN BY: Kathryn Michaelian Powers
DIRECTED BY: Allen Baron
GUEST STARS: Farrah Fawcett (Jill Munroe), Timothy Dalton (Damien Roth), Marilu Tolo (Carla), Michael DeLano (Michael), Richard Roat (Mr. Nobbs), Jenny Neumann (Mrs. Nobbs)

Damien Roth, a jetset aristocrat and heir to several fortunes, moonlights as a daring jewel thief. Michael Leone, aware of Roth's "hobby," hires the Angels to protect his cousin, Carla, an opera singer who plans to wear the famous Blue Heron diamond during her performance. Tiffany, Kris and Kelly all fail in their attempt at seducing Damien. Kelly finds out why, after following Roth to a martial arts studio and meeting his workout partner—Jill Munroe!

Jill Munroe (Farrah Fawcett) battles jewel thief
Damien Roth (Timothy Dalton) in "Fallen Angel"

Kris picks up the trail, surprised and sad that her sister neglected to call after arriving in Los Angeles. She confronts Jill, who knows about Damien's shady past, and is prepared to become his accomplice in the theft of the Blue Heron.

COMMENTARY

During his briefing, Charlie describes Damien Roth, played by Timothy Dalton, as "a man with James Bond-ian tastes, means and charm." An appropriate description, since Dalton would later play 007 in *The Living Daylights* (1987) and *License to Kill* (1989). On the wrong side of the law here, Dalton is terrific as a dashing rogue who, according to Charlie, is "impervious to feminine wiles." "That sounds like a challenge!" responds Kris. As always, an Angel can convince the coolest customer to drop his guard; this time, it takes one that has already turned in her halo.

Jill, after winning the *Grand Prix* in Belgium, is back again, and Farrah Fawcett is featured in her best guest appearance since her first return. Only drawback—not one line of dialogue is exchanged between Farrah and Shelley Hack, who is one again reduced to playing an incidental supporting role.

EPISODE **74**: *Caged Angel*

ORIGINAL AIRDATE:	October 31, 1979
PRODUCED BY:	Elaine Rich
WRITTEN BY:	B.W. Sandefur
DIRECTED BY:	Dennis Donnelly
GUEST STARS:	Shirley Stoler (Big Aggie), Louise Sorel (Lily), Sally Kirkland (Lonnie), Rose Gregorio (Matron Wallace), Bonnie Keith (Coley), Tisha Sterling (Singer)

A security guard kills a thief during an armed robbery, who turns out to be a woman on furlough from a nearby prison. The victim's father hires the Angels to prove that his daughter participated in the robbery against her will. Since prison officials could be involved in the crime, the Angel assigned to go undercover can have no contacts or back-up. Kris agrees to take the assignment.

Once inside, Kris learns quickly that all the prisoners are forced to do the bidding of a gang led by "Big Aggie," a lifer with nothing to lose. She terrorizes Kris into participating in another heist. Information planted in her file identifies Kris as a former employee in a diamond brokerage, an obvious and tempting target for Aggie's gang. While the robbery is in progress, a prison administrator in on the scheme tells Aggie that Kris is a detective.

COMMENTARY

"Caged Angel," or "Angels in Chains, Part II," turns the spotlight on Kris, who was not around the first time Charlie's girls solved a case behind bars. Cheryl Ladd, whose petite build appears even more fragile next to the monstrous Shirley Stoler, takes her turn at a strip search and fumigation spray. If she was aware of the sequel-esque nature of the story, Ladd didn't recall paying much attention, describing the episode as "nonsense." "I was just doing my job at that point—trying to be as professional as I could, and then going home and dealing with my personal life" (Ladd was then in the midst of a divorce from husband David Ladd). Viewers didn't pay much attention, either—"Caged Angel" ranked 31st out of 65 shows in the Nielsen survey.

Apart from the traditional opening and closing scenes in the Townsend office, Kelly and Tiffany appear only once, masquerading as nuns to pass information to Kris in prison. Shelley Hack skewers the delivery of every line she has.

Besides Shirley Stoler, who played roles like Big Aggie countless times in her career, "Caged Angel" features memorable contributions from Louise Sorel, an Emmy-winning soap star, and Sally Kirkland, Oscar-nominated in 1987 for *Anna*.

EPISODE 75: *Angels On the Street*

ORIGINAL AIRDATE:	November 7, 1979
PRODUCED BY:	Edward J. Lakso
WRITTEN BY:	Edward J. Lakso;
STORY BY	Laurie Lakso
DIRECTED BY:	Don Chaffey
GUEST STARS:	Richard Lynch (Freddie), Ford Rainey (Mr. Harkins), Madlyn Rhue (Georgia), Nancy Fox (Sunny), Amy Johnston (Judy)

Tiffany (Shelley Hack) and Kelly (Jaclyn Smith) join a
prostitution ring in "Angels on the Street"

When Judy Harkins, the daughter of a music school owner, is physically
assaulted for no apparent reason by Freddie, a local pimp, the Angels are
called in to investigate. Kelly and Tiffany join Freddie's "stable," and discover that the mild-mannered, bespectacled Judy transforms herself at night
into a prostitute named Rose, to help pay the debts on her father's school.

COMMENTARY

Though it's no surprise to anyone that Judy turns out to be one of Freddie's
girls, Amy Johnston paints a vivid portrait of a frightened, confused casualty
of mental illness, that is effectively underscored by her theme song, "If I
Could See," composed by Ed Lakso.

"That episode showed me the kind of diversity that came with the
job," said Shelley Hack. "One week I had to play a nun, the next week I
was playing a prostitute!" Hack is at last integrated into the team, but the

timing could not be worse. Her effortless class, boarding school manner and impeccable diction do not lend themselves well to her portrayal of a bargain-priced streetwalker. Jaclyn Smith, however, after already proving Kelly's street credentials in several previous episodes, blends right in. Nancy Fox, Smith's childhood pal, also plays a hooker in her second series appearance.

EPISODE 76: *The Prince and the Angel*

ORIGINAL AIRDATE: **November 14, 1979**
PRODUCED BY: **Edward J. Lakso**
WRITTEN BY: **Edward J. Lakso; story by: Laurie Lakso**
DIRECTED BY: **Cliff Bole**
GUEST STARS: **Farrah Fawcett (Jill Munroe), Leonard Mann (Eric Railman), Jesse Doran (Edward Dain), Herb Braha (George Stanos), Karl Held (Paul Kohler)**

Eric Railman, a handsome crown prince, is traveling incognito in the United States to avoid the political assassins who tried to kill him in his homeland. Jill catches his eye in a haberdashery, and a flirtatious conversation leads to a lunch date, though Eric refuses to reveal his true identity. Eventually he tells her the truth, by which time the Angels have already deduced that Eric's bodyguards are in the employ of a rival political organization.

COMMENTARY

By this time, Farrah Fawcett's returns are notable only for their lack of fanfare. Though the barely-there story revolves around Jill's romance with the prince, blandly played by Leonard Mann, "The Prince and the Angel" may be the low point of the series' fourth season. Only in the first scene, in which original Angels Jill and Kelly shop in Beverly Hills for Charlie's birthday, is there any suggestion of the chemistry that sparkled in every first season episode.

At least Jill talks to Tiffany this time. "Everything Farrah touched was going sour, so it was no big deal getting her back," Lakso said. "She was actually willing to do another episode after fulfilling her contract, but it never happened."

EPISODE 77: *Angels On Skates*

ORIGINAL AIRDATE: November 21, 1979
PRODUCED BY: Robert Janes
WRITTEN BY: Michael Michelian and John Francis Whelpley
DIRECTED BY: Don Chaffey
GUEST STARS: René Auberjonois (Freddie Fortune),
Ed Begley, Jr. (Kenny Daniels), Roz Kelly
(Gert), Chris Mulkey (Reggie Martin),
Joanna Barnes (Julia Lathrop) Lory Walsh
(Rita Morgan)

Kelly and Kris teach Tiffany to be a "real Californian" by roller skating at Venice Beach. While admiring a young skating duo rehearsing for a competition, the Angels find themselves witnesses to a kidnapping in broad daylight. Rita Morgan is snatched in the middle of her routine and hustled into a waiting van. Her partner, Kenny Daniels, and the startled Angels give chase in vain. Kelly, Kris and Tiffany volunteer their efforts to track her down; during a search of Rita's apartment, they find a photograph of her with her father, whom Charlie recognizes as a wealthy businessman, recently deceased.

COMMENTARY

René Auberjonois, after putting Kelly in a trance in "The Seance" (#11), returns to the series as Freddie Fortune, the Flo Ziegfeld of roller disco. The kitsch highlight is a roller boogie production number featuring all three Angels on skates. Cheryl Ladd is by far the most adept—must be something in those Munroe genes. Also on wheels—guest stars Ed Begley, Jr. (*St. Elsewhere*), and Roz Kelly, best known as Fonzie's girlfriend Pinky Tuscadero on *Happy Days*.

EPISODE 78: *Angels on Campus*

ORIGINAL AIRDATE: November 28, 1979
PRODUCED BY: Robert Janes and Elaine Rich
WRITTEN BY: Michael Michelian
DIRECTED BY: Don Chaffey
GUEST STARS: Nita Talbot (Willamena), Richard Hill (Steve), Gary Collins (Dr. James Fairgate), Sandie Newton (Jennifer Thomas), Jo Ann Pflug (Mrs. Kay), David Hayward (Richard), Janice Heiden (Susan)

At Whitley College, two beautiful coeds from the same sorority disappear under mysterious circumstances. The alumni committee brings back former Kappa Omega Psi president Tiffany Welles to investigate. She returns to her old sorority house, while Kris enrolls at the college as a student.

Shelley Hack (right) finally gets a chance to showcase her character in "Angels on Campus."

When no ransom demands are made, Tiffany fears a murderer may be on the loose, but Charlie has a hunch that the girls are alive and victims of an equally sinister fate. The only common denominator among the missing girls is the crush they both had on Dr. James Fairgate, a handsome, charismatic English professor.

COMMENTARY

At last, Tiffany takes her turn in the spotlight, and Shelley Hack rises to the occasion with her best work on the series. The absence of a familial closeness between Tiff and her fellow detectives remains a liability, but here, flying solo, Hack delivers a credible, even polished performance. After the mishaps in some of her previous outings, it's a revelation.

Perennial nice guy Gary Collins is cast against type as he was on "Mother Angel" (#55). As the English teacher who's everybody's best friend, you know he's got to be the ringleader of white slave smugglers. The involvement of Miss Kay, the kindly housemother played by Jo Ann Pflug, is more of a surprise. David Doyle, too often left on the sidelines in the series' final seasons, makes the most of Bosley's romance with a college librarian played by Nita Talbot.

EPISODE 79: *Angel Hunt*

ORIGINAL AIRDATE: December 5, 1979
PRODUCED BY: Robert Janes
WRITTEN BY: Lee Sheldon
DIRECTED BY: Paul Stanley
GUEST STARS: Lloyd Bochner (Case), L.Q. Jones (Burdette), Paul Sylvan (Wilson)

Kris gets a distress call, supposedly from Charlie, asking the Angels to fly to Mexico on a case. After arriving on desolate Diablo Island, Kris, Kelly and Tiffany discover that they have been lured into a deathtrap by Malcolm Case, a vengeful game hunter sent to prison by Charlie ten years earlier.

Case calls Charlie, demanding his surrender, or he'll begin hunting Angels. Meanwhile, Case's would-be prey call upon their survival skills to find food and shelter. While Charlie and Bosley desperately work against time, the Angels capture Case. Realizing that Charlie may be on his way to their "rescue," they wonder if the chance has come at last to meet the boss.

COMMENTARY

Another bright spot in a disappointing year, "Angel Hunt" is also the first genuine team adventure since Sabrina gave up her company parking space. Stranded together on a desert island, Kelly and Kris finally get acquainted with their new partner, in scenes that should have been played weeks earlier. Though their interplay still seems somewhat forced, more episodes like this might have helped salvage the season.

"I always called that the 'kill the new Angel' show," recalled Shelley Hack, "because of the lions and tigers, and having me in the water, and so far up a tree that when they broke a limb they couldn't get me down."

Both here and in the previous week's "Angels on Campus," a belated attempt is made to develop the character of Tiffany Welles. Her observation that a peacock on the island is "not indigenous to this latitude, or even to this hemisphere," identifies Tiff as an intellectual now in search of adventures outside academia, and an attempt by the series to replace the smart Angel with the really smart Angel.

The story mines the best nuggets from *Robinson Crusoe* and *The Most Dangerous Game*, and the Angels' ever-fervent desire to see Charlie inaugurates an amusing final scene. The viewers at home, however, get one of their most revealing looks yet at the mysterious Mr. Townsend, who is glimpsed at a near-full profile. Lloyd Bochner, as psycho hunter Malcolm Case, joins the ranks of returning villains (see "Angels Belong In Heaven"—#57).

EPISODE 80: *Cruising Angels*

ORIGINAL AIRDATE: December 12, 1979
PRODUCED BY: Robert Janes and Elaine Rich
WRITTEN BY: B.W. Sandefur
DIRECTED BY: George McCowan
GUEST STARS: Peter Mark Richmond (Atamien), Rodolfo Hoyos (General Ranez), Reni Santoni (Holder), Gene Evans (Webner), Beverly Garland (Pat Justice)

The Wayward Angel, a yacht purchased by Charlie, is stolen prior to its maiden voyage and then, just as mysteriously, is returned the next day. The incident is dismissed at first as a prank, until the Angels discover a pirates' cache of gold bullion stashed in the hold. Bosley is trapped on the yacht when the pirates return for their fortune, until the Angels sail to the rescue.

COMMENTARY

Bosley assumes the role of head detective on this case, but most of the action takes place between the pirates and a rival band of mercenaries, with the Angels caught in the middle. Beverly Garland, former "Queen of the 'B' movies," plays Bosley's latest love interest and future felon, Pat Justice, and would later play Kate Jackson's mother in *Scarecrow and Mrs. King* (1983-87). And at last, Shelley Hack learns how to hold a gun like a detective, instead of a *Soldier of Fortune* cover girl.

EPISODE 81: *Of Ghosts and Angels*

ORIGINAL AIRDATE: **January 2, 1980**
PRODUCED BY: **Robert Janes**
WRITTEN BY: **Kathryn Michaelian Powers**
DIRECTED BY: **Cliff Bole**
GUEST STARS: **Paul Burke (Clifford Burke), Virginia Gregg (Mrs. Craig), Robin Mattson (Erica), R.G. Armstrong (Sebastian Craig), Frank Christi (George Harper)**

Tiffany is reunited with Erica, a recently married college friend who fears there is something sinister lurking in the Victorian mansion owned by her new husband, Paul Burke. Awakened from a nightmare by rattling at the window on the very first night of her visit, Tiffany follows the sound of laughter and music to an unplanned party downstairs. After the costumed guests don't acknowledge her presence, she is suddenly engulfed in darkness. A flash of lightning reveals that Tiffany is now alone in the room. She asks Kelly and Kris to help her solve the mystery.

The Angels are reluctant to believe that ghosts are responsible for Tiffany's experiences, and the threats to Erica's life. The maid warns that Paul's first wife, Madeline, died a violent, premature death, and will not allow a second Mrs. Burke to live in "her" house.

Kelly (Jaclyn Smith), Tiffany (Shelley Hack) and Kris (Cheryl Ladd)
attend a masquerade party in "Of Ghosts and Angels"

COMMENTARY

The Angels do *Rebecca*; "She'll never stand for any other woman in this house," says the stern-faced retainer, still loyal to her first mistress, to young Erica, played by soap star Robin Mattson. The story might have worked better had it not followed the same series formula whenever a friend of the Angels is engaged or recently married. By now, we all know the groom is going to be the guilty party, and sure enough, it happens again.

"Of Ghosts and Angels" makes an overdue attempt to delve into the background of Tiffany Welles, but it's too little, too late.

EPISODE 82: *Angel's Child*

ORIGINAL AIRDATE: January 9, 1980
PRODUCED BY: Edward J. Lakso
WRITTEN BY: Edward J. Lakso
DIRECTED BY: Dennis Donnelly
GUEST STARS: Simon Oakland (Sgt. Shanks), Michael Whitney (Stone), Michael Hershewe (Greg Shanks), Rick Casorla (Burke), Michael Allen Harris (Joe Willow)

The Angels work with the police to halt a series of appliance store robberies. Two of the thieves are apprehended, but one escapes after killing an officer. Later that night, the dead man's partner, Sgt. Gates, takes out his rage on his son, Greg. The next day, Kelly sees the after-effects of the beating, and tries to intervene, but Gates refuses all offers of help. Seeing no other alternative, Kelly takes him to court, and wins temporary custody of Greg. They return to her home, and find the escaped killer waiting.

COMMENTARY

The fourth season contains several socially relevant stories, that deal with issues such as drug abuse ("Avenging Angel"—#71), alcoholism ("Harrigan's Angel"—#87), and, in this story, child abuse. Since the first-season episode "To Kill An Angel" (#7), Kelly has always been portrayed as the detective with the strongest maternal instincts, so it's not surprising that Jaclyn Smith is featured here. Ironically, Kelly removes Greg from his abusive home, and then almost gets him killed by armed robbers! The episode ends with Sgt. Gates agreeing to seek counseling, and Greg agreeing to stay with Kelly indefinitely. He is never seen or referred to again.

Michael Whitney, last seen in "Angel on My Mind" (#56), plays another formidable guest-villain.

EPISODE 83: *One of Our Angels is Missing*

ORIGINAL AIRDATE: January 16, 1980
PRODUCED BY: Edward J. Lakso
WRITTEN BY: Robert S. Biheller and Dal Jenkins
DIRECTED BY: Allen Baron
GUEST STARS: Jonathan Goldsmith (Vic Devlin), Don "Red" Barry (Harry Silvers), Marc Alaimo (John Mackey), Bob Levine (Frank Harris), Warren Berlinger (Beck)

Three years ago, Vic Devlin and John Mackey pulled an elaborate jewel heist. Devlin got the jewels, Mackey got caught and sent to prison. After being released, he confronts Devlin for his half of the spoils; instead, Devlin shoots him and leaves town.

The Angels are hired by a bail bondsman, who stands to lose $50,000 after Devlin left California for Arizona. Kris, posing as a rich divorceé, is sent to Phoenix to lure him back. While she cozies up to the seedy con man, Mackey revives in the hospital, and reveals that Devlin is also wanted in the rape-murders of three women. Charlie relays the information to Kris, and orders her off the case, but she insists on finishing the job, even after her cover is exposed.

COMMENTARY

For the first time, an Angel disobeys an order from Charlie, as Kris vows to bring in Devlin despite being warned of his violent past. Writers Robert S. Biheller and Dal Jenkins had previously collaborated on episodes of *Bonanza* and *CHiPs*. "We came in with several storylines, and this was the one Ed Lakso decided on," Biheller recalls. "I thought it turned out okay."

EPISODE 84: *Catch A Falling Angel*

ORIGINAL AIRDATE: January 23, 1980
PRODUCED BY: Edward J. Lakso
WRITTEN BY: Edward J. Lakso
DIRECTED BY: Kim Manners
GUEST STARS: Elissa Leeds (Bess Hemsdale), Gary Wood (Joe Willis), Sully Boyar (Stiles), Eugene Butler (Hacker), R. Anthony Mannino (Trask), Robert Pierce (Seth Jeffers)

Bess Hemsdale, a farm girl seeking stardom in Hollywood, falls under the spell of Joe Willis, a fast-talking pornography mogul. Seth Jeffers, her boyfriend back in Tennessee, is killed by Joe's cronies after he pleads with Bess to return home. Seth's father hires the Angels to find those responsible for his son's death.

While Kris poses as a would-be actress "willing to do anything" to be in the movies, Kelly and Tiffany find Bess living in Willis's apartment. After watching several of his films, the Angels figure out the clandestine location where they are shot. Bess overhears Joe talking about a murder, and wants out. Willis plans to have her killed, now that he's convinced that Kris is ready to step in as his new leading lady.

COMMENTARY

Gary Wood, the only actor to work with every Angel line-up, has his best role here as sleazeball producer Joe Willis. Another new song by Ed Lakso, "Home," is performed by Lynne Marta.

EPISODE 85: *Homes, $weet Homes*

ORIGINAL AIRDATE: **January 30, 1980**
PRODUCED BY: **Elaine Rich**
WRITTEN BY: **William Froug;story by: Robert E. Lee and Ronald E. Osborn**
DIRECTED BY: **Allen Baron**
GUEST STARS: **Dick Gautier (Barry Kingsbrook), Sherry Jackson (Tina Fuller), Natalie Core (Mrs. Mayhew), Vito Scotti (Tyrone)**

The burglar alarm at a posh Beverly Hills mansion is turned off during an "open house," allowing a shrewd thief to purloin a collection of Egyptian jewelry worth more than $3 million. The Angels suspect Barry Kingsbrook, realtor to the rich and famous, whose gorgeous female agents sell houses and anything else a client might desire.

Kris joins the firm as an agent. Tiffany offers Kingsbrook a $2 million house listing, and proudly displays her valuable collection of historical letters. After Bosley approaches the real estate mogul about acquiring her collection, no questions asked, Kingsbrook takes the bait.

COMMENTARY

A terrific idea, not particularly well-executed. Lydia Cornell (*Too Close for Comfort*) can be glimpsed briefly as one of Kingsbrook's agents. Character actor Vito Scotti, who has appeared in countless guest spots on TV series from *The Dick Van Dyke Show* to *Bewitched*, adds another credit to his resumé here as Tyrone, a not-very-bright caterer. Kelly plays two different roles in the episode, meets Vito as both characters with little more than a change in hairstyle, and he doesn't recognize her. The poodle in their first scene together was played by Jaclyn Smith's poodle, Albert, who even gets screen credit for the performance. Albert appeared once previously on the series, in the first-season episode "Consenting Adults" (#10).

Dick Gautier, another familiar face from the sitcoms *Get Smart* and *When Things Were Rotten*, has the episode's best line, when Kris visits Kingsbrook in his office: "Let's get into the hot tub and talk about your future with the company."

EPISODE 86: *Dancing Angels*

ORIGINAL AIRDATE: **February 6, 1980**
PRODUCED BY: **Edward J. Lasko**
WRITTEN BY: **Edward J. Lakso**
DIRECTED BY: **Dennis Donnelly**
GUEST STARS: **Cesar Romero (Elton Mills), Norman Alden (P.J. Wilkes), John Lansing (Steve), Lee Delano (Al Norman), Dawn Jeffory (Jenny), Brad Maule (Joe Fairgate), Jason Kincaid (Billy), Lindsay Bloom (Sally Fairgate)**

Joe Fairgate and his sister, Sally, are the favorites in a ballroom dance contest, until Sally disappears. Joe hires the Angels, whose investigation centers on Steve Ames, a hotheaded competitor determined to win the contest at any cost, and the owners of the dance club, who have ties to organized crime. After the bandsinger has a public argument with Ames, he is found dead in the alley behind the club. Later, Sally Fairgate is found murdered on the beach.

COMMENTARY

With the series now deep into its fourth season, the search for new and interesting settings in which to drop the Angels has become more challenging, which explains this venture into the cutthroat world of competitive ballroom dancing. Cheryl Ladd and Jaclyn Smith look right at home on the dancefloor, but couple number five, Tiffany and Bosley, probably won't make the cut for *Dirty Dancing II*.

Despite the ludicrous climax, in which the suave Latin bandleader played by Cesar Romero kills two people because they don't like "Moonlight Serenade," "Dancin' Angels" still makes for an entertaining hour of escapism, thanks to a bountiful collection of big band songs delivered with corny charm by Jason Kincaid and Dawn Jeffory, and several notables filling out the guest roles; in addition to Romero, soap fans will recognize *General Hospital*'s Brad Maule, who plays Joe Fairgaite. It's a standard client role consisting of two brief scenes, but Maule makes them both count. Lindsay Bloom plays Joe's sister, and though Norman Alden's face may not be familiar, his voice will be known to fans of several cartoons, including *Underdog*.

EPISODE 87: *Harrigan's Angel*

ORIGINAL AIRDATE: February 20, 1980
PRODUCED BY: Edward J. Lakso
WRITTEN BY: Edward J. Lakso
DIRECTED BY: Don Chaffey
GUEST STARS: Howard Duff (Harrigan), Ed Nelson
(George Starrett), Michael Cavanaugh
(Felber), Robert Englund (Belkin),
Charles McDaniel (Mathews)

A microelectronics firm owned by George Starrett is hit by a mysterious wave of break-ins and thefts, but Starrett is only willing to engage the Angels if they work alongside the detective he had previously hired, a grizzled alcoholic known only as Harrigan. The team is not impressed with their new partner, but Kris volunteers to keep him occupied while Kelly and Tiffany go to work.

COMMENTARY

From the more than forty scripts he contributed to *Charlie's Angels*, Edward J. Lakso calls "Harrigan's Angel" his personal favorite. "The name came from a horse called Harrigan's Angel, and I knew that was a good sign, even though he finished seventh," Lakso said.

Admittedly, there wasn't much of a case to crack, but the detective work takes a backseat here to the wonderful relationship between the rumpled, inebriated Harrigan, splendidly played by Howard Duff, and his reluctant female partners. "You mean I've got to work with girls?" is Harrigan's first reaction to the alliance, but by episode's end he has become as beloved to the Angels, especially Kris, as good old Bos. "I was thrilled when we got Howard Duff, because he's a wonderful actor. And the chemistry with Cheryl worked right from the start," Lakso said.

Ed Lakso's script and Duff's performance combine to create the most memorable non-recurring character of the series, and one that was scheduled for a return appearance in the fifth season, and a possible spin-off series. When *Charlie's Angels* was canceled, so were any plans for Harrigan. Duff's delightful rapport with Cheryl Ladd is both funny and poignant, and the Angels get to battle Freddy Krueger as Robert Englund makes a guest appearance. "All of a sudden I had something to play that was exciting," recalled Ladd of the script. "That was one of the high points of that year for me." "Harrigan's Angel" is not only a good show for the season—it's the only episode of the post-Farrah and Kate Jackson era that deserves to be ranked with the very best *Angels* adventures. It's a shame so many people had stopped watching by then.

EPISODE 88: *An Angel's Trail*

ORIGINAL AIRDATE: February 27, 1980
PRODUCED BY: Robert Janes
WRITTEN BY: Wayne Cruseturner
DIRECTED BY: Dennis Donnelly
GUEST STARS: Farrah Fawcett (Jill Munroe), L.Q. Jones (Sam Mason), Tracey Walter (Clint Mason), John Dennis Johnston (Harley Mason)

Jill Munroe accidentally witnesses a robbery and murder at a gas station on a backwoods country road, and becomes a hostage in the getaway. Before he dies, the station owner identifies the killer as Sam Mason, a dangerous career criminal. News of Jill's abduction reaches the Townsend Agency. The Angels join in the search, though Charlie cautions them to expect the worst.

The police are convinced that Mason is headed for Mexico, but Tiffany finds a Mormon trail not designated on most maps of the area, and believes Mason may be traveling in the opposite direction.

COMMENTARY

"An Angel's Trail" is the sixth and final episode in which Farrah Fawcett rejoins the Angels. As in "The Prince and the Angel" (#76), a potential special occasion is squandered on a routine chase story. Fans who looked forward to the interaction between Jill and her former teammates will be particularly disappointed—she shares a ten-second moment with sister Kris, and not one single scene with Kelly or Tiffany.

EPISODE 89: *Nips and Tucks*

ORIGINAL AIRDATE: **March 5, 1980**
PRODUCED BY: **Elaine Rich**
WRITTEN BY: **B.W. Sandefur; story by B.W. Sandefur and Cory Applebaum**
DIRECTED BY: **Don Chaffey**
GUEST STARS: **Louis Jourdan (Dr. Paul Redmont), Tab Hunter (Bill Maddox), Corinne Michaels (Angela), Barbara Iley (Elena), Lisa Shure (Julie), Joanna Pettet (Barbara Brown)**

Dr. Paul Redmont, a renowned cosmetic surgeon, is coerced into giving a wealthy and dangerous criminal a new face, and the freedom of movement that goes with it. The Angels are hired to infiltrate the doctor's Health and Beauty Clinic to discover the man's real identity. Tiffany joins the staff as a post-operative nurse, and Bosley checks in as a patient. While trying to stay above the suspicion of the gangster they are there to investigate, the Angels must also contend with Redmont's mistress, an expert with explosives.

COMMENTARY

Dull from start to finish, "Nips and Tucks" might have been saved if Louis Jourdan had hummed a few bars of "Gigi" during surgery.

EPISODE 90: *Three For the Money*

ORIGINAL AIRDATE: **March 12, 1980**
PRODUCED BY: **Edward J. Lakso**
WRITTEN BY: **Lee Sheldon**
DIRECTED BY: **George McCowan**
GUEST STARS: **Vincent Baggetta (Harley Dexter), Lee Terri (Professor McKendrick), Michael Pataki (De Sousa), William Wellman, Jr. (Gibel), Richard John Miller (Mike Lloyd), Carol Bruce (Mrs. Pattison), Conrad Bachman (Senator Langston)**

Harley Dexter, a clever con man and money launderer for an eastern syndicate, has bilked three people out of their life savings. The Angels set up an elaborate, triple-pronged sting operation to recover all the stolen money.

Tiffany, posing as an aide to a senator that has made public threats against Dexter, suggests to the con man that her boss could overlook his activities for a sizable campaign contribution. While Harley contemplates the offer, Kelly approaches him with a truckload of Mayan art treasures, worth several times the asking price of $100,000. After having the merchandise authenticated by "Professor" Bosley, Dexter agrees to the purchase. Kris, a damsel in distress thanks to a stalled Rolls Royce, persuades Harley to give her a lift home. The next day, it is Harley's car that's missing, along with a stash of syndicate money hidden inside. As the Angels' machinations converge, Harley Dexter is left dazed and confused, and penniless.

COMMENTARY

"Three for the Money" is the best of the Angel cons, and is the first story played more for laughs than action since "Pretty Angels All in a Row" (#25). An ingenious medley of subterfuge comes together in a humorous closing scene, in which all three Angels turn up, tag team style, at Dexter's hotel room to hang him out to dry.

Tiffany's portrayal of a senator's aide is an ideal showcase for Shelley Hack's fashion plate chic, and is the kind of undercover role that she should have been assigned more often.

EPISODE 91: *Toni's Boys*

ORIGINAL AIRDATE:	April 2, 1980
PRODUCED BY:	Robert Janes
WRITTEN BY:	Kathryn Michaelian Powers;
STORY BY	Powers and Robert Janes
DIRECTED BY:	Ron Satlof
GUEST STARS:	Barbara Stanwyck (Antonia McQueen), Bruce Bauer (Matt Parrish), Bob Seagren (Bob Sorenson), Stephen Shortridge (Cotton Harper), Robert Loggia (Michael Durano), Roz Kelly (Jade Allen), Andy Romano (Riso), Tricia O'Neil (Anne Moore)

The cast of the proposed Charlie's Angels spin-off, Toni's Boys:
Bruce Bauer, Stephen Shortridge, Barbara Stanwyck, and Bob Seagren.

At Tiffany's birthday party, the Angels are almost killed by a bomb planted in a giftwrapped box. At Charlie's insistence, the Angels become clients of "Toni's Boys," three dashing detectives led by the feisty Antonia McQueen. The two teams join forces, but after the Angels are captured by the would-be assassin, it's Toni's Boys to the rescue.

COMMENTARY

Plunging ratings had already placed *Charlie's Angels* on the path toward cancellation, but the series' pop culture profile was still high enough to inspire a spin-off attempt, in which three handsome male detectives are given marching orders from a sophisticated, older woman. Hollywood legend Barbara Stanwyck plays Antonia McQueen, an old friend of Charlie's who runs a detective agency she inherited from her late husband. Her field agents, "Toni's Boys," are Cotton Harper, a champion rodeo rider and roper (big help in Los Angeles), Matt Parrish, a master of disguises and weapons, and Bob Sorenson, a former U.S. Olympic champion, but of what we're never told.

Stanwyck's friendship with Aaron Spelling dates back to 1956, when he wrote a script for her about a female sheriff for Dick Powell's *Zane Grey Theater*. "She liked it so much, she started calling many people of influence at other studios, telling them to hire me," Spelling recalled in his autobiography, *A Prime-Time Life*. Stanwyck also introduced Spelling to fashion designer Nolan Miller, whose creations would become a staple on such Spelling shows as *Dynasty* and *Models, Inc.*

Cheryl Ladd remembered the experience of working with Stanwyck as "fascinating." "I don't know why she was doing the show, but it was a wonderful experience just to have been around her and to watch her work."

The idea is cute for one story—all the key contacts on this case just happen to be females, who ogle Toni's Boys the way the Angels turn heads in their interrogations, but there isn't much chemistry between the Boys, and ABC's decision to pass on the series seems appropriate.

Roz Kelly makes a quick return to the show after appearing in "Angels on Skates" (#77), and Robert Loggia, who menaced the Angels in the first season adventure "The Killing Kind" (#6) returns to cause more trouble (though not in the same role). The most surprising moment occurs in the first scene when, after four years of reliable service, Kelly's yellow Mustang is blown to bits.

EPISODES 92
AND 93: *One Love . . . Two Angels*

ORIGINAL AIRDATE: April 30, 1980 (part one);
May 7, 1980 (part two)
PRODUCED BY: Elaine Rich
WRITTEN BY: B. W. Sandefur
DIRECTED BY: Dennis Donnelly
GUEST STARS: Ray Milland (Oliver Barrows), Patrick Duffy
(Bill Cord), Robert Reed (Glenn Staley),
Lynne Marta (Linda), Simon Scott (Richard
Carver), William Mims (Sam Worden),
Harry Townes (Harmon), Nancy Fox (Eva)

Kelly Garrett, who was orphaned as an infant, receives a visit from attorney
Bill Cord, who is convinced that she's Margaret Barrows, the daughter of
multi-millionaire hotelier Oliver Barrows. Kelly flies to San Diego to meet
the man who may be her father, and begins a romance with the handsome
attorney. After a joyful reunion, Barrows dies of an apparent heart attack
two days later.

What Kelly does not know is that Oliver was poisoned by his nephew,
Glenn Staley. Deep in debt, Staley promised to deliver Barrows' San Diego
hotel to a developer with syndicate ties. Hoping the murder of Oliver would
solve the problem, Glenn is now faced with the necessity of killing the new
heiress. Kelly, meanwhile, is still uncertain about her real heritage, and hires
Kris, Tiffany and Bosley to find proof. Tiffany joins Kelly in San Diego to
study the Barrows family history, while Kris follows up on Bill Cord's investigation. In the course of their collaboration, Bill and Kris fall in love.

COMMENTARY

Although a backstory was created for all of the Angels, only Kelly's life before
Charlie was ever explored in any detail on the series. Her childhood at the
St. Agnes Home for Orphans in Texas was first mentioned in "Target: Angels"
(#7) and is examined again for this two-hour season finale.

The first genuine conflict between Angels since the series began is
prompted by *Dallas*'s Patrick Duffy, who qualifies for true man-among-men

status by romancing two Angels at once. Other able support is provided by Ray Milland as Kelly's possible father, Robert Reed as the desperate nephew (Mr. Brady a double murderer? Say it ain't so!), and Lynne Marta, whose voice has been heard often on the series performing the music of writer-producer Edward J. Lakso. Nolan Miller, who provided the wardrobe for *Dynasty*, works his magic here with a succession of spectacular gowns for the suddenly-wealthy Kelly Garrett.

Season Five
1980-1981

Jaclyn Smith (Kelly Garrett)

Cheryl Ladd (Kris Munroe)

Tanya Roberts (Julie Rogers)

David Doyle (John Bosley)

John Forsythe (Charlie Townsend)

EPISODE 94: *Angel in Hiding*

ORIGINAL AIRDATE:	November 30, 1980
PRODUCED BY:	Edward J. Lakso
WRITTEN BY:	Edward J. Lakso
DIRECTED BY:	Dennis Donnelly
GUEST STARS:	Jack Albertson (Edward Jordan), Christopher Lee (Dale Woodman), David Hurst (Stovich), Vic Morrow (Harry Stearns), Don Stroud (Jimmy Joy), Kitty Ruth (Louise)

Jody Mills, a would-be model reduced to working in a seedy amateur photography studio, is found murdered in an alley behind the studio. Her father hires the Angels, who begin an investigation of Jody's roommate, Julie Rogers. Kris learns that Jody may have bought drugs from Julie on the night of her death. A computer check reveals that Ms. Rogers also has a police record.

Kelly and Kris go undercover as models in the Woodman Agency, where Julie and Jody both worked at one time. When another model from the agency commits suicide, the Angels visit the site at the same time as Julie and her friend, Harry Stearns. After shots are fired and Harry is killed, Julie admits that she has been working undercover with the police to gather evidence against Dale Woodman, who is using his modeling agency as a front for prostitution and drug trafficking. One of Woodman's clients, businessman Edward Jordan, also frequents the photography studio where Jody was killed. Kris is hired as a model, and quickly learns that Jordan has more on his mind than photography.

COMMENTARY

"Tiffany's decided to stay east for awhile," is all the explanation given for the departure of Shelley Hack, continuing an Angel tradition of quick goodbyes that began with Farrah Fawcett. The mistake made last season of not giving the new Angel a personality until her fourth or fifth episode is corrected this time; Julie Rogers, sporting a seen-it-all demeanor and a colorful line of tough talk, makes an impressive and memorable first entrance.

Tanya Roberts's debut is more poised and confident than that of Shelley Hack, but to be fair the script actually gave her something to do, where Hack was almost forgotten on the *Love Boat*. Julie's ride through a parking garage on the hood of a speeding car is a terrific action scene. Roberts actually performed the stunt, though the car was not moving as fast as it seemed. "They figured it was the show's last year, so if she dies, she dies!" said Roberts, laughing.

Once again, the *Angels* begin a new year with a two-hour, guest star-filled adventure; former *Chico and the Man* star Jack Albertson, who looks so feeble that it's hard to believe he could swat a fly without keeling over, plays a pervert shutterbug who manages to chase and strangle a healthy young woman. Vic Morrow ("Angels in Vegas"—#47) returns for his second season opener, and Christopher Lee adds another villain role to his crowded resume` as the unflappable Dale Woodman.

EPISODE 95: *To See an Angel Die*

ORIGINAL AIRDATE: November 30, 1980
PRODUCED BY: Edward J. Lakso
WRITTEN BY: Edward J. Lakso
DIRECTED BY: Dennis Donnelly
GUEST STARS: Jane Wyman (Eleanor Willard),
Cameron Mitchell (Tom Grainger),
Gary Frank (Tom Grainger, Jr.), Katie Hanley
(Charlene Grainger)

Trouble follows the Angels on their Hawaiian vacation, when Kris is kidnapped by Tom Grainger and his two devoted children. Grainger holds Kris responsible for the death of his wife; during her stint with the San Francisco Police, Mary Grainger was arrested by Kris on a prostitution charge, and later hanged herself in prison.

With the assistance of psychic Eleanor Willard, Kelly and Julie trace Kris's whereabouts, just as the abducted Angel makes her own plans to escape.

COMMENTARY

The first of five episodes set in Hawaii, "To See an Angel Die" originally aired immediately after the two-hour season premiere, as part of a three-hour, "Night With the Angels" extravaganza. The plot is similar to "Angel In a Box" (#63), but benefits from the appearance of Jane Wyman as psychic Eleanor Willard. "That was the beginning of her comeback. She told Aaron she wanted to work again, and he told me to write something for her," Lakso said. The following year, she joined the cast of the primetime soap opera *Falcon Crest*. "While we were on the set, we got the results of the presidential election," Lakso recalled. "A guy came running up and said 'Reagan won—he's the president. Jane, his ex-wife, said, 'Finally, he did something right.'"

EPISODE 96: *Angels of the Deep*

ORIGINAL AIRDATE: December 7, 1980
PRODUCED BY: Robert Janes
WRITTEN BY: Robert George
DIRECTED BY: Kim Manners
GUEST STARS: Patti D'Arbanville (Bianca Blake),
Antonio Fargas (Blackie), Gary Lockwood
(Claude), Sonny Bono (Walrus), Moe Keale
(Chin), Bradford Dillman (Tony Kramer),
Anne Francis (Cindy Lee), Soon-Teck Oh
(Lt. Torres)

Julie and her friend Bianca Blake are attacked while scuba diving for sunken treasure. They are rescued by the Coast Guard, but while Julie calls the police, Bianca disappears. The Angels investigate, and discover that Julie had been diving near a spot where a shipment of marijuana had been stashed, and later stolen.

COMMENTARY

The Bikini-meter is propelled to record highs during the Angels' sojourn in Hawaii, but the change in locale also pays dividends in the volume of outdoor location shooting, and larger-scale action sequences. The high-gloss production values and roll call of recognizable guests give "Angels of the Deep" a made-for-TV movie ambience. Patti D'Arbanville plays the shady Bianca with zest, Anne Francis has a better one-scene appearance here than her wasted role in "Pom Pom Angels (#53)," and Sonny Bono is hilarious as a burned-out beatnik whose dialogue consists almost solely of the phrase, "Far out, man!"

There is a comfort level in the mix of the veteran Angels with Tanya Roberts that was not achieved with Shelley Hack until midseason the previous year, which explains the welcome return to team stories over solo adventures. Julie Rogers, however, is not living up to the potential of her debut. The streetwise wildcat has already been domesticated.

EPISODE 97: *Island Angels*

ORIGINAL AIRDATE: **December 14, 1980**
PRODUCED BY: **Robert Janes**
WRITTEN BY: **Robert George, story by Robert I. Holt**
DIRECTED BY: **Don Chaffey**
GUEST STARS: **Richard Jaeckel (Bud Fisher), Barbi Benton (Toni Green), Lyle Waggoner (Jack Barrows), Don Knight (Frederick Ober), Keye Luke (Lin), Randolph Mantooth (Mark Williams), Carol Lynley (Lisa Gallo), Soon-Teck Oh (Lt. Torres)**

Eric Nelson, the head of an international peace organization, is the target of an unsuccessful assassination attempt in Athens by a terrorist group known as the Red Circle. Every indication points to another attempt at the next stop on his speaking tour—Honolulu. Julie, having witnessed a Red Circle shooting in Istanbul, is brought in by the police to identify one of the killers at the airport. Arriving in a group of singles club tourists, he is recognized by Julie and captured easily.

The ease of his apprehension prompt the police and the Angels to suspect that a second assassin may have slipped past security. Posing as journalists with "Single Life" magazine, Bosley and Kelly race against time to expose the guilty party before Nelson's arrival.

COMMENTARY

Agatha Christie meets *Fantasy Island*, as viewers watch a parade of familiar TV Land stars deplane in Honolulu and try to guess which one is a killer. The Angels are assisted in sifting through the suspects by Lt. Torres, a recurring character in the Hawaii stories, and by a bikini-clad Barbi Benton, who certainly displays all the attributes of a fourth Angel.

EPISODE 98: *Waikiki Angels*

ORIGINAL AIRDATE: January 4, 1981
PRODUCED BY: Robert Janes
WRITTEN BY: B. W. Sandefur
DIRECTED BY: Dennis Donnelly
GUEST STARS: Dan Haggerty (Bo Thompson), Patrick Wayne (Steve Walters), Rex Holman (Lee Dain), Denise Dubarry (Marti), Christopher Goutman (David), Richard Anderson (Sam Knight), Edd Byrnes (Ted Burton), Soon-Teck Oh (Lt. Torres)

When the daughter of Congressman Sam Knight is kidnapped, and her husband seriously injured after a run-in on the beach with three men driving dune buggies, the Angels go undercover as lifeguards. The incident is the latest in a rash of assaults on private beaches, masterminded by the sadistic Bo Thompson. After rescuing the congressman's daughter during a phony ransom offer, Kelly and Kris head back to the beach as bait to catch the kidnappers.

COMMENTARY

A milestone of sorts is achieved in this adventure, nicknamed "Hell's Angels Go Hawaiian" by Julie; during the lifeguard training scene, all three Angels appear in bikinis in the same frame for the first and only time in the series. To listen to the Angels' critics, you would think such an occurrence happened every week!

Despite such pleasing visuals, the attempt to inject new life in a five-year old series with a change in locale has now started to wear off. Even the travelogue shots of beaches and roaring surf and volcanoes get boring after awhile, and the limitations in possible storylines have started to outweigh the advantages in wardrobe.

Still, "Waikiki Angels" is the most interesting of the road trip shows, primarily due to Dan Haggerty's performance as creepy lowlife Bo Thompson. Haggerty, best known as good guy *Grizzly Adams*, understands that the most frightening villains are the most outwardly kind and soft-spoken. Patrick (son of John) Wayne plays a lifeguard, and Richard Anderson, who gave Steve Austin his marching orders on *The Six Million Dollar Man*, plays Congressman Sam Knight.

EPISODE 99: *Hula Angels*

ORIGINAL AIRDATE: **January 11, 1981**
PRODUCED BY: **Robert Janes**
WRITTEN BY: **Robert George**
DIRECTED BY: **Kim Manners**
GUEST STARS: **Gene Barry (Steve Moss), Patch MacKenzie (Amy), Shawn Hoskins (Donna), Branscombe Richmond (Bob Ahuna), Pat Crowley (Marion Moss), Joanna Cassidy (Stacy Parrish), Soon-Teck Oh (Lt. Torres)**

Steve Moss, the owner of a popular Hawaii nightclub, is kidnapped and held for a $1 million ransom. Moss's wife hires the Angels, but warns them that Steve has a long list of enemies. When the ransom isn't paid, a dancer is abducted from the club, and a warning is left that more kidnappings will follow. Julie and Kris join the floorshow.

The angels enjoy the Hawaiian nightlife in "Hula Angeles."

COMMENTARY

Jaclyn Smith is the only Angel with professional dancing credits on her resumé, but Cheryl Ladd and Tanya Roberts are assigned the undercover roles in Moss's nightclub. Ladd, as she already proved in "Angels In the Wings" (#32) (opposite Gene Barry, who appears here as well) and "Dancing Angels" (#86), is more than capable—her hula has gotten even better than it was in "Angels in Paradise" (#23). "It's easy," brags Kris to Julie, "you just have to have the right equipment!" Julie Rogers certainly has the right equipment, but she's no Ginger Rogers (more like Fred Rogers, if the truth be told). Pat Crowley, who seduced Bosley in "Angels in Waiting" (#66) returns as a less than trustworthy client.

EPISODE 100: *Moonshinin' Angels*

ORIGINAL AIRDATE: January 24, 1981
PRODUCED BY: Elaine Rich
WRITTEN BY: B. W. Sandefur
DIRECTED BY: Kim Manners
GUEST STARS: Andrew Duggan (Hackshaw), George Loros (Max Lacy), Dennis Fimple (George Bartlett), Steve Hanks (Bobby Dan Bartlett), Miriam Byrd-Nethery (Flo Bartlett), Tisch Raye (Melinda Catlin), Dabbs Greer (Bluford Catlin)

New York businessman Max Lacy reignites a 100-year-old feud between the Catlin and Bartlett clans of Gifford County, hoping to take over their lucrative bootleg whiskey market. The Angels infiltrate the warring families—Kris talks herself into a job as the Catlins' new stillmaster, Kelly is hired as a driver for the Bartletts—and convince them to join forces against Lacy and his underworld partners.

COMMENTARY

Those seeking the low point of the series' five-year run need look no further than this dreadful episode, in which the Angels return from Hawaii and land in *Dukes of Hazzard* territory. The very idea that two backwoods families who haven't trusted anyone outside their kin for 100 years would hire two outsiders on sight is beyond ludicrous, and hardly the only problem in B. W. Sandefur's cliché-ridden script. The only saving grace is a fiddle and steel guitar arrangement of the *Charlie's Angels* theme that plays beneath the nonsense.

EPISODE 101: *He Married An Angel*

ORIGINAL AIRDATE: January 31, 1981
PRODUCED BY: Edward J. Lakso
WRITTEN BY: Edward J. Lakso
DIRECTED BY: Don Chaffey
GUEST STARS: David Hedison (John Thornwood), Beege Barkett (Monica Regis), Harold J. Stone (Joe Fenell), Eloise Hardt (Barbara Stone)

John Thornwood, a handsome San Francisco con man, defrauds two spinsters of their $100,000 inheritance and skips town. The women pursue him to Los Angeles and hire the Angels to retrieve the money.

Thornwood is already setting up his next mark, art gallery owner Monica Regis, when the Angels trace him to a new luxury housing complex. Kris takes the apartment next door, and stages an argument with Bosley that establishes her as a con artist with a similar taste for the good life. Impressed, Thornwood offers to cut her in on his next scheme. The Angels plan to spring their trap on schedule, but worry about the effect the truth will have on Monica Regis, a shy, plain girl who has fallen in love for the first time. Instead of simply exposing Thornwood as a fraud, they decide to use his own tactics against him.

COMMENTARY

"He Married an Angel" is another deft sting operation in the tradition of "Three For the Money" (#90), right down to the gratifying payback scene when the con man is stared down by the Angels and their clients. David Hedison is terrific as the smooth-talking John Thornwood, and Cheryl Ladd plays her scenes on the other side of the law with a wicked dazzle. "It was a funny premise and a good show, but I had a hell of a time with the casting," said Lakso. "We hired a plain-looking girl to play the gallery owner, which is what we needed, but she walked on the set the next day after a complete makeover, and she looked too pretty! I told her she couldn't play the role that way, but her ego wouldn't allow her to play a plain girl. We had to replace her."

EPISODE 102: *Taxi Angels*

ORIGINAL AIRDATE: **February 7, 1981**
PRODUCED BY: **Robert Janes**
WRITTEN BY: **Robert George**
DIRECTED BY: **John Peyser**
GUEST STARS: **Norman Alden (Jake Barnett), Sally Kirkland (Laurie Archer), David Pritchard (Tom Archer), Robert Costanzo (Mac Gossett), Scott Brady (Sarge)**

The Archer Taxicab Company is subjected to a series of threatening phone calls and attacks, culminating with the explosion of a bomb in a cab that nearly kills its driver. Hired by company owners Tom and Laurie Archer, the Angels receive their undercover assignments—Julie becomes the new dispatcher, Kelly is hired as a new driver, Kris poses as a waitress at a popular cabbie hangout. Their prime suspect is "Sarge," a delusional ex-soldier who experiences World War II flashbacks.

COMMENTARY

The show, like the Archer Taxicab Company, is running out of gas, but there are still a few fun moments created before the axe fell. The sequence in which Kelly debates a New York cab driver about the merits of their respective hometowns is a gem, and it's fun to see Kris back on roller skates again. Sally Kirkland ("Caged Angel"—#74) makes her second series appearance.

EPISODE 103: *Angel On the Line*

ORIGINAL AIRDATE: **February 14, 1981**
PRODUCED BY: **Edward J. Lakso**
WRITTEN BY: **Edward J. Lakso**
DIRECTED BY: **Kim Manners**
GUEST STARS: **Tisha Sterling (Mary), Diane McBain (Penny), Paul Cavonis (Harry Stark), Bruce Watson (Edward Ford), Brad Maule (Bartender)**

At the Hotline Club, where all the tables are numbered and connected by private phones, two women are threatened with death by a deranged caller. One of them meets the stalker in the parking lot, and is killed by an oncoming car while making her escape. Her friend hires the Angels, who return to the club as customers. The killer chooses Kelly as his next victim, but the Angels are unable to trace his whereabouts. They suspect that the club's featured performer, Margo the Hypnotist, knows something about the case, but even the Angels are not prepared when the startling truth is revealed.

COMMENTARY

A case that becomes personal after Kelly is terrorized by a psychotic stalker, "Angel On the Line" generates slasher movie tension. The toughest Angel is on the receiving end of a genuinely terrifying onslaught, and Jaclyn Smith plays the moment with conviction. Anyone paying attention will pick up on the clues that point to Margo the Hypnotist, so the *Crying Game*-like revelation is not exactly a shock. Female impersonator Jim Bailey, whose recreations of Barbra Streisand and Judy Garland played to packed houses across the country, was hired to play Margo, but had to withdraw due to a scheduling conflict. Bruce Watson, however, carries off a dual role with campy flamboyance, and deserves serious consideration as the Angels' most twisted adversary.

Real clubs like the Hot Line had their 15 minutes of fame at the time "Angel On the Line" was aired. The use of telephones to call people at tables across the room seems a precursor to the online coffee houses of today, in which people do the same thing via computer.

EPISODE 104: *Chorus Line Angels*

ORIGINAL AIRDATE: February 21, 1981
PRODUCED BY: Edward J. Lakso
WRITTEN BY: Edward J. Lakso
DIRECTED BY: David Doyle
GUEST STARS: Michael Callan (Darian Mason), Mark Slade (John Summers), Pamela Peadon (Marcia Howard), Mary Doyle (Ruth Traina), Nancy Fox (Nancy Swenson), Lee Travis (Jessica Thorpe)

The choreographer and lead dancer of a lavish new Las Vegas musical mysteriously disappear. An investor, Ruth Traina, hires the Angels to discover who is trying to sabotage the production, and why. Kelly joins the ranks of the chorus line, with Julie in tow as her agent/manager, while Kris schmoozes her way into the heart of producer Darian Mason, as a reporter for the "Omaha Dance Review." Mason's interest in Kris proves short-lived when she uncovers his role in the kidnappings.

COMMENTARY

"Chorus Line Angels" gave David Doyle an opportunity to direct his first episode. "He always wanted to try his hand at it, so I decided to give him a shot," said producer Ed Lakso.

Earlier episodes, including "Pretty Angels All In A Row" (#25), "Angels in the Wings" (#32) and "Angels in Vegas" (#47), had allowed Jaclyn Smith to display her dance skills, but this was the first time she was given a showcase worthy of her talent. Unfortunately, the story that unfolded between musical numbers was rather uninteresting. There were the usual suspects—the over-eager choreographer, the chorus line dancer with the secret past—but none of them were developed sufficiently to warrant any genuine suspicion.

The resolution of the case comes surprisingly early after a lackluster action sequence, clearing the way for an extended musical finale. The scene is replayed again, as the teaser, probably in an attempt to fill time. Michael Callan ("The Vegas Connection"—#17) once again plays a slimy villain. Previous guest-stars Nancy Fox and Lee Travis were also on hand to fill out the chorus line.

EPISODE 105: *Stuntwoman Angels*

ORIGINAL AIRDATE: February 28, 1981
PRODUCED BY: Edward J. Lakso
WRITTEN BY: Edward J. Lakso
DIRECTED BY: Dennis Donnelly
GUEST STARS: Denny Miller (Jeff Stanowich), Pat Cooper (Jonathan Tobias), Beth Schaffel (Ellen Travers), Gerald O'loughlin (Jake Webner)

A modern-day "Robin Hood," complete with crossbow and costume, terrorizes a movie set where an Errol Flynn remake is being shot. Jonathan Tobias, an exasperated executive for Mammoth Studios, hires the Angels to find out the identity of the man behind the mask. Charlie enrolls the Angels in stunt training school, where they learn how to withstand the bumps and bruises of stuntwork.

After establishing their cover, the Angels report to work on the set of "Marian and Her Merry Maids," where they meet actress Ellen Travers and her disgruntled husband, Jeff. Ellen and the director are wounded by arrows fired by the mad archer, before the Angels discover that two different Robin Hoods are stalking the set.

COMMENTARY

During the series' first season, "Angels in Chains" writer Robert Earll offered a stuntwoman-themed story treatment that was never approved. Five seasons later, the concept was revisited; "I enjoyed writing this one, because I liked working on the Errol Flynn aspect," said Ed Lakso. "It had a nice feel."

The Angels work well as a team in this episode; Tanya Roberts contributes several comic one-liners, expressing Julie's fear of stuntwork, but why are Kris and Kelly so apprehensive? Didn't they get proper training at the police academy?

Denny Miller, a frequent bit player on the series, turns in a memorable performance as the husband with the identity crisis, and Gerald O'loughlin, who costarred with Kate Jackson for four seasons on *The Rookies*, turns up two years too late for a reunion. Several exteriors from the 20th Century Fox lot were used throughout the episode, including Stage 8, where *Charlie's Angels* was filmed.

EPISODE 106: *Attack Angels*

ORIGINAL AIRDATE: June 3, 1981
PRODUCED BY: Elaine Rich
WRITTEN BY: B. W. Sandefur
DIRECTED BY: Kim Manners
GUEST STARS: Eric Braeden (John Reardon), Darleen Carr (Darlene Warden), David Sheiner (Robert Carver), Dr. Joyce Brothers (Dr. Lantry), Barbara Luna (Cynthia Weaver)

Two top officials at Western Techtronics die mysteriously, and one of the remaining board members, Steve Briggs, suspects foul play. He hires the Angels to investigate. Kelly and Kris join the corporate world as junior executives; Julie is hired by the Reardon Group, headed by the charismatic John Reardon. Ostensibly a temp agency, Reardon actually uses hypnotic control over his employees, involving them in murder in his attempt to take over Western Techtronics. Julie falls under Reardon's spell, and is ordered to kill Steve Briggs.

COMMENTARY

The first-ever fight scene pitting Angel vs. Angel is staged when a hypnotized Julie squares off against Kris and Kelly. It's a short but well-choreographed battle that, for a moment anyway, restores Julie to the tough streetfighter image she created in her debut episode. Eric Braeden, who worked with Ed Lakso on *Combat* and is best-known as Victor Newman on *The Young and the Restless*, plays the type of intimidating character he thrives at, but he is no match for the formidable Julie, who must have watched some *Avengers* reruns before taking a job at the Reardon Group.

EPISODE 107: *Angel On a Roll*

ORIGINAL AIRDATE: June 10, 1981
PRODUCED BY: Edward J. Lakso
WRITTEN BY: Edward J. Lakso
DIRECTED BY: Dennis Donnelly
GUEST STARS: Mark Pinter (Ted Markham), Rick Casorla (Hank), Joseph Sirola (Boris), Robert Rockwell (Harrison), Noah Keen (Bank President)

Computer designer Ted Markham, who specializes in automatic teller machines, quits his job, and simultaneously twelve different banks are relieved of the cash in their machines. The banks retain the Angels to trace the lost money, which luckily is denominated in serialized $100 bills. Kris is assigned to trail Markham and procure one of the bills as evidence. Happy to have an attractive woman to help him spend his money, Markham takes Kris on a gambling spree that begins at a Los Angeles card club, and culminates at the blackjack tables in Las Vegas. Kris realizes that she must lure him back to California for capture, but after a fun-filled weekend, she isn't sure if she really wants to!

COMMENTARY

A return to the solo *Angel* stories of the previous season, "Angel On a Roll" works only because of its tweaking of the familiar formula of Angel romances with nice guys who turn out to be snakes. For the first time, there is a genuine moment of doubt as to whether a compassionate Kris will turn the charismatic, bad-but-not-really-bad Ted Markham into the authorities.

EPISODE 108: *Mr. Galaxy*

ORIGINAL AIRDATE: June 17, 1981
PRODUCED BY: Elaine Rich
WRITTEN BY: Mickey Rich
DIRECTED BY: Don Chaffey
GUEST STARS: Roger Callard (Ron Gates), Dick Bakalyan (Artie Weaver), Ric Drasin (Chuck Wilde), Danny Barr (Joseph Ruskin), Selena Hansen (Bonnie Keith), Karen Haber (Sally)

The Angels infiltrate the world of male bodybuilding, when attempts are made on the life of one of the competitors. Ron Gates, an ex-boxer now hoping to become "Mr. Galaxy," is almost killed by sabotaged weightlifting equipment, and later by a hotwired jacuzzi.

Julie gets a job at the Mid Valley Health Club, to investigate Gates' chief competitor, Chuck Wilde. Kelly goes undercover as a staff writer for "Health Fare" magazine, but her cover is blown after she meets Danny Barr, a mafia-type businessman who links her with the Townsend Agency.

COMMENTARY

Not much to draw on here, although Danny Barr has one amusing line when he sees Kris with her gun drawn—"What have we here, Wonder Woman?" Though they spend a lot of time picking locks and searching offices, the Angels don't really save the day this time, leaving the heavy lifting to the bodybuilders. Since the series was coming to an end, they decided to take it easy.

"The bodybuilders loved the show. They were much more exhibitionistic, and into posing, than the Angels ever were!" said Tanya Roberts. "Critics said we were in front of mirrors all the time with our hair and makeup? These guys were in front of the mirror like you never saw in your life!"

EPISODE 109: *Let Our Angel Live*

ORIGINAL AIRDATE: June 24, 1981
PRODUCED BY: Edward J. Lakso
WRITTEN BY: Edward J. Lakso
DIRECTED BY: Kim Manners
GUEST STARS: Gary Wood (Joe Danworth), George Ball
(Dr. Jackson), Michael Whitney (Police Officer)

During a routine stake-out, Kelly and Bosley corner Joe Danworth, a suspect who has made off with $200,000 of his company's money. Danworth fires a gun concealed beneath his jacket, seriously injuring Kelly. After an enraged Bosley takes out the gunman, Kelly is rushed to the hospital in critical condition.

The other Angels are summoned, and Charlie enlists a specialist to consult with the surgical team. Kris, Julie and Bosley keep a vigil after being told that Kelly has a 50-50 chance of survival. While waiting for the outcome of her surgery, the trio reminisce about past cases, and Bosley tells the girls that they must decide, "whatever happens," if it was all worth it. They offer no regrets for their chosen occupation.

COMMENTARY

Although the cast and crew had known that "Let Our Angel Live" would be *Charlie's Angels'* last episode, the series still could not bring itself to actuate the long-hoped-for face to face meeting between Charlie and his Angels. Their brush in the hospital had some measure of finality, but the audience could be forgiven for feeling cheated.

During the Angels' reminiscences of past cases, Kris recalls the time Bosley went undercover in a hospital. The episode was "Terror on Ward One" (#18) from the first season, before Kris had actually joined the team. Perhaps her sister called her later with the details!

"It was a very emotional time," recalled director Kim Manners. "We had our own little world on Stage 8 for four and a half years, and it was coming to an end. It was a very difficult episode to shoot."

The Charlie's Angels Merchandise Gallery

Television merchandising was at its peak during the 1970s, and no series was in greater demand than *Charlie's Angels*. Never before had a series or its stars gathered so much attention in such a short amount of time. Its popularity actually prompted three different toy companies to produce dolls on both the actresses and their series characters, an industry first.

In 1977, Hasbro Industries devoted a $2.5 million dollar advertising campaign to promote their *Charlie's Angels* dolls, featuring Jill, Kelly and Sabrina. Mego Toys, famous for their line of superhero and celebrity dolls, followed suit by producing a Farrah Fawcett and Jaclyn Smith doll under the actresses' real names. "We make Hasbro's Jaclyn Smith doll look like a piece of crap," a Mego spokesman boasted to *Us* magazine in 1977. But Hasbro's dolls became the second biggest item sold during the 1977 holiday season, (they were outsold only by Mattel's gooey green mystery substance, known as Slime). More than two million dolls were sold within months. The Mego Farrah Fawcett doll finished the holiday season in sixth place.

Farrah Fawcett's decision to leave the show after the first season put some companies in a quandary as to whether they should continue to market products with the images of the three original angels. "We manufactured a prototype lunchbox with Farrah's likeness on it," an Aladdin spokeswoman said in 1979; "then after we manufactured the test issue, we found out she would not be returning and that was the season the lunchbox would be out. We felt that since she would not be with the series by then, it may not sell, so the prototype box as well as all designs connected with the item were destroyed."

When Cheryl Ladd replaced Farrah Fawcett, she soon became immortalized in plastic as well, as Hasbro expanded their doll line with the addition of Kris Munroe, and Mattel introduced a Cheryl Ladd doll and a Kate Jackson doll. Jackson had reportedly turned down negotiations with Mego a year earlier for a doll bearing her name and likeness. A *Charlie's Angels* lunchbox was released by Aladdin with the newest Angels, and Topps Chewing Gum Company, the leader in sports and non-sports trading cards, released four series of *Charlie's Angels* trading cards. This was Topps most popular non-sports series in terms of mass appeal, and the first to reach four issues.

In 1977-78, Farrah Fawcett became a major marketing commodity in her own right. Items bearing her image were very successful; among the most popular were rugs, pillows, bean bag chairs, and notebooks. Prior to starring in *Charlie's Angels*, Farrah had a small part in the science fiction cult classic, *Logan's Run* (1976). That was reason enough for MGM to jump on the Farrah bandwagon; they licensed T-shirts, coffee cups, posters, puzzles and beach towels all bearing the image of Fawcett and the *Logan's Run* logo.

ALADDIN INDUSTRIES

Lunchbox and thermos (Kelly, Kris, Sabrina)

Brunch bag and thermos (Kelly, Kris, Sabrina)

AZOULAY

Charlie's Angels jeans
Designer jeans with "Angels" logo on back pocket.

BALLANTINE BOOKS

Charlie's Angels paperback books
Based on series episodes.

#1 Series Pilot
#2 "The Killing Kind"
#3 "Angels on a String"
#4 "Angels in Chains"
#5 "Angels on Ice"

BI-RITE ENTERPRISES

Charlie's Angels posters   Size: 23" x 35"

Charlie's Angels 1976	(Jill, Kelly, Sabrina)
Charlie's Angels 1977-78	(Kelly, Kris, Sabrina)
Charlie's Angels 1978 Collage	(Kelly, Kris, Sabrina)
Charlie's Angels 1979	(Kelly, Kris, Tiffany)
Jaclyn Smith as "Kelly"	(White Bikini)
Farrah Fawcett Majors as "Jill"	(Collage)

"Kelly" of *Charlie's Angels*	(Collage)
"Sabrina" of *Charlie's Angels*	(Collage)
Cheryl Ladd as "Kris"	(Collage)
Charlie's Angels poster put-ons	9" x 9" Laminated Stickers
Charlie's Angels 1977-78	(Kelly, Kris, Sabrina)
Charlie's Angels Collage 78	(Kelly, Kris, Sabrina)
"Sabrina" of *Charlie's Angels*	(Collage)
"Kelly" of *Charlie's Angels*	(Collage)
Cheryl Ladd as "Kris"	(Collage)

COLLEGEVILLE COSTUMES

Halloween costume

"Sabrina" mask—available in small, medium, and large sizes.

COLORFORMS CORPORATION

Charlie's Angels colorforms adventure set (Kelly, Kris, Sabrina)

Colorforms kit featuring plastic pieces of the Angels "that stick like magic," and accessories, with playboard and booklet.

CORGI CORPORATION

Charlie's Angels custom van (Kelly, Kris, Sabrina)

Metal custom van with "Angels" logo on the sides and swinging doors.

Charlie's Angels junior van (Kelly, Kris, Sabrina)

Small metal "matchbox" size van with "Angels" logo on sides.

DUN PRODUCTIONS

Charlie's Angels in Hawaii Magazine

Souvenir magazine dedicated to the season two premiere episode, filmed on location in Hawaii.

FLEETWOOD TOYS

Angels beads

Plastic beads featuring each individual Angel in the center packaging. Produced in versions featuring both Jill and Kris.

Pendants

Long full-length figural pendant of each individual Angel on a long chain. Produced in versions featuring both Jill and Kris.

Jewelry set (Jill, Kelly, Sabrina)

Heart-shaped necklace with each individual Angel featured, plus earrings and ring.

Jewels and case (Kelly, Kris, Sabrina)

Plastic heart-shaped jewelry box with Angels logo, necklace, bracelet and earrings.

Beauty set

Plastic comb and hand mirror set, featuring each individual Angel on the mirror backing. Produced in versions featuring both Jill and Kris.

Charlie's Angels 'Talk Time' (Jill, Kelly, Sabrina)

Plastic play princess telephone with the Angels faces on the phone, with address book and pencil.

Dresser set (Jill, Kelly, Sabrina)

Plastic dresser ornament, small brush, comb and mirror with each individual Angel on the ornament and mirror.

Jewelry set

Four plastic bracelets, earrings, necklace and heart-shaped clip featuring each individual Angel. Produced in versions featuring both Jill and Kris.

Hair dryer

Small plastic play hair dryer, brush, comb and two rollers. Produced in versions featuring both Jill and Kris.

Charlie's Angels '3-D Viewer' (Kelly, Kris, Sabrina)

Plastic viewer with four showcards featuring 24 scenes.

'Angels' cosmetics' (Kelly, Kris, Sabrina)
Plastic play perfume bottles, compact, lipstick and accessories.

Charlie's Angels sunglasses with case (Jill, Kelly, Sabrina)
Plastic sunglasses with plastic case featuring all three Angels.

Shoulder bag (Jill, Kelly, Sabrina)
Red and white trimmed plastic shoulder bag with "Angels" logo.

Charlie's Angels 'Travelers' (Jill, Kelly, Sabrina)
White plastic coin purses with "Angels" logo

Headband and jewelry set
Plastic necklace, earrings and headband all accented with the "Angels" logo. Produced in versions featuring both Jill and Kris.

Charlie's Angels 'elegant jewels' (Kelly, Kris, Sabrina)
Elegant bracelet, earrings and "cameo" pin.

GLJ Toy Co.

Charlie's Angels toy fashion watch (Jill, Kelly, Sabrina)
Plastic watch with movable "Angels" logo that works like a real watch.

Gottlieb & Co.

Charlie's Angels pinball machine
(Kelly, Kris, Sabrina)
Solid-state, four player, pinball machine with electronic scoring.

H-G Toys, Inc.

Puzzles (standard size) 10" x 14" ,
150-piece fully interlocking puzzles.
"Angels" (Jill, Kelly, Sabrina)
"On the Job" (Jill, Kelly, Sabrina)
"In Action" (Jill, Kelly, Sabrina)
"Portrait" (Kelly, Kris, Sabrina)
"Montage" (Kelly, Kris, Sabrina)
"The Girls" (Kelly, Kris, Sabrina)

Giant puzzle—14" x 36" 250-piece
fully interlocking puzzle
(Jill, Kelly, Sabrina)

New *Charlie's Angels* puzzle (Kelly, Kris, Sabrina)—16" x 20",
500-piece, fully interlocking, puzzle. Hawaiian scene.

Poster art kit
Art kit that includes two 18" x 24" posters to color and five colored markers. Produced in versions featuring both Jill and Kris.

Deluxe poster art kit (Jill, Kelly, Sabrina)
Boxed art kit that includes three 18" x 24" posters
to color and six colored markers.

Charlie's Angels beauty hair care set

Set includes battery operated hair blower, rollers, comb, brush, mirror with "Angels" photo on back, hairstyling tips, mini photos and poster. Produced in versions featuring both Jill and Kris.

Charlie's Angels cosmetic beauty kit
(Jill, Kelly, Sabrina)

Set includes swivel mirror with "Angels" photo on back, makeup bag, play makeup and fragrance
bottles, lipstick, manicure set and beauty care tips.

Charlie's Angels fashion dress-up set (Kelly, Kris, Sabrina)

Set includes purse, high heel shoes, belt, sunglasses, necklace, play watch, ring and fashion tips.

HASBRO INDUSTRIES

Charlie's Angels dolls

8 1/2" fully posable dolls with "Twist and Turn" waist and hair that can be styled (Jill, Kris, Kelly, Sabrina).

Charlie's Angels dolls gift set

Boxed set of three dolls, (Jill, Kelly, and Sabrina, or Kelly, Kris, Sabrina)

Fashion costume assortment (produced in versions featuring both Jill and Kris)

"Night Caper"—pink gown and robe
   with marabou trim plus sandals.
"Peasantry"—gold trim pants and bolero, tie-blouse scarf and boots.
"Moonlight Flight"—silver gown with marabou accents plus white sandals.
"Gaucho Pizazz"—gaucho, turban, boots and a fur coat.
"Russian Roulette"—mink-look hat coat, belt and boots.
"Black Magic"—metallic dress, jacket, headband and sandals.

"Gold Coast" editions fashion assortment (Kelly, Kris, Sabrina)

"Golden Whispers"—white eyelet dress with fringed shawl, gold choker
   and sandals.
"Golden Intrigue"—gold lamé trenchcoat, scarf, belt and boots.
"Golden Goddess"—golden swimsuit, slacks, and sarong belt, plus sandals.
"Golden Marathon Girl"—silky plum jogging outfit with gold trim,
   plus sneakers.
"Golden Sport"—sporty red matching shorts and jacket, gold lined top,
   and boots.
"Golden Pro"—tennis dress with gold trim, shorts, visor sneakers, and
   knee socks.

Flying skateboard adventure

Costume featuring cut-off jeans, shirt, sneakers and a real miniature skateboard, produced in versions featuring both Jill and Kris.

Escapade outfits (Jill, Kelly, Sabrina)

Two complete adventure outfits, plus action gear in a deluxe boxed set.

"Slalom Caper"—leotard, parka, hat caftan, sandals, ski boots, skis, poles, goggles, binoculars.

"River Race"—leotard, bolero, scarf, boots, backpack, raft, oar, flashlight and walkie-talkie.

"Underwater Intrigue"—leotard, lamé gown, turban, sandals, tank, mask, flippers and spear.

Fashion tote (Kelly, Kris, Sabrina)

Cylindrical pink fashion tote carries dolls and wardrobe. Includes three hangers.

Adventure van (Kelly, Kris, Sabrina)

Deluxe custom van with T-bar roof and bucket seats. Accessories include parson's table, director's chair, camera, binoculars, and earphones.

Hide-a-way house

Three-level home complete with barbecue area, living area and sundeck. Accessories include work-out mat, director's chair, couch, bed, fireplace, bar and bar stool. Produced in versions featuring both Jill and Kris.

Paint-by-numbers set (Kelly, Kris, Sabrina)

Deluxe version—9 acrylic paints and 3 pictures.
Standard version—6 acrylic paints and 2 pictures.

ILLCO TOYS

Pocketbook radio

AM Radio with microphone amplifier for communications, morse code button and earplug. Pocketbook with "Angels" logo on side for carrying (Jill, Kelly, Sabrina).

Wrist radio

Solid-state micro sound AM radio, with "Angels" logo (Jill, Kelly, Sabrina).

L.J.N. TOYS

Walkie-talkies

Five-transistor circuitry walkie-talkies with Morse code/ signal beeper and "Angels" logo (Jill, Kelly, Sabrina)

MILTON BRADLEY

Charlie's Angels game, "Jill" and "Kris" Versions

Board game featuring die-cut figures of the Angels and gameboard, produced in versions featuring both Jill and Kris. Object: Be the first to capture the culprit with your team.

MONTY CARDS

Charlie's Angels trading cards

One-hundred card set printed in Holland featuring the first five Angels.

PARADISE PRESS

Charlie's Angels Official Poster Monthly Magazine (Kelly, Kris, Sabrina)

Issues # 1, 2 and 3 featuring stories, facts and photos on the series and a pull-out poster.

PHOTO-LITH INTERNATIONAL

Iron-on transfers

Charlie's Angels (Sabrina, Jill, Kelly)
New *Charlie's Angels* (Sabrina, Kelly, Kris)
Charlie's Angels (Sabrina, Kelly, Kris)
Charlie's Angels 'Glitter' (Kelly, Kris, Tiffany)
Farrah Fawcett as "Jill"
Kate Jackson as "Sabrina"
Jaclyn Smith as "Kelly"
"Charlie's Sabrina"
"Charlie's Kelly"
Cheryl Ladd as "Kris"

PLACO TOYS

Target Set

Knock-down target featuring "Angels" logo, with 2 safety guns and 6 darts. Produced in versions featuring both Jill and Kris.

REVELL, INC.

Mobile unit van,

1/25-scale plastic model kit, produced in versions featuring both Jill and Kris.

Snap-together van,

1/32-scale plastic snap-together model kit, featuring Kelly, Kris, Sabrina.

SHARIN TOY CO.

Charlie's Angels Cubemensional puzzle

Cardboard cube squares that are interchangeable and can form up to sixteen different puzzle scenes. Features Kelly, Kris, Sabrina

STAFFORD PEMBERTON PUBLISHING CO.

Charlie's Angels annuals

Hardcover books with stories, comics, puzzles and photos.

Gift book/1978   Jill, Kelly, Sabrina

1979 Issue	Kelly, Kris, Sabrina
1980 Issue	Kelly, Kris, Sabrina
1981 Issue	Kelly, Kris, Tiffany

Charlie's Angels puzzles, #2078 "Jill" versions only
(red border, 250 large-piece 17" x 12" puzzles)

A. "Sabrina, Jill, Kelly"   B. "Sabrina"   C. "Jill"   D. "Kelly"

Charlie's Angels puzzles, #9079 "Kris" versions Only
(pink border, 250 large-piece 17" x 12" puzzles)

A. "Sabrina, Kelly, Kris"   B. "Sabrina"   C. "Kelly"   D. "Kris"

Charlie's Angels Coloring Book "Kris" Version Only

Charlie's Angels Press-Out Book "Kris" Version Only

Charlie's Angels Children's Book "Kris" Version Only

Charlie's Angels Doll Dressing Book Cut-out Doll, Clothes to Fit

A. "Sabrina"   B. "Kelly"   C. "Kris"

STUART HALL COMPANY, INC.

School supplies

Notebook, 10-1/2" x 8", themebook, 11" x 8-1/2", themebook. Three-ring binder, and portfolio, all featuring Kelly, Kris, Sabrina

THERMO SERV INC.

Coffee cups, beer mugs, drinking tumblers

Each set depicts individual shots of Kris, Kelly, and Sabrina.

TOPPS CHEWING GUM COMPANY, INC.

Bubble gum cards

Series 1—#1–55
Cards featuring Jill, Kelly, Sabrina.
Series 2—#56–121
Cards featuring Jill, Kelly, Sabrina.
Series 3—#122–187
Cards featuring Kelly, Kris, Sabrina.
Series 4—#188–253
Cards featuring Kelly, Kris, Sabrina.

Bubble gum stickers

Series 1—#1–11	Stickers featuring Jill, Kelly, Sabrina.
Series 2—#12–22	Stickers featuring Jill, Kelly, Sabrina.
Series 3—#23–33	Stickers featuring Kelly, Kris, Sabrina.
Series 4—#34–44	Stickers featuring Kelly, Kris, Sabrina.

THE TOY FACTORY

Paper dolls

14" Die-cut figures of Jill, Kelly, and Sabrina, with cut-out paper clothes and accessories.

Playset, "Jill" version

Cardboard playset that includes posable figures of the Angels, cars, house interior, helicopter, speed boat, dune buggy, hidden rock cave with cliff house, cabana and pool.

TRAVEL TOY CORPORATION

Three-piece Luggage Set, "Jill" and "Kris" versions

Boxed all vinyl constructed set includes larger size train case, models case and day tripper

Deluxe 3-piece luggage set, "Jill" and "Kris" versions

Larger boxed all vinyl constructed set includes larger train case, models case and day tripper.

Three-piece luggage set, "Kris" version

Shrink-pack all vinyl constructed set includes overnighter, train case and shoulder tote.

Backpack, "Kris" version

All vinyl constructed backpack with "quick-lock" straps and "Angels" photo.

Rainy Day Set, "Kris" version

Water repellent set includes 20" umbrella with "Angels" logo,
rain hat and shoulder tote with "Angels" photo.

Wallet, "Kris" version

Sturdy vinyl wallet with change purse, picture holders and compartment.

WESTERN PUBLISHING COMPANY

Golden all-Star book, featuring Jill, Kelly, Sabrina

Illustrated "comic-type" Book, with three different stories.

Magic slate, featuring Kelly, Kris, Sabrina

Classic write-on, peel-off paper saving slate with plastic writing instrument.

Cast Merchandise Not Related to the Series:

AMT

Farrah's Foxy Vette model kit

AMERICAN PUBLISHING CORPORATION

Puzzle depicting the famous red swimsuit poster image of Farrah Fawcett.
Two different sizes. Smaller puzzles feature other Farrah poster images, designated as "Flower" and "Super."

BEAR FACTORIES LTD.

Iron-on transfers featuring Farrah Fawcett ("Swimsuit," "Flower," "Super"), Jaclyn Smith ("Bed"), and Kate Jackson ("Scarf")

CRAFTMASTER

Farrah Fawcett poster pen set

DARGIS ASSOCIATES

Logan's Run posters featuring Farrah Fawcett as Holly. Two styles.

DAWN PRODUCTS

Logan's Run coffee cups and tumblers, featuring Farrah Fawcett as Holly. Red and blue Styles

FRANCO LTD.

Logan's Run beach towels, featuring Farrah Fawcett as Holly; two designs (close-up and full body)

GADWAR

Farrah "The Fawcett" necklace

MATTEL, INC.

Cheryl Ladd doll

Kate Jackson doll

TV star women's fashions (designed for Mattel dolls)
"Interview at Home"
"TV Awards Night"

"Racing Adventure Scene"
"Producer's Party"
"Season Premiere Party"
"Rehearsal Time"

MEGO CORPORATION

Farrah Fawcett doll / Farrah Fawcett Fashions
"Boogie Blues", "Visions" "Knockabouts", and "Highlights".
Farrah's Dressing Room Playset
Farrah's Glamour Center
Farrah's Styling Center
Jaclyn Smith Doll

NATIONAL BLANK BOOK CO.
Notebooks

Farrah Fawcett ("Swimsuit", "Flower", "Super")

Kate Jackson ("Scarf")

Jaclyn Smith ("Bed")

Cheryl Ladd ("Ms. Ladd")

The Official Farrah Fawcett Fan Club Kit

The Official Cheryl Ladd Fan Club Kit

PRO ARTS POSTER COMPANY
Posters

Farrah Fawcett
"Swimsuit"
"Flower"
"Super"
"L.A. Farrah"
"Paisley"
"Mrs. Majors"
"Blue"
"Giant" Farrah

Jaclyn Smith
"Bed"
"Ms. Smith"
"Pink"
"Gold"

Kate Jackson
"Scarf"
"Ms. Jackson"
"Super"

Cheryl Ladd
"Robe"
"Ms. Ladd"
"Lace"
"Giant"
"Black"

THERMO SERV
Three Farrah Fawcett coffee cups, tumblers and beer mugs, in styles designated as "Swimsuit", "Flower", and "Super."

WESTERN GRAPHICS
Posters

Shelley Hack "Raincoat"

Tanya Roberts "Bikini"

ZODIAC DESIGNS

Three Farrah Fawcett pillows, styles named as "Swimsuit," "Flower," and "Super." Available in small and large sizes. The company also manufactured bean bag chairs and rugs in the same three varieties.

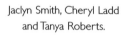

Jaclyn Smith, Cheryl Ladd
and Tanya Roberts.

The Charlie's Angels Swimsuit Guide

*C*HARLIE'S ANGELS WILL FOREVER BE REMEMBERED AS THE ORIGINATOR OF "Jiggle TV." Long before the days of *Baywatch*, the original girl-watching series dubbed "The Bod Squad" has been celebrated and criticized for presenting its angelic actresses underdressed when they went undercover. In 1976, *TV Guide* critic Robert MacKenzie summed up the series as being mainly about skin: "Yards of bare shoulders, bare legs, tummies and hair—gobs of it, tumbling over those bare shoulders."

After 109 episodes and countless costume changes, just how often were all six of Charlie's dazzling detectives scantily clad? How many times did Farrah fend off the culprit in her bathing suit, or Kate Jackson discover incriminating evidence wearing no more than a towel? The results may surprise you. Out of 109 episodes, only 32 featured the actresses in revealing attire.

For each appropriate episode, the chart below lists Angel appearances in bikinis, one-piece swimsuits, and towels. A (!) next to an entry indicates an extra-special cheesecake moment. This chart may put the critics' term "jiggle T.V." to rest.

EPISODE	BIKINI	SWIMSUIT	TOWEL
Pilot	Kelly (!)		Kelly
Mexican Connection (#2)	Kelly	Jill	Jill
Night of the Strangler (#3)	Kelly		Kelly
Angels in Chains (#4)			Sabrina (!)
			Jill (!)
			Kelly (!)
The Killing Kind (#6)	Kelly		Jill
			Kelly
Angel Trap (#13)	Kelly		
Angels on a String (#15)	Kelly		
Angels in Paradise (#23)	Kelly		
	Kris (!)		
Pretty Angels all in a Row (#25)	Kris		Kelly
			Kris
Angel Flight (#26)			Kelly
			Kris
Magic Fire (#33)			Kris
Angels on Horseback (#35)		Kelly (!)	
		Kris (!)	
Game, Set, Death (#36)			Kris
Hours of Desperation (#37)			Kelly
Diamond in the Rough (#38)		Kris	
Angels in the Backfield (#39)			Kris
Little Angels of the Night (#43)	Kelly	Kris	
	Kris (!)		
Angel Come Home (#48)		Kris	

EPISODE	BIKINI	SWIMSUIT	TOWEL
Angel on High (#49)	Kris (!)		
Angels in Springtime (#50)			Sabrina
			Kelly
			Kris
Love Boat Angels (#69)	Kris (!)	Kelly (!)	
		Tiffany	
Caged Angel (#74)			Kris
Angels on Campus (#78)			Tiffany
Angel Hunt (#79)		Kelly	
		Kris	
		Tiffany	
One of Our Angels is Missing (#83)	Kris	Kris	
Homes $weet Homes (#85)		Kris	
Angel in Hiding (#93)	Julie	Kelly	
		Kris	
To See an Angel Die (#94)	Julie (!)		
Angels of the Deep (#95)	Kelly (!)		
	Kris (!)		
	Julie (!)		
Island Angels (#96)	Kris	Kelly	
	Julie	Julie	
Waikiki Angels (#97)	Kelly (!)	Kelly	
	Kris (!)	Kris	
	Julie (!)	Julie	
Hula Angels (#98)	Kris	Kelly	
	Julie	Kris	
		Julie	

A Complete List of Angels' Credits

Farrah Fawcett

Television Series

1975-76	*Harry O*
1976-77	*Charlie's Angels*
1991	*Good Sports*

Television Appearances

1969	*The Flying Nun* ("Marcello's Idol")
1969	*I Dream of Jeannie* ("See You in C-U-B-A")
1969	*I Dream of Jeannie* ("My Sister the Homewrecker")
1970	*The Flying Nun* ("Armondo and the Pool Table")
1970	*The Partridge Family* ("The Sound of Money")
1970	*The Young Rebels* ("Dangerous Ally")
1971	*Inside O.U.T.* (Pilot)
1973	*The Girl with Something Extra* ("How Green was Las Vegas")
1974	*McCloud* ("The Colorado Cattle Caper")
1974	*Marcus Welby, MD*
1974	*The Six Million Dollar Man* ("The Rescue of Athena One")
1974	*Apple's Way* ("First Love")
1974	*The Six Million Dollar Man* ("The Peeping Blonde")
1975	*S.W.A.T.* ("The Steel-Plated Security Blanket")
1976	*The Six Million Dollar Man* ("The Golden Pharoah")
1976	*The Six Million Dollar Man* ("Nightmare in the Sky")
1976	*Battle of the Network Stars*

1981	*The Fall Guy*
1995	*The Larry Sanders Show*
	("Eight")
1997	*Johnny Bravo*
	("Johnny Meets Farrah Fawcett")
1997	*Farrah Fawcett: All of Me*

Television Movies

1971	*The Feminist and the Fuzz*
1973	*The Great American Beauty Contest*
1974	*The Girl Who Came Giftwrapped*
1975	*Murder on Flight 502*
1981	*Murder in Texas*
1984	*The Red Light Sting*
1984	*The Burning Bed*
1986	*Between Two Women*
1986	*Nazi Hunter: The Beate Klarsfeld Story*
1987	*Poor Little Rich Girl: The Barbara Hutton Story*
1989	*Double Exposure: The Margaret Bourke-White Story*
1989	*Small Sacrifices*
1992	*Criminal Behavior*
1994	*The Substitute Wife*
1995	*Children of the Dust*
1996	*Dalva*
1999	*Silk Hope*

Film

1969	*Love is a Funny Thing*
1970	*Myra Breckinridge*
1976	*Logan's Run*
1978	*Somebody Killed Her Husband*
1979	*Sunburn*
1980	*Saturn 3*
1981	*The Cannonball Run*
1986	*Extremities*
1989	*See You in the Morning*
1995	*Man of the House*
1997	*The Apostle*
1997	*The Lovemaster*
1998	*The Brave Little Toaster Goes to Mars* (voice only)

Kate Jackson

Television Series

1970-71	*Dark Shadows*
1972-76	*The Rookies*
1976-79	*Charlie's Angels*
1983-87	*Scarecrow & Mrs. King*
1988-89	*Baby Boom*

Television Appearances

1972	*The Jimmy Stewart Show*
1972	*The New Healers*
	(Pilot)
1972	*Bonanza*
	("One Ace too Many")
1972	*Movin' On*
	(Pilot)
1978	*The San Pedro Beach Bums*
	("The Angels and the Bums")
1992	*Boys of Twilight*
	("Shadow of a Shadow")
1993	*Arly Hanks*
	(Pilot)
1997	*Ally McBeal*
	("The Kiss")
1998	*Dead Man's Gun*
	("Death Warrant")
1999	*Twice in a Lifetime*
	("Double Exposure")

Television Movies

1973	*Satan's School for Girls*
1974	*Death Cruise*
1974	*Killer Bees*
1975	*The Shrine of Lorna Love*
1975	*Death Scream*
1977	*James at 15*
1979	*Topper*

1981	*Inmates: A Love Story*
1981	*Thin Ice*
1983	*Listen to Your Heart*
1990	*The Stranger Within*
1992	*Quiet Killer*
1992	*Homewrecker* (Voice Only)
1993	*Adrift*
1993	*Empty Cradle*
1994	*Armed and Innocent*
1994	*Justice in a Small Town*
1995	*The Silence of Adultery*
1995	*The Cold Heart of a Killer*
1996	*Panic in the Skies*
1996	*A Kidnapping in the Family*
1997	*What Happened to Bobby Earl?*
1998	*Sweet Deception*
2000	*Satan's School for Girls*

Film

1971	*Night of Dark Shadows*
1972	*Limbo*
1977	*Thunder & Lightning*
1981	*Dirty Tricks*
1982	*Making Love*
1989	*Loverboy*

Jaclyn Smith

Television Series

1976-1981	*Charlie's Angels*
1989-1990	*Christine Cromwell*

Television Appearances

1970	*The Partridge Family*
	"When Mother Gets Married"
1973	*McCloud*
	"Showdown at the End of the World"
1974	*Fools, Females and Fun*
	"Is there a Doctor in the House?"
1975	*McCloud*
	"The Man with the Golden Hat"
1975	*Get Christie Love*
	"A Fashion Heist"
1975	*Switch*
	"Pilot"
1975	*Switch*
	"The Old Diamond Game"
1975	*Switch*
	"The Late Show Murders"
1975	*Switch*
	"Death Heist"
1975	*The Rookies*
	"Go Ahead and Cry"
1976	*The Wonderful World of Disney*
	"The Whiz Kid and the Carnival Caper"
1977	*Battle of the Network Stars*
1977	*The San Pedro Beach Bums*
	"The Angels and the Bums"
1977	*The Love Boat*
	"A Tasteful Affair"
1977	*The Hardy Boys Mysteries*
	"Mystery of the Hollywood Phantom"

Television Movies

1972	*Probe*
1977	*Escape From Bogen County*
1978	*The Users*
1980	*Nightkill*
1981	*Jacqueline Bouvier Kennedy*
1983	*Rage of Angels*
1984	*George Washington*
1984	*Sentimental Journey*
1984	*The Night They Saved Christmas*
1985	*Florence Nightingale*
1986	*Rage of Angels: The Story Continues*
1988	*Windmills of the Gods*
1988	*The Bourne Identity*
1989	*Settle the Score*
1990	*Danielle Steele's Kaleidoscope*
1991	*Lies Before Kisses*
1991	*The Rape of Dr. Willis*
1992	*In the Arms of a Killer*
1992	*Nightmare in the Daylight*
1992	*Love Can Be Murder*
1994	*Cries Unheard: The Donna Yaklich Story*
1994	*Danielle Steele's Family Album*
1996	*My Very Best Friend*
1997	*Married to a Stranger*
1998	*Before He Wakes*
1999	*Freefall*
1999	*Three Secrets*
2000	*Navigating the Heart*

Film

1969	*Goodbye, Columbus*
1970	*The Adventurers*
1974	*The Bootleggers*
1985	*Dejé Vu*

Cheryl Ladd

Television Series

1970	*Josie and the Pussycats* (Singing voice only)
1972	*The Ken Berry "WOW" Show*
1972-73	*Search*
1977-1981	*Charlie's Angels*
1994-97	*One West Waikiki*

Television Appearances

1973	*Ironside* "A Game of Showdown"
1973	*The Partridge Family* "Double Trouble"
1974	*Harry O* "Such Dust as Dreams are Made of"
1974	*Streets of San Francisco* "Blockade"
1974	*Happy Days* "A Date with Cindy Shea"
1975	*Switch* "Death by Resurrection"
1977	*Police Woman* "Silky Chamberlain"
1977	*Police Story* "Prime Rib"
1977	*Code R*
1977	*The Fantastic Journey* "The Innocent Prey"
1977	*The San Pedro Beach Bums* "The Angels and the Bums"
1977	*Battle of the Network Stars*
1979	*The Cheryl Ladd Special*
1980	*Cheryl Ladd: Looking Back, Souveniers*
1982	*Cheryl Ladd: Scenes from a Special*
1983	*Cheryl Ladd: Fascinated*
1997	*Ink* "The Black Book"
1999	*Jesse* "Crazy White Female"

Television Movies

1972	*Alexander Zwo*
1973	*Satan's School for Girls*
1979	*When She Was Bad*
1983	*Kentucky Woman*
1983	*Grace Kelly*
1983	*The Hasty Heart*
1985	*Romance on the Orient Express*
1985	*A Death in California*
1986	*Danielle Steele's Crossings*
1987	*Deadly Care*
1988	*Bluegrass*
1989	*The Fullfillment of Mary Gray*
1990	*Jekyll & Hyde*
1990	*The Girl Who Came Between Them*
1990	*Crash: The Mystery of Flight 1501*
1991	*Danielle Steele's Changes*
1991	*Locked Up: A Mother's Rage*
1992	*Dead Before Dawn*
1993	*Broken Promises: Taking Emily Back*
1994	*Dancing with Danger*
1996	*A Tangled Web*
1997	*Kiss and Tell*
1997	*The Haunting of Lisa*
1998	*Every Mother's Worst Fear*
1998	*Perfect Little Angels*
1999	*Michael Landon: The Father I Knew*

Film

1971	*Chrome and Hot Leather*
1974	*Evil in the Deep* (aka *The Treasure of Jamaica Reef*)
1983	*Danielle Steele's Now and Forever*
1984	*Purple Hearts*
1989	*Millennium*
1990	*Lisa*
1992	*Poison Ivy*
1998	*Permanent Midnight*
1999	*A Dog of Flanders*

Shelley Hack

Television Series

1979-1980	*Charlie's Angels*
1983	*Cutter to Houston*
1986-87	*Jack and Mike*

Television Appearances

1980	*The Love Boat* "Dumb Luck"
1993	*Sequest DSV* "To Be or Not to Be"
1994	*L.A. Law* "Whose San Andreas Fault is it, Anyway"
1997	*Diagnosis Murder* "Looks Can Kill"
1998	*Tales From the Crypt* "The Assassin"

Television Movies

1979	*Death Car on the Freeway*
1982	*Vanities*
1983	*Trackdown: Finding the Goodbar Killer*
1983	*Found Money*
1984	*Single Bars, Single Women*
1985	*Kicks*
1989	*Bridesmaids*
1990	*A Casualty of War*
1992	*Taking Back My Life:* *The Nancy Ziegenmeyer Story*
1993	*Not In My Family*
1993	*Perry Mason:* *The Case of the Wicked Wives*
1995	*Falling From the Sky–Flight 174*
1996	*Frequent Flyer*

Film

1977	*Annie Hall*
1978	*If Ever I See You Again*
1983	*The King of Comedy*
1986	*Troll*
1987	*The Stepfather*
1989	*Blind Fear*
1992	*The Finishing Touch*
1992	*Me, Myself and I*
1996	*House Arrest*

Tanya Roberts

Television Series

1980-81	*Charlie's Angels*
1996	*Hotline*
1998-	*That 70'S Show*

Television Appearances

1980	*VEGA$*
	"Ladies in Blue"
1982	*The Love Boat*
	"Past Perfect Love"
1982	*Fantasy Island*
	"The Ghost's Story"
1994	*Burke's Law*
	"Who Killed Nick Hard?"
1995	*Silk Stalkings*
	"Til Death Do Us Part"
1997	*High Tide*
	"Girl on the Run"

Television Movies

1978	*Zuma Beach*
1979	*Pleasure Cove*
1980	*Waikiki*
1983	*Mickey Spillane's Mike Hammer:*
	Murder Me, Murder You

Film

1975	*Forced Entry*
1976	*The Yum Yum Girls*
1978	*Fingers*
1979	*Racquet*
1979	*California Dreamin'*
1979	*Tourist Trap*
1982	*The Beastmaster*
1983	*Hearts and Armour*

1984	*Sheena*
1985	*A View to a Kill*
1987	*Body Slam*
1989	*Purgatory*
1990	*Night Eyes*
1990	*Legal Tender*
1991	*Inner Sanctum*
1991	*Almost Pregnant*
1992	*Sins of Desire*
1995	*Deep Down*

CD ROM

1996	*Pandora's Box*

About the Authors

.vid Hofstede has written eight books, including *Holly-wood Heroes* (1994), *The Dukes of Hazzard* (1998), and *Slammin'!* (1999). He writes a film column for *Cowboys & Indians* magazine, and has contributed dozens of articles on entertainment and pop culture to a variety of national publications. He lives in Las Vegas, Nevada.

Jack Condon is famous as the world's foremost collector of *Charlie's Angels* memorabilia. He has been profiled in *People* magazine, and has been featured on the *E!* Entertainment network, and the television series *Showbiz Today*, *The Vicki Lawrence Show*, *Treasures in Your Home*, and *Extra*. His collection contains over 8,000 items, including several rare, one-of-a-kind artifacts, 3,000 photos, and more than 50,000 newspaper clippings. He lives in Sherman Oaks, California.

If you enjoyed this book, check out
my Web site and let me know.

— Jack Condon

WWW.CHARLIESANGELSFAN.COM